D0708057

* **remove make-up with petroleum jelly...**

* **soothe an aching back with mustard...**

* **protect pot plants with bubble wrap...**

* **keep aphids off rosebushes with banana skins...**

* **use vinegar to make perfect poached eggs...**

* **repair your leaky garden hose with a toothpick...**

EXTRAORDINARY
USES
FOR ORDINARY
THINGS

OVER 1800 WAYS TO SAVE MONEY AND TIME
USING 178 COMMON HOUSEHOLD ITEMS

Reader's
Digest

Published by The Reader's Digest Association Limited
London • New York • Sydney • Montreal

CONTENTS

* Denotes a **SUPER ITEM**: A household item with an amazingly large number of uses.

YOUR COMPLETE A-Z GUIDE

A

Address labels

- **Tag a bag** Address labels aren't just for sticking on envelopes. They can be an effective, inexpensive way of making sure lost items stand a chance of finding their way home. Place an address label – covered with a small piece of sticky tape or clear packing tape to prevent wear – inside a laptop computer bag, glasses case, gym bag, rucksack and all items of luggage.

- **Label electronic equipment** Few people bother to take out insurance on their collection of personal electronics equipment, but replacing an expensive digital camera, camcorder or MP3 player can cost serious money. A tape-covered address label conspicuously placed on your equipment may be sufficient to ensure its safe return.

- **Hang on to your umbrella** A well-made umbrella can last for years, but that's no use if it gets left behind at the cinema or on a bus or train. Minimise the risk of your loss becoming someone else's gain by sticking an address label on the umbrella handle and wrapping it once around with clear packing tape. This will protect the label from the elements and general wear and tear and make it considerably more difficult to remove.

- **Secure school supplies** It is one of the universal truths of parenthood: children are forever losing pencil cases, folders, markers and other school supplies. You may be able to reduce the losses by fixing address labels with a piece of transparent tape to the contents of your child's school bag and backpack.

- **Identify items for repair** Do you feel anxious when you take stereo equipment or another precious item into a repair shop? You may feel better if you place an address label on the base or some other unobtrusive, undamaged area. Note: This practice is not recommended for all personal treasures – you may not want to label paper documents, paintings, photos and other personal items.

Adhesive plaster

- **Remove a splinter** If a splinter is too tiny or too deep to remove with tweezers, cover it with adhesive plaster. Leave for about three days, then remove the tape and the splinter should come out painlessly.

- **Reduce your hat size** If your hat is a bit too big, wrap layers of adhesive plaster around the sweatband until you have the perfect fit.

- **Get a grip on tools** Adhesive plaster has the right texture for wrapping around tool handles. It gives a positive, comfortable grip and it's highly absorbent so the tool won't become slippery if your hand sweats. As you wrap the handle, overlap each winding by about half a tape width, using several layers to get the best grip. Here are some useful applications:

  - Screwdriver handles are sometimes too narrow and slippery to grip well when you are driving in or removing stubborn screws. Wrap adhesive plaster around the handle until it feels comfortable in your hand – this is especially useful if you have arthritis in your fingers as you won't have to grip so tightly.

  - When plumbers want to cut a pipe in a spot that's too tight for their hacksaw frame, they remove the blade and wrap one end of it well to form a handle, making a mini-hacksaw.

did you **KNOW?**

In the 1920s, Josephine Dickson, an accident-prone US housewife, inspired the invention of the Band-Aid plaster. Her husband, Earle, who tended her wounds, stuck small squares of sterile gauze onto adhesive tape, covered it with a layer of crinoline, and rolled it back up so that Josephine could cut off and apply the ready-made bandages herself. His employer, Johnson & Johnson, soon began producing the first Band-Aids. When Earle died in 1961, by then a member of the board of directors, sales exceeded $30 million (£20 million) a year.

Alka-Seltzer

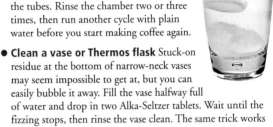

- **Clean a coffee maker** Fill the water chamber of a coffee maker with water and drop in four Alka-Seltzer tablets. When the Alka-Seltzer has dissolved, put the coffee maker through a brew cycle to clean the tubes. Rinse the chamber two or three times, then run another cycle with plain water before you start making coffee again.

- **Clean a vase or Thermos flask** Stuck-on residue at the bottom of narrow-neck vases may seem impossible to get at, but you can easily bubble it away. Fill the vase halfway full of water and drop in two Alka-Seltzer tablets. Wait until the fizzing stops, then rinse the vase clean. The same trick works for cleaning glass Thermos flasks.

- **Clean glass cookware** Don't scour stubborn stains off ovenproof glass cookware. Just fill the container with water, add up to six Alka-Seltzer tablets and let it soak for an hour. Then wipe away the stains.

- **Clean the toilet** The citric acid in Alka-Seltzer combined with its fizzing action makes it an effective toilet-bowl cleaner. Simply drop a couple of tablets into the bowl and leave for about 20 minutes. After a quick scrub with a toilet brush the bowl will be gleaming.

- **Clean jewellery** Drop dull-looking jewellery in a glass of fizzing Alka-Seltzer for a couple of minutes. It will sparkle and shine when you pull it out.

- **Unblock and deodorise the kitchen sink**
  Get almost instant results by dropping a couple of Alka-Seltzer tablets down the plug hole. Then pour in a cup of vinegar. Wait a few minutes and then run the hot-water tap at full force to clear the blockage. This is also a good way to eliminate unpleasant odours in the sink.

- **Soothe insect bites** If an insect bite is persistently itchy, drop two Alka-Seltzer tablets into half a glass of water. Dip a piece of cotton wool into the glass and apply it to the bite.
  WARNING: don't do this if you are allergic to aspirin, which is a key ingredient in Alka-Seltzer.

- **Attract fish** Avid anglers know that fish are attracted to bubbles. If you use a hollow plastic tube jig on the line, just break off a piece of Alka-Seltzer and slip it into the tube. The jig will produce an enticing stream of bubbles as it sinks.

(**SCIENCE** FAIR)
An Alka-Seltzer rocket

You will need a plastic canister with a lid that fits tightly inside the canister (canisters with lids that fit around an outside lip won't work), stiff paper, sticky tape and scissors. To make the rocket's body, wrap a piece of paper around the canister with the canister's open end facing out of the bottom of the tube. Tape the paper in place. Make a nose cone from a piece of stiff paper. Trim it along the bottom and tape it onto the top of the rocket. To launch, fill the canister about half full with refrigerated water – vital to a successful lift off. Add two Alka-Seltzer tablets. Put on the lid, set the rocket on the ground and stand back. The gas will quickly build up pressure in the canister, causing the canister lid to pop off and the rocket to launch several feet into the air.

Aluminium cans

- **Create a Chinese lantern** Mark two lines around a clean empty can, about 2.5cm from the top and bottom. With a sharp craft knife, make vertical cuts about 1.5cm apart between the lines. Make a cut across the bottom of two adjacent strips to make an opening for a candle. Gently press down on the can to make the strips bend in the middle. Insert a tea-light through the opening. Tuck the cut ends of the opening strips inside the can. Finally, attach a hanging loop to the ring pull. Spray-paint the can before cutting if you want to make different-coloured lanterns.

- **Make planters more portable** Don't strain your back moving a planter loaded with heavy soil. Reduce the amount of soil and lighten the load by first filling a third to a half of the planter with empty, upside-down aluminium cans. Then add the soil and plants. The rustproof aluminium cans make the planter lighter and help it to drain well.

- **Protect young plants** Remove both ends of a can (a soup or coffee can, depending on the size you need) and push it into the earth as a collar to protect young garden plants from cutworms (the caterpillars of noctuid moths).

- **Keep track of bulbs and seedlings** Remove the top and bottom of a can and cut plant labels from the remaining aluminium sheet. Write on them with a ballpoint or marker pen and attach them to plant stakes or pots to identify the variety and colour of your plants.

- **Make Christmas decorations** Cut the top and bottom from several empty cans, then slit and flatten the cylinder. Cut simple shapes such as stars. Use a ballpoint pen to draw designs on the wrong side. Decorate with stick-on jewels or transparent glass paint. Make a hole and add a wire for hanging.

Aluminium foil...

...in the kitchen

- **Keep rolls and bread warm** To lock in the oven-fresh warmth of homemade rolls or bread for a dinner party or picnic, wrap the freshly baked goods in a napkin and place a layer of aluminium foil underneath. The foil will reflect the heat to keep the bread warm and soft for quite some time.

- **Bake a perfect piecrust** Keep the edges of piecrusts from getting burnt by covering them with strips of aluminium foil.

- **Decorate a cake** Make a disposable icing bag out of a piece of heavy-duty aluminium foil. Roll it into a tube and fill it with soft icing. As a bonus, there's no icing bag to clean.

- **Make an extra-large salad bowl** If you are making a large salad but don't have a bowl big enough to toss it, simply line the kitchen sink with aluminium foil and you should have plenty of room to mix it up.

A **...in the kitchen**

- **Preserve steel-wool pads** To stop a used steel-wool pad from turning into a rusty mess, wrap it in foil and place it in the freezer. You can also lengthen the life of steel-wool soap pads by crumpling up a sheet of foil and placing it under the steel wool in its dish or container. (Don't forget to periodically drain off the water that collects at the bottom of the dish.)

- **Scrubbing pans** If you don't have a scrubbing pad or brush to hand, crumple up a handful of aluminium foil and use it to scrub your pots and pans.

- **Make novelty cake tins** For a teddy bear birthday cake, a Valentine's Day heart cake, a Christmas tree cake or whatever shaped cake the occasion may call for, you can use aluminium foil. Just form a double thickness of heavy-duty aluminium foil into the desired shape inside a large cake tin.

- **Soften up brown sugar** To get hardened brown sugar flowing free again, chip off a piece, wrap it in aluminium foil and bake it in the oven at 150°C (gas mark 2) for 5 minutes.

TIP foil-eating acidic foods

Think twice before using aluminium foil to wrap left-over food, especially if it is dripping with tomato sauce. Very acidic or salty foods such as lemons, grapefruits, ketchup and pickles accelerate the oxidation of aluminium and can actually 'eat' through foil with prolonged exposure. This can also leach aluminium into the food, which can affect its flavour and may pose a health risk. If you want to use foil for foods with acidic ingredients, cover it first with a layer or two of plastic wrap or greaseproof paper to prevent the sauce from coming into contact with the foil.

...around the house

- **Clean silver and jewellery** If your silverware has become dulled and blackened, try an ion exchange, a molecular reaction in which aluminium acts as a catalyst. Line a pan with a sheet of aluminium foil, fill it with cold water and add 2 teaspoons of salt. Put the silverware in, let it sit for 2-3 minutes, then rinse off and dry. To brighten dull jewellery, use an aluminium foil-lined pan and hot water. Mix in a tablespoon of bleach-free powdered laundry detergent (not liquid) such as Dreft. Let the jewellery soak for a minute. Rinse well and air-dry.

- **Stop silverware from tarnishing** Store freshly cleaned silverware on top of a sheet of aluminium foil to stop it from tarnishing. For long-term storage, first tightly cover each piece in a clear plastic wrap – be sure to squeeze out as much air as possible – then wrap in foil and seal the ends.

- **Improve the efficiency of radiators** Get more heat out of radiators without spending more money. Tape heavy-duty aluminium foil onto a piece of cardboard with the shiny side of the foil facing out. The radiant heat waves will bounce off the foil into the room instead of being absorbed by the wall behind the radiator. If your radiators have covers, attach a piece of foil under the top of the cover as well.

- **Keep pets off furniture** If your pet keeps jumping onto the sofa, place a piece of aluminium foil on the seat cushions. After one attempt at settling down on the noisy surface, your pet will no longer consider it a comfy place to snooze.

- **Protect a child's mattress** To spare the mattress, especially if you don't have a plastic protector, lay several sheets of aluminium foil across the width of the mattress and cover them with a large beach towel. Replace the mattress pad or mattress cover and the bottom sheet.

...around the house

- **Hide worn spots on a mirror** Disguise small flaws on a mirror's reflective surface by putting a piece of aluminium foil, shiny side facing out, on the back of the glass. Attach it with strips of masking tape to the backing behind the mirror or to the frame.

- **Sharpening scissors** Use clean, leftover pieces of foil to sharpen up dulled scissors. Smooth the foil out and then fold the strips into several layers and start cutting against the 'pad' with the scissors. Seven or eight passes should be enough.

- **Move furniture** To slide large furniture over a smooth floor, place small pieces of aluminium foil under the feet to increase traction. Place it dull side down as the shiny side is less slippery.

- **Fix loose batteries** The springs that hold batteries in place can lose their tension, causing the current to be intermittent. Fold a small piece of aluminium foil to make a pad that will take up the slack. Place the pad between the battery and the spring.

...in the laundry

- **Speed up ironing** When you iron, the board sucks up much of the iron's heat – so you may have to make several passes to remove creases. To speed up the process, place some aluminium foil under the ironing board cover. The foil will reflect the heat, allowing you to smooth creases more quickly.

- **Clean your iron** To remove a build-up of spray starch on the iron, run the hot iron over a piece of aluminium foil.

- **Attach a patch** If you are using an iron-on patch to fix a hole, put a piece of aluminium foil under the hole to stop it from sticking to the ironing board. You can just slip it out when you have finished ironing.

...in the garden

- **Put some bite in a mulch** To keep hungry insects and slugs away from cucumbers and other vegetables, mix strips of aluminium foil in with the mulch.

- **Make a sun box for plants** Plants tend to bend towards light. To light your plants from all sides, make a sun box. Remove the top and one side from a cardboard box and line the other sides and bottom with aluminium foil, shiny side out, taping or gluing it in place. Place your plants in the box close to a window.

- **Build a seed incubator** To give plants grown from seed a head start, line a shoe box with aluminium foil, shiny side up, allowing about 5cm of foil to extend out over the sides. Make several drainage holes in the bottom, penetrating the foil, then fill the box to slightly more than halfway with potting compost and plant the seeds. The foil inside the box will absorb heat to keep the seeds warm as they germinate, while the foil outside the box will reflect light onto the young shoots. Place the box near a sunny window, keep the compost moist and watch them grow.

- **Improve outdoor lighting** Brighten up outdoor electrical lighting by making a foil reflector to put behind the light. Attach the reflector to the fixture with a few strips of electrical tape or gaffer tape – but do not apply tape directly to the bulb.

did you **KNOW?**

Have you ever wondered why aluminium foil has one side that's shinier than the other? The different shades of silver result from the final rolling process in its manufacture, when two layers of foil pass through the rolling mill simultaneously. The sides in contact with the mill's heavy, polished rollers come out shiny, while the inside layers retain a dull or matt finish. The shiny side is better for reflecting light and heat, but both sides are equally good for wrapping food or lining grills.

...in the garden

- **Protect tree trunks** Mice, rabbits and other animals often feed on the bark of young trees during winter. A cheap and effective deterrent is to wrap lower tree trunks with a double layer of heavy-duty aluminium foil in late autumn. Be sure to remove the foil in spring.

- **Scarecrows and other birds** Are hungry birds eating all the fruit on your trees? Dangle strips of aluminium foil from the branches using monofilament fishing line. Even better, hang some foil-wrapped seashells from the branches. As the wind blows them about, they will add a bit of noise to startle the birds and keep them away from the ripening fruit.

- **Grow untangled cuttings** Help plant cuttings to grow up strong and uncluttered by starting them in a container covered with a sheet of aluminium foil. Make a few holes in the foil and insert the cuttings through the holes. As an added bonus, the foil slows evaporation, so you will need to add water less frequently.

TIP Prevent sunscald on trees

Wrapping young tree trunks with a couple of layers of aluminium foil during the winter can help prevent sunscald, a condition that damages the bark of some young thin-barked trees – especially fruit trees, ashes, limes, maples, oaks and willows. The problem occurs on warm winter days when the sun's rays reactivate dormant cells underneath the tree's bark. The subsequent drop in night-time temperatures kills the cells and can injure the tree. In most areas, you can remove the aluminium wrapping in early spring.

...in the great outdoors

- **Keep wasps away from sweet drinks** Tightly cover the top of your glass with aluminium foil. Poke a straw through it and enjoy your drink in peace.

- **Make an impromptu picnic platter** When you need a disposable platter for a picnic or buffet supper, just cover a piece of cardboard with heavy-duty aluminium foil.

- **Keep matches dry** Wrap matches in aluminium foil to keep them from getting damp or wet on camping trips.

- **Improvise a frying pan** If you don't want to take a frying pan on a camping trip, make your own. Place a forked stick centrally over two layers of heavy-duty aluminium foil and wrap the edges of the foil tightly around the forked branches. Leave some slack in the foil between the forks. Invert the stick and depress the centre to hold food for frying.

- **Make a barbecue drip pan** To keep meat drippings from falling onto the barbecue, make a drip pan out of a few layers of heavy-duty aluminium foil. Shape it freehand or use a baking pan as a mould (remove the pan once you have finished). Don't forget to make the drip pan slightly larger than the meat on the grill.

- **Clean a barbecue grill** After the last steak is cooked and while the coals are still red-hot, lay a sheet of aluminium foil over the grill to burn off any remaining food deposits. The next time you use the barbecue, crumple up the foil and use it to scrub off the burned food before you start cooking.

- **Keep your toes warm when camping** Wrap some large stones in aluminium foil and heat them by the campfire. Wrap them in towels and put them in the bottom of your sleeping bag.

- **Keep a sleeping bag dry** Place a piece of heavy-duty aluminium foil under your sleeping bag to stop the moisture seeping through.

...for the DIY-er

- **Make a flexible funnel** Double up a length of heavy-duty aluminium foil and roll it into the shape of a cone – you can bend the aluminium foil to reach awkward holes, like the oil-filler hole tucked against the engine of a lawnmower.

- **Re-attach a vinyl floor tile** If a vinyl floor tile has become detached, reposition it on the floor, lay a piece of aluminium foil on top and run a hot clothes iron over it until you can feel the glue melting underneath. Put something heavy on top of the tile to weigh it down while the glue resets. This technique also works well to smooth out unsightly bulges and straighten curled seams in sheet-vinyl flooring.

- **Keep paint off doorknobs and handles** When painting a door, use aluminium foil to wrap the doorknobs to keep paint away from them. Overlap the foil onto the door when you wrap the knob, then run a sharp craft knife around the base of the knob to trim the foil. You will be able to paint right up to the edge of the knob.

- **Keep a paintbrush wet** If you have stopped painting but want to continue later, don't clean the brush – just squeeze out the excess paint and wrap it tightly in aluminium foil (or plastic wrap). Secure the foil tightly at the base of the handle with a rubber band. For extended wet-brush storage, place the wrapped brush in the freezer. Defrost the brush before you paint.

- **Line roller trays** Lining a roller tray with aluminium foil works just as well as a bought liner and is a lot cheaper.

did you **KNOW?**

Some people still ask for tinfoil when they want to wrap up leftovers. Household foil was made only of tin until 1947, when aluminium foil was introduced, eventually replacing tinfoil in the kitchen drawer.

- **Make an artist's palette** Tear off a length of heavy-duty aluminium foil, crimp up the edges and you have a ready-to-use palette. For a more stylish solution, cut a piece of cardboard into the shape of a palette, including a thumb-hole and cover it with foil. If you already have a wooden palette, cover it with foil before each use and then remove it when you have finished.

- **Prevent paint from forming a skin**
When you open a half-used tin of paint, you will typically find a skin of dried paint on the surface. You can prevent this by putting a piece of aluminium foil under the can and tracing around it. Cut out the circle and drop the foil disc onto the paint surface. Then take a deep breath, blow into the can and quickly put the top in place. The carbon dioxide in your breath replaces some of the oxygen in the can, and helps to keep the paint from drying.

- **Reflect light for photography** Professional photographers use reflectors to throw extra light on their subject. To make a reflector, lightly coat a large piece of heavy cardboard with glue and cover it with aluminium foil, shiny side out. You can make one single reflector, as large as you like, or, for easy storage and carrying, it is more useful to make three panels and then join them together with gaffer tape. That way they will stand up by themselves and can be easily folded for handy storage. Attach string handles on the back of the two end pieces for carrying.

- **Give a shine to chrome** For sparkling electrical appliances such as kettles and toasters, gold-club shafts and older car bumpers, crumple up a handful of aluminium foil with shiny side out and apply some elbow grease. If you rub really hard, the foil will even remove rust spots. Note: some 'chrome' on new cars is actually plastic – so check before you rub with aluminium foil.

Aluminium pie dishes

- **Create a centrepiece** Make a quick centrepiece for a special dinner party by securing a tall, thick candle or a few church candles to an aluminium pie dish by melting some wax from the bottom of the candles onto the dish. Add a thin layer of water or sand and cover it completely with rose petals or seashells.

- **Contain the mess from children's projects** Glitter is notorious for turning up in the corners and crevices of your home long after your child's masterpiece has been discarded. Cut down on the mess by using an aluminium pie dish to enclose projects that involve working with glitter, beads, spray paint and feathers.

- **Make trays for craft supplies** Bring some order to your children's – or your own – inventory of crayons, beads, buttons, sequins, pipe cleaners and other craft items by sorting them in aluminium pie dishes. To secure materials when storing the tins, cover each with a layer of plastic wrap.

- **Keep insects out of pet dishes** Use an aluminium pie dish filled with about 1cm of water to create a metal moat around your pet's food dish. It should keep marauding ants and other small insects at bay.

- **Train your pet** If Rover or Fluffy has a tendency to leap up on the sofa or kitchen worktop, leave a few aluminium pie dishes along the edges of the worktop or back of the sofa when you're not at home. The resulting loud rattling noise will give him a good scare when he jumps up on top of them and should stop him from doing it again.

- **Keep squirrels and birds off fruit trees** Scare away furry and feathered thieves with a few dangling aluminium pie dishes. String them up in pairs so they will make some noise and you shouldn't have to worry about finding any half-eaten apples or plums come autumn.

- **Store sanding discs and other items** As they are highly resistant to corrosion, aluminium pie dishes are excellent for storing sanding discs, hacksaw blades and other hardware accessories in the workshop. Cut a dish in half and attach it (with staples or gaffer tape around the edges) open side up to a peg board.

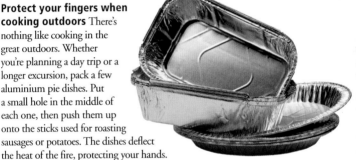

- **Protect your fingers when cooking outdoors** There's nothing like cooking in the great outdoors. Whether you're planning a day trip or a longer excursion, pack a few aluminium pie dishes. Put a small hole in the middle of each one, then push them up onto the sticks used for roasting sausages or potatoes. The dishes deflect the heat of the fire, protecting your hands.

(KIDS' STUFF)
Making ice ornaments

Keep children busy indoors on a cold, winter day by making ice ornaments that you can hang on a tree outside. You need an aluminium pie dish, some water, a piece of heavy string or a shoelace, and a mix of decorative – preferably biodegradable – materials such as dried flowers, dried leaves, pine cones, seeds, shells and twigs.

Let the children arrange the materials in the pie dish. Then fold the string or shoelace in half and place it in the dish. The fold should hang over the edges of the tin, while the two ends meet in the centre. Slowly fill the pan with water, stopping just below the rim. You may have to place an object on the string to keep it from floating to the top.

If the temperature outside is below freezing, simply put the pan on the doorstep to freeze. Otherwise, pop it into the freezer. Once the water has frozen solid, remove the pie dish and let your children hang it up outside.

Apples

- **Roast a juicy chicken** If your roast chicken tends to be tough and dried out, stuff an apple inside the bird before cooking it. Remove the apple once the chicken has cooked.

- **Keep cakes fresh** Store cake alongside half an apple. It will help the cake to maintain its moisture much longer than keeping it in the fridge or in a cake tin.

- **Ripen green tomatoes** Quickly ripen tomatoes by placing them, along with a ripe apple, in a paper bag for a couple of days. For best results, try to maintain a ratio of about five or six tomatoes to every apple.

- **Soften up hardened brown sugar** Brown sugar becomes hard when exposed to humidity. Place an apple wedge in a self-sealing plastic bag with the sugar. Seal, leave in a dry place for a day or two, and your sugar will be soft enough to use.

- **Absorb salt in soups and stews** If you've added too much salt when cooking, simply drop a few apple (or potato) wedges into the pan. Cook for another 10 minutes or so, remove the wedges, and the excess salt will have been absorbed.

did you **KNOW?**

The old saying 'One bad apple spoils the barrel' is close to the truth. Apples are among a diverse group of fruits, including apricots, avocados, bananas, blueberries, cantaloupes and peaches, that produce ethylene gas, a natural ripening agent. So the increased level of ethylene produced by a single rotten apple can significantly accelerate the ageing process of the other apples around it.

Ethylene-producing fruits can be useful if you want to help to speed the ripening process, but they can also have unwanted effects. Placing a bowl of ripe apples or bananas too close to freshly cut flowers, for instance, can cause them to wilt. And if potatoes are sprouting buds too soon, they may be too close to the apples.

Ashes

- **Clean glass woodburning-stove doors** Mix ashes with a little water, and rub over the surfaces of the doors with a damp cloth. Rinse with a wet sponge, then dry with a clean cloth.

- **Use as plant food** Wood ashes have a high alkaline content and trace amounts of calcium and potassium, which encourage blooms. If your soil is acidic, sprinkle ash around alkaline-loving plants, such as clematis, hydrangea, lilac and roses, in spring. (Avoid acid-lovers like rhododendrons and azaleas.) Be sparing when adding ashes to a compost pile; they can counteract the benefits of manure and other high-nitrogen materials.

- **Repel insects** Scatter ashes around the garden and on plants to deter worms, slugs, snails and soft-bodied insects. It sticks to their bodies and draws moisture from them.

- **Clean pewter and wood** Dip a damp, soft cloth into cigarette ash and rub it well over the item. It will turn darker at first, but the shine will return after a thorough rinse. Do the same to remove water spots and heat marks from wood furniture. Then add a shine with furniture polish.

- **Protect your fireplace floor** When cleaning the fireplace, leave a 2.5 to 5cm layer of ash under the andiron to reflect heat back up to the burning wood and protect your fireplace floor against hot embers. Be sure not to let the ashes clog up the space under the grate and block the airflow that a good fire needs.

TIP selecting firewood

For a hot-burning and long-lasting fire, ash, beech, hornbeam, hawthorn, crab apple and wild cherry are among the best woods. Green or wet woods and pine burn poorly and build up heaps of creosote (the leading cause of chimney fires) in the chimney. WARNING: Never burn pressure-treated wood (used for decking) as it contains chemicals that can be extremely harmful when burned.

Aspirin

- **Revive dead car batteries** If you get behind the wheel only to discover that the car battery has given up the ghost – and there's no one around to give you a jump start – you may be able to get the vehicle started by dropping two soluble aspirin tablets into the battery itself. The aspirin's acetylsalicylic acid will combine with the battery's sulphuric acid to produce one last charge. Even if this method is successful, you should always have the battery checked immediately by an experienced mechanic.

- **Remove perspiration stains** Before giving up hope of removing a stubborn perspiration stain from a smart white shirt, try this. Crush two aspirins and mix the powder in 100ml warm water. Soak the stained part of the garment in the solution for 2-3 hours.

- **Treat hard skin on feet** Soften hard callouses on your feet by grinding five or six aspirins into a powder. Make a paste by adding ½ teaspoon each of lemon juice and water. Apply the mixture to the affected areas, then wrap your foot in a warm towel and cover it with a plastic bag. Put your feet up for at least 10 minutes, remove the bag and towel and file down the softened callous with a pumice stone.

- **Restore hair colour** Swimming in a chlorinated pool can have a noticeable and often detrimental effect on your hair colouring if you have light-coloured hair. You can usually return your hair to its former shade by dissolving six to eight aspirins in a glass of warm water. Rub the solution thoroughly into your hair and let it set for 10–15 minutes. Rinse off and the greenish tinge should have gone.

- **Control dandruff** Keep a flaky scalp in check by crushing two aspirins to a fine powder and adding it to the normal amount of shampoo you use each time you wash your hair. Leave the mixture on your hair for 1-2 minutes, then rinse well and wash again with plain shampoo.

- **Dry up pimples** Even those of us who are well past adolescence can still get the occasional spot. Crush an aspirin and moisten it with a little water. Apply the paste to the pimple and let it sit for a couple of minutes before washing it off with soap and water. It will reduce the redness and soothe the sting. If the pimple persists, repeat the procedure as needed until it has gone.

- **Help cut flowers last longer** Put a crushed aspirin in water before adding flowers to a vase. Other household items that you can add to water to extend the life of flower arrangements include a multivitamin tablet, a teaspoon of sugar, a pinch of salt, bicarbonate of soda and even a copper coin. Don't forget to change the water in the vase every day if possible.

- **Give the garden first aid** Aspirin is not only a first-aid essential for you, but for the garden as well. Some gardeners use ground-up aspirin as a rooting agent or mix it with water to treat fungus conditions in the soil. But be careful when using aspirin around plants; too much can burn or damage the greenery. When treating soil, the typical dosage should be a half or a full aspirin tablet in a litre of water.

did you **KNOW?**

The bark of the willow tree is rich in salicin, a natural painkiller and fever reducer. In the 3rd century BC, Hippocrates used it to relieve headaches and pain. Later, many traditional healers, including Native Americans, used salicin-containing herbs to treat cold and flu symptoms. But it wasn't until 1899 that Felix Hoffmann, a chemist at the German company Bayer, developed a modified derivative, acetylsalicylic acid, better known as aspirin.

Aspirin

- **Remove egg stains from clothes** Scrape off as much of the egg as you can and then try to sponge out the rest with lukewarm water. Never use hot water – it will cook and set the egg. If that doesn't completely remove the stain, mix water and cream of tartar into a paste and add a crushed aspirin. Spread the paste on the stain and leave it for 30 minutes. Rinse well in warm water and the egg should be gone.

- **Soothe insect bites and stings** Control the inflammation caused by mosquito bites and bee stings by wetting your skin and rubbing an aspirin over the spot. WARNING: If you are allergic to bee stings – and have difficulty breathing, develop abdominal pains or feel nauseated following a bee sting – you must seek medical attention at once.

TAKE CARE

About 10 per cent of people with severe asthma are also allergic to aspirin – and, in fact, to all products containing salicylic acid, aspirin's key ingredient, including some cold medicines, fruits, food seasonings and additives. That jumps to 30 to 40 per cent for older asthmatics who also suffer from sinusitis or nasal polyps. Acute sensitivity to aspirin is also seen in a small percentage of the general population without asthma – particularly people with ulcers and other bleeding conditions. Always consult a doctor before using any medication and do not apply aspirin externally if you are allergic to taking it internally.

Baby oil

- **Remove a plaster** You can significantly lessen the 'ouch' factor when removing a plaster on a child by first rubbing some baby oil into the adhesive parts on top and around the edges. If you see the plaster working loose, let your child finish the job to help her overcome her fear. Adults who have sensitive or fragile skin may also want to try this.

- **Make your own bath oil** Add a few drops of your favourite scent to 50ml baby oil in a small plastic bottle. Shake well and add it to the bath.

- **Buff up golf clubs, stainless-steel sinks and chrome trim** Don't waste money on special cleaning kits for chrome-plated carbon steel golf club heads. Just keep a small bottle of baby oil in your golf bag along with a chamois cloth or towel. Dab a few drops of oil on the cloth and polish the head of the club after each round of golf. Do the same to buff up a dull-looking stainless-steel sink. Rub dry with a towel and repeat if necessary. This is also a terrific way to remove stains on the chrome trim of kitchen appliances and bathroom fixtures.

- **Slip off a stuck ring** Do you find that rings frequently get jammed on your fingers? Try this. First lubricate the ring area with a generous amount of baby oil. Then swivel the ring around to spread the oil underneath it. You should be able to slide the ring off with ease.

- **Clean a bath or shower** Remove dirt and built-up soap scum around a bath or shower enclosure by wiping surfaces with a teaspoon of baby oil on a moist cloth. Use another cloth to wipe away any leftover oil. Finally, spray the area with a disinfectant cleaner to kill any remaining germs. This technique is also great for cleaning soap film and watermarks off glass shower doors.

Baby oil

- **Shine stainless-steel sinks and chrome trim** Buff up a dull-looking stainless-steel sink by rubbing it down with a few drops of baby oil on a clean, soft cloth. Rub dry with a towel and repeat if necessary. This is also a terrific way to remove stains on the chrome trim of kitchen appliances and bathroom fixtures.

- **Polish leather bags and shoes** Just a few drops of baby oil applied with a soft cloth can add new life to an old leather bag or pair of patent-leather shoes. Don't forget to wipe away any oil remaining on the leather when you've finished.

- **Get scratches off dashboard plastic** Disguise scratches on the plastic lenses covering the indicators on the car dashboard by rubbing over them with a little baby oil.

- **Remove emulsion paint from skin** Do you get almost as much paint on your face and hands as you do on the walls when decorating? Quickly remove emulsion paint from your skin by first rubbing it with some baby oil, followed by a thorough wash with soap and hot water.

- **Treat cradle cap** To combat cradle cap, a common, somewhat unsightly, but usually harmless condition in babies, gently rub in a little baby oil and lightly comb it through your child's hair. If your child gets upset, comb it a bit at a time. Do not leave the oil on for more than 24 hours. Then, thoroughly wash the hair. Repeat the process in persistent cases. Note: if you notice a lot of yellow crusting or if the cradle cap has spread behind the ears or onto the neck, speak to a doctor before trying to treat it yourself.

Baby powder

- **Give sand the brush-off** Minimise the mess after a day at the seaside or in the sandpit by sprinkling some baby powder over sweaty, sand-covered children (and adults) before they enter the house. In addition to soaking up excess moisture, the powder makes sand incredibly easy to brush off.

- **Cool sheets in summer** Sprinkle a little baby powder between the sheets before getting into bed on warm summer nights – it will keep them – and you – beautifully cool and smooth.

- **Dry-shampoo your pet** Is the dog in need of a bath but you just don't have time to do it? In between proper shampoos, vigorously rub a handful or two of baby powder into your pet's fur. Let it settle in for a couple of minutes and follow up with a thorough brushing. Your dog should both look and smell much fresher. You can even occasionally 'dry shampoo' your own hair using the same technique.

- **Absorb grease stains on clothing** Frying foods can be a dangerous business – especially for clothes. If you get a splash of grease on your clothing, try dabbing the stain with some baby powder on a powder puff. Make sure you rub it in well and then brush off any excess powder. Repeat until the mark has completely disappeared.

- **Clean grimy playing cards** Here is a simple way to keep your playing cards from sticking together and getting grimy. Loosely place the cards in a plastic bag with some baby powder. Seal the bag and give it a good shake. When you remove the cards from the bag, they should feel fresh and smooth to the touch.

- **Slip on rubber gloves** Don't jam or squeeze your fingers into rubber gloves when the inner layer inside the gloves wears out. Instead, lightly dust your fingers with baby powder. The rubber gloves should slide on as good as new.

Baby powder

- **Dust off flower bulbs** Many gardeners use medicated baby powder to dust flower bulbs before planting them. Simply place 5-6 bulbs and 3 tablespoons of medicated baby powder in a sealed plastic bag and give it a few gentle shakes. The medicated-powder coating helps both to reduce the chance of rot and keep away moles, voles, grubs and other bulb-munching pests.

- **Remove mould from books** If some of your books have been stored in a less-than-ideal environment and have become mouldy or mildewed, this should help. First, let them thoroughly air-dry. Then, sprinkle some baby powder between the pages and stand the books upright for several hours. Afterwards, gently brush out the remaining powder from each book. They may not be as good as new, but they should be in a lot better shape than they were before.

did you **KNOW?**

Most ordinary baby powder is talc-based and not good for infants to breathe. In addition, the base material for talc is often extracted from environmentally sensitive regions and should be avoided for this reason.

Paediatricians often recommend using a cornflour-based powder – if one is needed at all – when changing nappies. Cornflour powder is coarser than talcum powder and does not have the health risks, but it may promote fungal infection and should not be applied in skin folds or to broken skin. An alternative 'natural' powder is available, based on powdered tapioca. Medicated baby powder includes zinc oxide added to either talcum powder or cornflour-based powder. It is generally used to soothe skin afflicted with nappy rash and to prevent chafing.

Baby wipes

- **Use for quick, on-the-move clean-ups** Baby wipes are brilliant for wiping your hands after filling the car with petrol, mopping up small spills and cooling a sweaty brow after exercise.

- **Recycle as dust cloths** Believe it or not, some brands of baby wipes – Huggies, for instance – can be laundered and reused as dusters and cleaning rags. Only 'mildly' soiled wipes should be laundered and you should always wash them at 60°C or above.

- **Remove stains from carpet, clothing and upholstery** Use a baby wipe to blot up coffee spills from a rug or carpet; it absorbs both the liquid and the stain. Wipes can also be effectively deployed when attacking various spills and drips on clothing and upholstered furniture.

- **Buff up the bathroom or kitchen** When you need to clean surfaces in a hurry, baby wipes are extremely good at cleaning off practically any engrained dirt or stains. Keep a dry cloth in your other hand to buff things up as you make your rounds.

- **Clean a PC keyboard** Shake out your computer keyboard to get rid of the dust and debris underneath and in between the keys. Then, use a baby wipe to remove the dirt that builds up on the keys themselves. Always turn off the computer or unplug the keyboard before you wipe the keys.

- **Soothe sunburn** You can cool sunburn temporarily by gently patting the area with a baby wipe. Baby wipes can also be used to treat cuts and scrapes. Although most wipes don't have any antiseptic properties, there's nothing wrong with using one for an initial cleansing before applying the proper medical treatment.

- **Remove make-up** It is one of the fashion industry's worst-kept secrets: many models consider a baby wipe to be their best friend when it is time to remove stubborn make-up from their faces, particularly black eyeliner.

Baby wipes containers

- **Organise your stuff** These plastic boxes are incredibly useful storage, and rectangular ones can be stacked as well. Use them to store everything from sewing supplies, coupons and craft and office supplies to old floppy disks, small tools, photos, receipts and bills. Label the contents of each with a marker on masking tape.

- **Make a first-aid kit** Gather up essential first-aid items (such as plasters, sterile gauze rolls and pads, adhesive tape, scissors and antibiotic cream) and use a rectangular baby wipes container to hold it all. Before you add your supplies, wash the container well – and rub the inside with surgical spirit after it dries.

- **Use as a decorative wool or string dispenser** A clean cylindrical wipes container makes a perfect dispenser for a roll of wool or string. Simply remove the cover, insert the roll and thread it through the slot in the lid, then reattach the cover. You can paint or paper over the container to give it a more decorative look.

- **Store plastic shopping bags** Bring order to the puffed-up chaos plastic bags create by storing them in a rectangular wipes containers. Each container will hold 40 to 50 bags if you squeeze the air out of them. A large rectangular tissue box – the kind with a perforated cutout dispenser – would also work.

- **Hold towels or rags in the workshop** A used baby wipes container is useful in the workshop for storing rags and paper towels – and to keep a steady supply on hand as needed. You can easily keep a full roll of detached paper towels or six or seven good-sized rags in each container.

TIP removing labels

Use a blow-dryer on a high setting to warm the labels on baby wipes containers and make them easier to pull off. You can get rid of adhesive by applying a little WD-40 oil or orange citrus cleaner.

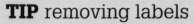

Balloons

- **Protect a bandaged finger** To keep a bandaged finger dry, slip a small balloon over it when doing dishes, bathing or even washing your hands. You'll find that the bandage stays secure, clean and dry.

- **Keep track of your child** Even if you keep close tabs on your kids, buy a little peace of mind by loosely tying a helium balloon to your child's wrist on a weekend shopping trip.

- **Make a party invitation** Inflate a balloon (using a pump if possible – it's more hygienic). Pinch off the end, but don't tie a knot in it. Write the invitation details on the balloon with a permanent marker, making sure the ink is dry before you deflate it. Send one to each guest. When your guests receive it, they'll have to blow it up to see what it says.

- **Transport cut flowers** Don't use awkward, water-filled plastic bags when travelling with freshly cut flowers. Fill a balloon with about 100ml water and slip it over the cut ends of your flowers. Wrap a rubber band several times around the mouth of the balloon to keep it from slipping off.

- **Use as a hat mould** To keep the shape in a freshly washed knitted cap or cloth hat, fit it over a balloon, inflated to the size of the owner's head while it dries. Use a piece of masking tape to keep the balloon attached to a worktop or railing.

- **Keep a punch bowl cool** To keep a party punch bowl cold and well filled, pour juice into several balloons using a funnel and place them in the freezer. When you are ready, peel the latex off the ice and periodically drop a couple of the ice spheres into the punch bowl.

- **Mark a campsite** Take several helium-filled balloons to attach to your tent on your next camping holiday. They'll make it easier for your party to locate your tent or to spot it from a distance.

Balloons

- **Make an ice pack** To make a flexible ice pack that you can use for everything from icing a sore back to keeping food cold in a cooler, fill a large, durable balloon with as much water as you need and put it in the freezer. You can even mould it into specific shapes – for example, put it under something flat if you want a flat ice pack for your back.

- **Repel unwanted garden visitors** Old deflated shiny metallic balloons from past birthday parties can be put to work in the garden. Cut them into vertical strips and hang them from poles around the vegetables and on fruit trees to scare off invading birds, rabbits and squirrels.

(SCIENCE FAIR)
Inflate a balloon the fun way

Use the gas produced by mixing bicarbonate of soda and vinegar to blow up a balloon. First, pour 100ml vinegar into the bottom of a narrow-neck bottle or jar. Then insert a funnel into the mouth of an average-sized balloon, and fill it with 5 tablespoons bicarbonate of soda. Carefully stretch the mouth of the balloon over the opening of the bottle, then gently lift it up so that the bicarbonate of soda empties into the vinegar at the bottom of the bottle. The fizzing and foaming you see is actually a chemical reaction between the two ingredients. This reaction results in the release of carbon dioxide gas – which will soon inflate the balloon.

Bananas

- **Polish silverware and leather** Using a banana skin is actually an excellent way to put the shine back into both silverware and leather. First, remove any of the leftover stringy material from the inside of the skin, then just start rubbing the inside of the peel on the leather or silver. When you've finished, buff with a paper towel or soft cloth.

- **Brighten up houseplants** Wipe down each leaf with the inside of a banana skin. It will quickly remove all the grime on the leaves' surface.

- **Make a face mask** Use a banana as a natural moisturising face mask to leave your skin looking and feeling softer. Mash a medium-sized ripe banana into a smooth paste, then gently apply it to your face and neck. Leave it to set for 10-20 minutes, then rinse it off with cold water. Another popular mask recipe calls for 50g plain yoghurt, 2 tablespoons honey and a medium-sized, mashed banana. Simply mix and apply.

- **Make a frozen banana lolly** Peel and cut four ripe bananas in half across the middle. Stick a wooden ice-lolly stick into the flat end of each piece. Place them on a piece of greaseproof paper and put it in the freezer. Serve a few hours later. For a more indulgent treat, dip the frozen bananas in 200g melted butterscotch or chocolate (you could also add chopped nuts or shredded coconut), then re-freeze.

- **Tenderise a roast** Banana leaves are commonly used in many Asian countries to wrap meat while it is cooking to make it more tender. Some people also believe that the banana itself has this ability. Next time you are worried that a roast may turn out a bit tough, try softening it up by adding a ripe, peeled banana to the roasting pan as it cooks.

Bananas

- **Deter aphids** If aphids are attacking garden plants, they will soon disappear if you bury dried or cut banana skins a few centimetres deep around the base of the aphid-prone plants. Don't use whole skins or the bananas themselves; squirrels, rats, mice and other animals will dig them up as a tasty treat.

- **Use as fertiliser or mulch** Bananas and their skins are rich in potassium – an important nutrient for both people and plants. Dry out banana skins in the winter and, in early spring, grind them in a food processor or blender to make a mulch. It can be spread around or near new plants and seedlings to give them a healthy start. Many cultivars of roses and other plants, like staghorn ferns, also benefit from the nutrients in banana skins; just cut up them up and use them around established plants.

- **Add to compost pile** With their high content of potassium and phosphorus, whole bananas and their skins are extremely useful additions to any compost pile. The fruit will break down especially fast in hot temperatures. But don't forget to remove any glued-on tags from the skins and be sure to bury the bananas deep within the compost – otherwise they may simply turn out to be a welcome meal for a foraging four-legged visitor.

- **Attract butterflies and birds** Bring more butterflies and bird species to the garden by putting out overripe bananas (and other fruits such as mangoes, oranges and papayas) on a raised platform. Punch a few holes in the bananas to make the fruit more accessible to the butterflies. The fruit is also likely to attract more bees and wasps as well, so make sure that the platform is well above head level and not centrally located. You may want to remove the remaining food before sunset, to discourage visits from nocturnal scavengers.

Basters

- **Transfer paints and solvents** Avoid spills by making a baster a permanent addition to a workshop for transferring paints, solvents, varnishes and other liquid chemicals from a large container into a smaller one.

- **Cure a musty-smelling air conditioner** A musty odour blowing out of an air conditioner is probably caused by a clogged drain hole. Unscrew the front of the unit and find the drain hole – it is usually under the barrier between the evaporator and compressor, or underneath the evaporator. Use a bent wire hanger to clear away any obstacles in the hole or use a baster to flush it clean. Use the baster to remove any water that may be pooling up at the bottom of the unit to gain access to the drain.

- **Fix a leaky refrigerator** A blocked drain tube is the most likely cause of water leaking inside a fridge. This plastic tube runs from a drain hole in the back of the freezer compartment along the back of the fridge and drains into an evaporation pan underneath. Try forcing hot water through the drain hole in the freezer compartment with a baster. If you can't get to the drain hole, try disconnecting the tube on the back to blow water through it. After clearing the tube, pour a teaspoon of bleach into the drain hole to prevent a re-occurrence of algae spores, the probable cause of the blockage.

TAKE CARE

Never use your kitchen baster for tasks such as cleaning out a fish tank or spreading or transferring chemicals. Get a number of basters to keep around the house specifically for non-cooking chores. Label each one with a piece of masking tape to make sure you always use the same baster for the same task.

Bath oil

- **Remove glue from labels or plasters** Get rid of sticky adhesive marks from plasters, price tags and labels by rubbing them away with a bit of bath oil on a cotton-wool ball. It works brilliantly on glass, metal and most plastics.

- **Use as a hot-oil treatment** Heat 100ml bath oil mixed with 100ml water on the High setting in the microwave for 30 seconds. Place the solution in a deep bowl and soak your fingers or toes in it for 10-15 minutes to soften cuticles or hard skin on your feet. After drying, use a pumice stone to smooth callouses or a file to push down cuticles. Finish by rubbing in hand cream until fully absorbed.

- **Loosen chewing gum from hair and carpeting** If chewing gum gets into hair or into the carpet, rub a liberal amount of bath oil into the gum. It should loosen it up enough to comb out. On a carpet, test the oil on an inconspicuous area before applying.

- **Remove scuff marks** It is easy to remove scuff marks from patent-leather shoes or handbags. Apply a bit of bath oil to a clean, soft cloth. Gently rub in the oil, then polish with a dry towel.

- **Clean grease or oil from skin** Before you use a heavy-duty grease remover, try this. Rub a few squirts of bath oil onto your hands, then wash them in warm, soapy water. It works and it's a lot easier on the skin than harsh chemicals.

- **Slide together pipe joints** If you can't find any all-purpose lubricating oil or WD-40 when you're trying to join pipes together, try bath oil instead – a few drops should provide sufficient lubrication to fit your pipe joints together with ease.

Beans (dried)

- **Treat sore muscles** If a bad back or tennis elbow is acting up, a hot beanbag may be the cure. Place a couple of handfuls of dried beans in a cloth shoe bag, an old sock or a folded towel (tie the ends tightly) and microwave it on High for between 30 seconds and 1 minute. Let it cool for a minute or two, then apply it to your aching muscles.

- **Make a beanbag** Pour 200-300g dried beans into an old sock, shaking them down to the toe section. Tie a loose knot and tighten it up as you work it down against the beans. Then cut off the remaining material about 2.5cm above the knot. You now have a beanbag for throwing, juggling. Or you can use it as a squeeze bag for exercising the muscles in your hands.

- **Practise your percussion** Make a homemade percussion shaker or maraca. Add 100g dried beans to a small plastic jar, or a drink or juice can – even an empty coconut shell. Cover any openings with adhesive or gaffer tape. You can use the rattle at sporting events or as a dog-training tool (try giving it a couple of shakes when the dog misbehaves).

- **Decorate a jack-o'-lantern** Increase the fright potential of a Halloween jack-o'-lantern by gluing on various dried beans for the eyes and teeth.

- **Use as playing pieces** The racing car, Scottie dog and all their companions on the Monopoly board go missing all too frequently. But dried beans work well as replacement pieces for everything from Cluedo to Snakes and Ladders to Bingo.

Beer

- **Use as setting lotion** Mix 3 tablespoons of flat beer in 100ml warm water. Shampoo your hair and rub in the solution. Let it set for a few minutes, then rinse it off.

- **Soften up tough meat** Tenderise a tough, inexpensive cut of stewing meat by marinating it in beer overnight in the fridge. If you have less time, soak it in a can of beer for about an hour before cooking or put the beer in a slow cooker with the meat.

- **Polish gold jewellery** Get the shine back in solid gold jewellery (without any gemstones) by pouring a little lager onto a soft cloth and rubbing it on gently. Polish off with a dry cloth.

- **Clean wood furniture** Use flat beer to clean wooden furniture. Just wipe it on with a soft cloth and then off with another dry cloth.

- **Make a trap for slugs and snails** Slugs and snails find beer irresistible. If you're having problems with them, bury a container, such as a clean, empty juice container cut lengthways in half, where you've seen the pests, and pour in about half a can of warm beer. Leave it overnight to make your own irresistible 'slug pub'.

- **Remove coffee or tea stains from rugs** Pour a little beer on top of the stain. Rub it in lightly and the stain should disappear. You may have to repeat the process a couple of times.

did you **KNOW?**

Beer brewing, along with bread making, is probably the most ancient form of manufacturing. The Chinese brewed beer some 5,000 years ago and the ancient Babylonians perfected the art – a tablet in New York's Metropolitan Museum records the production of several different types of beer. Beer brewing in Australia began around 1794, encouraged by a government anxious to prevent the excessive consumption of rum.

Bicarbonate of soda...

...in the kitchen

- **Tenderise meat** To soften a tough cut of meat, rub it down with bicarbonate of soda. Let it sit in the refrigerator for 3-5 hours and rinse it thoroughly before cooking.

- **Soak out fish smells** Get rid of fishy smells by soaking raw fish for about an hour in the fridge in 2 tablespoons bicarbonate of soda in a litre of water. Rinse well and pat dry before cooking.

- **Rid your hands of food odours** Remove smells, such as garlic or fish, from your hands by wetting them and vigorously rubbing with about 2 teaspoons bicarbonate of soda. The smell should wash off with the powder.

- **Reduce acids in tomato-based sauces or coffee** Sprinkle in a pinch of bicarbonate of soda while cooking (or, for coffee, before brewing). Bicarbonate of soda can also counteract the taste of vinegar if you add too much. But don't overdo the bicarb or the combination will start foaming.

B

...in the kitchen

- **Bake better beans** Add a pinch of bicarbonate of soda to baked beans as they are cooking to reduce their gassy properties.

- **Use as yeast substitute** Use powdered vitamin C (or citric acid) and bicarbonate of soda instead of yeast. Just mix in equal parts in the same quantity as the yeast required. As a bonus, the dough does not need to rise before baking.

- **Clean baby bottles and accessories** Avoid expensive solutions and soak baby bottles, teats and brushes overnight in hot water and 200g bicarbonate of soda. Rinse thoroughly and dry before using. Alternatively, boil bottles in a pan of water with 3 tablespoons bicarbonate of soda for 3 minutes.

- **Clean a chopping board** Keep a wooden or plastic cutting board clean by scrubbing it with a paste made from 1 tablespoon each of bicarbonate of soda, salt and water. Rinse thoroughly.

- **Clear a blocked drain** Pour in 200g bicarbonate of soda followed by 200ml hot vinegar (heat in the microwave for 1 minute). Give it several minutes to work, then add 1 litre boiling water. Repeat if necessary. If you know the drain is blocked with grease, use 100g each of bicarbonate of soda and salt followed by 200ml boiling water. Let the mixture work overnight; then rinse with hot tap water in the morning.

- **Boost the potency of washing-up liquid** Add 2 tablespoons bicarbonate of soda to your usual amount of washing-up liquid and watch it cut through grease.

- **Make your own dishwasher detergent** If you have run out of dishwasher detergent or tablets, make your own by mixing 2 tablespoons bicarbonate of soda with 2 tablespoons borax. You may be so pleased with the results that you will switch for good.

- **Deodorise the dishwasher** Sprinkle 100g bicarbonate of soda on the bottom of the machine between wash loads. To

freshen it fully, pour in 200g bicarbonate of soda and run the empty machine through a complete rinse cycle.

- **Remove coffee and tea stains from china** Dip a moist cloth in bicarbonate of soda to form a stiff paste and gently rub the cups and saucers. Rinse clean and dry well.

- **Clean a microwave** To clean splashes inside a microwave, put a solution of 2 tablespoons bicarbonate of soda in 200ml water in a microwave-safe container and cook on High for 2-3 minutes. Remove the container, then wipe down the microwave's moist interior with a damp paper towel.

- **Remove residue on the inside of a Thermos** Mix 50g bicarbonate of soda in 1 litre water and pour into the Thermos. If necessary, scrub with a bottle brush to loosen things up and let it soak overnight. Rinse clean before using.

- **Freshen up the fridge or kitchen bin** Empty the fridge or bin, then sprinkle bicarbonate of soda on a damp sponge and scrub inside, including, in the fridge, the shelves and compartments. Rinse with a clean, wet sponge or paper towel and let dry. To keep smelling fresh, put an opened box of powder inside the fridge after cleaning or sprinkle a little bicarbonate of soda into the bottom of the bin before inserting the bag.

TIP no baking powder on hand?

If you have run out of baking powder, you can usually substitute 2 parts bicarbonate of soda mixed with 1 part each cream of tartar and cornflour. To make the equivalent of 1 teaspoon baking powder, mix ½ teaspoon bicarbonate of soda with ¼ teaspoon cream of tartar and ¼ teaspoon cornflour. The cornflour slows the reaction between the acidic cream of tartar and the alkaline bicarbonate of soda so that, like commercial baking powder, it maintains its leavening power for longer.

...in the kitchen

- **Freshen a sour-smelling sponge or towel** Soak the kitchen sponge or dishcloth overnight in 2 tablespoons bicarbonate of soda and a couple of drops of anti-bacterial washing-up liquid dissolved in 450ml warm water. In the morning, squeeze it out and rinse with cold water. It should smell completely fresh.

- **Clean burned or scorched pots and pans** Simply fill the burned pan a quarter full with water, boil it and add 5 tablespoons bicarbonate of soda. Turn off the heat and let the powder settle for a few hours or overnight. The burned-on mess will virtually slide off.

- **Remove burned-on food from your iron cookware** Boil 1 litre water with 2 tablespoons bicarbonate of soda in the dirty pan for 5 minutes. Pour off most of the liquid, then lightly scrub with a plastic scrubbing pad. Rinse well, dry and season with a few drops of olive oil.

- **Clean nonstick cookware** Boil 200ml water mixed with 2 tablespoons bicarbonate of soda and 100ml vinegar in the dirty pan for 10 minutes. Then wash in hot, soapy water. Rinse well, let dry, then season with a bit of vegetable oil.

- **Remove stains and scratches on worktops** If a kitchen worktop is covered with stains or small knife cuts, use a paste of 2 parts bicarbonate of soda to 1 part water to 'rub out' most of them. For stubborn stains, add a drop of chlorine bleach to the paste. Immediately wash the area with hot, soapy water to prevent the bleach from causing fading.

- **Get rid of grease stains on the hob or splashback** Wet the stains with a little water and cover with a little bicarbonate of soda. Rub off with a damp sponge or towel.

- **Shine up a stainless-steel sink and chrome trim**
  Sprinkle the sink with bicarbonate of soda. Then rub it down with a moist cloth, moving in the direction of the grain. To polish dull chrome trim on the kettle and toaster, pour a little bicarbonate of soda onto a damp sponge and rub over the chrome. Let it dry for an hour or so, then wipe down with warm water and dry with a clean cloth.

- **Clean an automatic coffee maker** Every two weeks or so, brew a pot of 1 litre water mixed with 50g bicarbonate of soda, followed by a pan of clean water. Use an old toothbrush to scrub the plastic basket with a paste of 2 tablespoons bicarbonate of soda and 1 tablespoon water. Rinse thoroughly with cold water when you have finished. Do this and you will never drink bitter or weak coffee again.

- **Care for metal coffee pots and teapots** Remove mineral deposits by filling them with a solution of 200ml vinegar and 4 tablespoons bicarbonate of soda. Bring the mixture to a boil, then simmer for 5 minutes. Alternatively, boil 1 litre water with 2 tablespoons bicarbonate of soda and the juice of half a lemon. Rinse with cold water when finished. To remove exterior stains, wash pots with a plastic scouring pad in a solution of 50g bicarbonate of soda in 1 litre warm water. Follow with a cold-water rinse.

did you **KNOW?**

Bicarbonate of soda is the main ingredient in many commercial fire extinguishers. You can use it straight out of the box to extinguish small fires throughout your home.

Keep a box near the cooker and barbecue so you can throw on a few handfuls to quell a flare-up. In the case of a grease fire, first turn off the heat, if possible, and try to cover the fire with a pan lid. Be careful not to let the hot grease splatter you.

Keep a box in the garage and inside your car to quickly extinguish mechanical or car-interior fires. Bicarbonate of soda will also snuff out electrical fires and flames on clothing, wood, upholstery and carpeting.

...around the house

- **Wash wallpaper** Brighten up your wallpaper by wiping with a sponge moistened in a solution of 2 tablespoons bicarbonate of soda in 1 litre water. To remove grease stains, make a paste of 1 tablespoon bicarbonate of soda and 1 teaspoon water. Rub it on the stain, leave it to set for 5-10 minutes, then rub off with a damp sponge.

- **Deodorise rugs, carpets and furniture** Remove odours, such as vomit or cigarette smoke, from carpets, rugs and furniture by lightly sprinkling them with bicarbonate of soda. Let it settle in and sit for 15 minutes to a couple of hours or so, then vacuum off.

- **Freshen musty drawers and cupboards** Put bicarbonate of soda sachets to work on persistent musty odours. Fill the toe of a clean sock with 3-4 tablespoons powder, tie a knot about 2cm above the bulge and either hang it up or place it in an unobtrusive corner. Use a few sachets in large spaces like wardrobes and attic storage areas. Replace them every other month if needed. This treatment will also get rid of the strong smell of mothballs.

(KIDS' STUFF)
Making watercolour paints

Make watercolour paints for your children using ingredients from the kitchen. (1) In a small bowl, combine 3 tablespoons each of bicarbonate of soda, cornflour and vinegar with 1½ teaspoons liquid glucose (available from a pharmacist). (2) Wait for the fizzing to subside, then separate the mixture into several small containers or jar lids. (3) Add eight drops of food colouring to each batch and mix well. Put a different colour in each batch or combine colours to make new shades. Children can either use the paints right away, or wait for them to harden, in which case, they'll need to use a wet brush before painting.

- **Clean up baby accidents** Keep some bicarbonate of soda in your nappy bag and if a child vomits, brush off any solid matter, moisten a washcloth, dip it in a bit of bicarbonate of soda and dab the spot. The odour (and the potential stain) will soon be gone.

- **Remove wine and grease stains from carpet** Blot up as much of the liquid as possible with a paper towel, then sprinkle a liberal amount of bicarbonate of soda over the spot. Leave it to absorb the stain for at least an hour, then vacuum up the remaining powder.

- **Polish silver and gold jewellery** To remove built-up tarnish, make a thick paste with 50g bicarbonate of soda and 2 tablespoons water. Apply with a damp sponge and gently rub, rinse and buff dry. To polish gold jewellery, cover with a light coating of bicarbonate of soda, pour some vinegar over it and then rinse clean.
    WARNING: do not use this technique with jewellery containing pearls or gemstones, as it could damage their finish and loosen the glue.

- **Remove yellow stains from piano keys** Mix a solution of 50g bicarbonate of soda in 1 litre warm water. Apply to each key with a damp cloth (place a thin piece of cardboard between the keys to avoid seepage). Wipe again with a cloth dampened with plain water and buff dry with a clean cloth. (You can also clean piano keys using lemon juice and salt.)

- **Remove stains from a brick fireplace surround** You may need to use a bit of elbow grease, but it is possible to clean smoke stains from fireplace bricks by washing them with a solution of 100g bicarbonate of soda added to 1 litre warm water.

- **Remove crayon marks from walls** Take a damp rag, dip it in some bicarbonate of soda and lightly rub the offending marks. They should come off with a minimal amount of effort.

...around the house

- **Remove white marks on wood surfaces** Make a paste of 1 tablespoon bicarbonate of soda with 1 teaspoon water to remove white marks caused by hot cups or sweating glasses. Gently rub the spot using a circular motion until it disappears. Use the minimum amount of water.

- **Give a shine to marble-topped furniture** Revitalise a marble top by washing it with a soft cloth dipped in a solution of 3 tablespoons bicarbonate of soda and 1 litre warm water. Let it stand for 15-30 minutes, rinse with plain water and wipe dry.

(KIDS' STUFF)
Invisible ink

Here's how to send a message or draw a picture with invisible ink. Mix 1 tablespoon each of bicarbonate of soda and water. Dip a toothpick or paintbrush in the mixture and write your message or draw a picture on a piece of white paper. Let the paper and the 'ink' dry completely. To reveal your message or picture, mix 6 drops food colouring with 1 tablespoon water. Dip a clean paintbrush into the solution and lightly paint over the paper.

...in the medicine cabinet

- **Fight nappy rash** Soothe nappy rash by adding a couple of tablespoons bicarbonate of soda to a lukewarm – not hot – bath. If the rash persists or worsens after several treatments, however, consult a doctor.

- **Control your dandruff** To get dandruff under control, wet your hair and rub a handful of bicarbonate of soda vigorously into your scalp. Rinse thoroughly and dry. Do this every time you normally wash your hair, but only use bicarbonate of soda, not shampoo. Your hair may feel somewhat dried out at first. But after a few weeks your scalp will start producing natural oils, leaving your hair softer and free of flakes.

- **Combat cradle cap** Cradle cap is a common and typically harmless condition in many infants. Make a paste of about 3 teaspoons bicarbonate of soda and 1 teaspoon water. Apply it to your baby's scalp about an hour before bedtime and rinse it off the following morning. Do not use with shampoo. You may need to apply it several nights running before the cradle cap recedes. (Note: you can also treat cradle cap using baby oil. See page 30.)

- **Treat minor burns** Quickly pour some bicarbonate of soda into a container of ice water. Soak a cloth and apply it to the burn. Keep applying the solution until the burn no longer feels hot. This treatment will also prevent many burns from blistering. (If you have no bicarb, keep the burn under cold running water for 10-20 minutes.)

- **Make a salve for bee stings** Take the pain from a bee sting – fast. Make a paste using 1 teaspoon bicarbonate of soda mixed with several drops of cool water and let it dry on the affected area.

    WARNING: many people have allergic reactions to bee stings. If you have difficulty breathing or notice a dramatic swelling, get medical attention at once.

- **Cool off sunburn and other skin irritations:**

    - To get quick relief from the pain of sunburn, soak a couple of gauze pads or large cotton balls in a solution made up of 4 tablespoons bicarbonate of soda mixed in 200ml water and apply it to the affected areas.

    - To ease a bad burn on your legs or torso – or to relieve the itching of chicken pox – take a lukewarm bath with 250-500g bicarbonate of soda added to the running water.

...in the medicine cabinet

● To ease razor burns, dab your skin with cotton wool soaked in a solution of 1 tablespoon bicarbonate of soda in 200ml water.

● To combat a case of athlete's foot, you can deploy wet or dry bicarbonate of soda. First, try dusting your feet (along with your socks and shoes) with dry bicarbonate of soda to dry out the infection. If that doesn't work, try making a paste of 1 teaspoon bicarbonate of soda and ½ teaspoon water and rubbing it between your toes. Let it dry and wash off after 15 minutes. Dry your feet thoroughly before putting on your shoes.

● To soothe heat rash – itchy red bumps, particularly on your neck, chest, armpits and groin, caused by sweat that can't evaporate when the pores become blocked – add a few tablespoons of bicarbonate of soda to a bath and have a long soak. You can also apply it directly to the rash to absorb sweat.

● To find temporary relief from itching inside a plaster cast, especially in the heat of summer, use a hair dryer – on the coolest setting – to blow a little bicarbonate of soda down the edges of the cast. Note: ask someone to help you, to avoid getting the powder in your eyes.

...in the bathroom

● **Remove mineral deposits from a showerhead**
Cover the head with a heavy-duty sandwich-size bag filled with 50g bicarbonate of soda and 200ml vinegar. Loosely fasten the bag with adhesive tape or a large twist tie (it needs to be loose so some of the resultant gas can escape). Leave for about an hour. Then remove the bag and turn on your shower to wash off any remaining debris. Not only will the deposits disappear, but the showerhead will be bright and shiny again.

- **Absorb bathroom odours** Keep the bathroom smelling fresh by placing a dish filled with 100g bicarbonate of soda either on top of the toilet cistern or on the floor behind the toilet. You can make up your own bathroom freshener by filling small dishes with equal parts of bicarbonate of soda and your favourite bath salts.

- **Make the toilet bowl sparkle** Pour 250g bicarbonate of soda into the cistern once a month. Leave it overnight, then give it a few flushes. This will clean the cistern and the bowl. You can also pour several tablespoons of bicarbonate of soda directly onto stains in the bowl and scrub well. Wait a few minutes, then flush.

- **Use as a gargle or mouthwash** Gargle with 1 teaspoon bicarbonate of soda in half a glass water. The bicarbonate of soda will neutralise any odours on contact. Used as a mouthwash, bicarbonate of soda will also relieve pain from mouth ulcers.

- **Scrub teeth and clean dentures** Dip your wet toothbrush into bicarbonate of soda (a natural alternative to commercial toothpaste) and brush and rinse as usual. To clean retainers, gum shields and dentures, use a solution of 1 tablespoon bicarbonate of soda in 200ml warm water. Soak for 30 minutes. Rinse well.

- **Clean and freshen toothbrushes** Make a solution of 50g bicarbonate of soda and 50ml water. Soak the brushes overnight every week or two. Rinse thoroughly before use.

- **Remove product build-up from hair** Add 1 tablespoon bicarbonate of soda to your hair while shampooing. Do this at least once a week. Note: it may lighten the colour of your hair.

- **Clean combs and brushes** Make a solution of 600ml warm water and 2 teaspoons bicarbonate of soda. Swirl combs and brushes to loosen debris between the teeth, then let them soak for about half an hour. Rinse well and dry before using.

- **Use as an anti-perspirant** For an effective, all-natural deodorant, apply about a teaspoon of bicarbonate of soda with a powder puff under each arm. You should stay fresh and dry all day.

B

...in the bathroom

- **Soothe tired, smelly feet** Make a footbath of 4 tablespoons bicarbonate of soda in 1 litre warm water. The bicarbonate of soda will relax your feet and remove the sweat and lint that gather between your toes. Regular bicarb footbaths can also be an effective treatment for persistent foot odour.

- **Deodorise shoes and trainers** Liberally sprinkle bicarbonate of soda in the shoe and leave overnight. Discard the powder in the morning. (Note: be careful using bicarbonate of soda on leather shoes, as repeated applications can dry them out.)

- **Make reusable 'odour eaters'** Fill the toes of old socks with 2 tablespoons bicarbonate of soda. Knot them and stuff the socks into each shoe at night. Remove in the morning.

...in the laundry

- **Remove mothball smell from clothes** If your clothes have come out of storage reeking of mothballs, add 100g bicarbonate of soda during the washing machine's rinse cycle to get rid of the smell.

- **Boost liquid detergent and bleach** It may sound like a cliché, but adding 100g bicarbonate of soda to your usual amount of liquid detergent really will give you 'whiter whites' and brighter colours. The bicarbonate of soda also softens the water, so you can use less detergent. Adding 50g bicarbonate of soda to a white cotton wash also increases the potency of the bleach, so you need only half the usual amount.

- **Get chemicals out of baby clothing** Avoid harsh detergents and wash your baby's new clothes with some mild soap and 100g bicarbonate of soda to remove any chemicals.

- **Rub out perspiration and other stains** Pre-treat clothes with a paste made from 4 tablespoons bicarbonate of soda and 50ml warm water. For really bad perspiration stains, let the paste dry for about 2 hours before washing. Rub out tar stains by applying the paste and washing in plain bicarbonate of soda. For grimy collar stains, rub in the paste and add a bit of vinegar as you are putting the shirt in the wash.

- **Wash mildewed shower curtains** Clean a mildewed plastic shower curtain in the washing machine with two bath towels on a low temperature setting. Add 100g bicarbonate of soda to the detergent during the wash cycle and 100ml vinegar during the rinse cycle. Let it drip-dry; never put it in a tumble dryer.

...for the DIY-er

- **Use as a de-icer** Salt and commercial de-icer formulations can stain and eat away at concrete paths and patios. For an equally effective, but completely harmless way to melt ice on steps and paths during cold winter months, try sprinkling them with generous amounts of bicarbonate of soda. You can also add a bit of sand for better traction.

- **Give decking the weathered look** Make a solution of 400g bicarbonate of soda mixed in 4 litres water. Use a stiff brush to work the solution into the wood, then rinse with cool water.

- **Tighten cane chair seats** Cane and wicker seats can sag with age, but it is possible to tighten them up again easily. Just soak two cloths in a solution of 100g bicarbonate of soda in 1 litre hot water. Saturate the top surface of the caning with one cloth, while pushing the second up against the bottom of the caning to saturate the underside. Use a clean, dry cloth to soak up the excess moisture, then put the chair in the sun to dry.

...for the DIY-er

- **Clean car-battery terminals** Scrub the terminals clean using an old toothbrush and a mixture of 3 tablespoons bicarbonate of soda and 1 tablespoon warm water. Wipe off with a wet towel and dry with another towel. Once the terminals have fully dried, apply a little petroleum jelly around each terminal to deter future corrosive build-up.

- **Remove tar from a car** Make a soft paste of 3 parts bicarbonate of soda to 1 part water and apply to the tar spots with a damp cloth. Let it dry for 5 minutes, then rinse clean.

- **Keep a humidifier odour-free** Eliminate the musty smell from a humidifier by adding 2 tablespoons bicarbonate of soda to the water each time you change it. Note: check first with the owner's manual or consult the manufacturer of the unit before trying this.

...for your pet

- **Make a deodorising dog shampoo** If your dog is getting a bit dirty and smelly, rub a few handfuls of bicarbonate of soda into his coat and give it a thorough brushing. It will remove the smell and leave his coat shiny and clean.

TIP how long does bicarb last?

To test if your bicarbonate of soda is still good, just pour out a small amount – a little less than a teaspoon – and add a few drops of vinegar or fresh lemon juice. If it doesn't fizz, it is time to replace it. A sealed box of bicarbonate of soda has an average shelf life of 18 months, while an opened box lasts six months.

- **Wash inside your pet's ears** If your pet is constantly scratching its ears, it could indicate an irritation or ear mites. Use a cotton wool ball dipped in a solution of 1 teaspoon bicarbonate of soda in 1 cup warm water to gently wash the inside of the ears to ease the itch (and wipe out any mites).

- **Keep insects away from pets' dishes** Place a border of bicarbonate of soda around your pet's food bowls to keep away insects. (It won't harm your pet if it laps up a little, although it won't like the bitter taste.)

- **Deodorise a cat-litter tray** Don't waste money on expensive deodorised cat litter, just put a thin layer of bicarbonate of soda under ordinary litter to absorb the odour. Or mix bicarbonate of soda with the litter as you are changing it.

...in the garden

- **Clean plastic garden furniture** Most commercial cleaners are too abrasive to be used on plastic garden furniture. Clean the furniture with a wet sponge dipped in bicarbonate of soda and avoid scratches. Wipe and rinse well.

- **Keep weeds out of paving cracks** Simply sprinkle handfuls of bicarbonate of soda onto the concrete and sweep it into the cracks. The added sodium will make it much less hospitable to dandelions and their friends.

- **Use as plant food** Give flowering, alkaline-loving plants, such as clematis, delphiniums and dianthus, an occasional shower in a mild solution of 1 tablespoon bicarbonate of soda in 2 litres water. They'll show their appreciation with fuller, healthier blooms.

Bleach

- **Remove mould and mildew** Bleach and ammonia are useful for removing mould and mildew both inside and outside the home. However, the two should never be used together. Bleach is especially suited for the following chores:

  - Wash mildew out of washable fabrics. Wet the mildewed area and rub in some powdered detergent. Wash the garment in the hottest water setting permitted by the manufacturer, using 100ml chlorine bleach. If the garment can't be washed in hot water and bleach, soak it in a solution of 50ml oxygen bleach (labelled 'all fabric') in 4 litres warm water for 30 minutes before washing in the machine.

  - Remove mould and mildew from tiling grout. Mix equal parts of chlorine bleach and water in a spray bottle and spray it over the grout. Let it sit for 15 minutes, then scrub with a stiff brush and rinse off. You can also do this just to make your grout look whiter.

  - Rid a rubber shower mat of mildew. Soak in a solution of 25ml chlorine bleach in 4 litres of water for 3-4 hours. Rinse well.

  - Get mildew and other stains off unpainted cement, patio stones or stucco. Mix a solution of 200ml chlorine bleach in 8 litres water. Scrub vigorously with a stiff brush and rinse. If any stains still remain, scrub again using 100g washing soda (this is sodium carbonate, not bicarbonate of soda) dissolved in 8 litres warm water.

  - Remove mildew from painted surfaces. Add 50ml chlorine bleach to 400ml water. Brush on mildewed areas. Let the solution set for 15 minutes, then rinse. Repeat as necessary.

- **Sterilise second-hand toys** Soak used, waterproof toys for 5-10 minutes in a solution of 150ml bleach, a few drops of antibacterial washing-up liquid and 4 litres warm water. Rinse well, then air-dry, preferably in sunlight.

- **Shine white porcelain** Place several paper towels over the porcelain item (or across the bottom of the porcelain sink) and carefully saturate them with undiluted bleach. Do this in a well-ventilated area on a work surface protected by heavy plastic. Let it soak for 15 minutes to half an hour, then rinse and wipe dry with a clean towel. Note: do not try this with antiques; you can diminish their value or cause damage. And never use bleach on coloured porcelain, because the colour will fade.

- **Make a household disinfectant spray** To make a good, all-purpose disinfectant, mix 1 tablespoon bleach in 4 litres hot water. Then fill a clean, empty spray bottle and use it (sprayed onto a paper towel) to clean worktops, tablecloths, garden furniture – basically, wherever it's needed.

    WARNING: do not to use it in the presence of ammonia or other household cleaners.

- **Increase cut flowers' longevity** Freshly cut flowers will stay fresh longer if you add ¼ teaspoon bleach per litre of water to the vase. Another popular recipe calls for 3 drops bleach and 1 teaspoon sugar in a litre of water. This will also keep the water from getting cloudy and inhibit the growth of bacteria.

- **Clean butchers' blocks, chopping boards and wooden worktops** Scrub with a brush dipped in a solution of 1 teaspoon bleach diluted in 2 litres water. Scrub in small circles and do not saturate the wood. Wipe

TAKE CARE

Never mix bleach with ammonia, lye, rust removers, oven or toilet-bowl cleaners or vinegar. Any combination can produce toxic chlorine gas fumes, which can be deadly. Some people are even sensitive to the fumes of undiluted bleach itself. Always make sure you have adequate ventilation in your work area before you starting pouring.

Bleach

with a damp paper towel, then immediately buff dry with a clean cloth. Note: never use furniture polish or any household cleaner to clean a butcher's block, chopping board or worktop.

- **Brighten up glassware** For sparkling glasses and dishes, add a teaspoon of bleach to your soapy dishwater as you're washing glassware. Be sure to rinse well and dry with a soft towel.

- **Sterilise garden tools** If you have used a pair of secateurs to cut a diseased stalk off a rose bush, avoid spreading the disease. Washing them with 100ml bleach in a litre of water will sterilise a tool for its next use. Let the tool air-dry in the sun, then rub on a few drops of oil to prevent rust.

- **Clean plastic outdoor furniture** Wash each item with mild detergent mixed with 100ml bleach in 4 litres water. Rinse it clean, then air-dry.

- **Kill weeds in paths and patios** Pour undiluted bleach into cracks and crevices. After a day or two, simply pull them out and the bleach will stop them from coming back. Be careful not to get bleach on grass or plants bordering the paths.

- **Get rid of moss and algae** To remove slippery moss and algae from brick, concrete or stone paths, scrub them with a solution of 150ml bleach in 4 litres water.

TAKE CARE

Some people prefer not to use bleach when cleaning their toilets, fearing that lingering ammonia from urine – especially in households with young children – could result in toxic fumes. Unless you are sure there is no such problem, you may want to stick with ammonia for this job.

Borax

- **Clean windows and mirrors** When you want to get windows and mirrors spotless and streak-free, wash them with a clean sponge dipped in 2 tablespoons borax dissolved in 600ml water.

- **Rub out heavy sink stains** Get rid of stubborn stains – even rust – on a stainless steel or porcelain sink. Make a paste with 200g borax and 50ml lemon juice. Put some of the paste on a cloth or sponge and rub it into the stain, then rinse with running warm water. The stain should wash away with the paste.

- **Sterilise a waste disposal unit** A waste disposal is a great convenience but can also be a breeding ground for mould and bacteria. To maintain a more hygienic unit, pour 3 tablespoons borax down the drain every couple of weeks and let it sit for an hour. Then turn on the disposal unit and flush it with hot water from the tap.

- **Clean your toilet** Here is a good way to disinfect a toilet bowl and leave it glistening without having to worry about dangerous or unpleasant fumes. Use a stiff brush to scrub it with a solution of 100g borax in 4 litres water.

(KIDS' STUFF)
Making slime

Help children brew up some gooey, stretchy 'slime'. Mix 200ml water, 200ml white glue and 10 drops food colouring in a medium bowl. In a larger bowl, dissolve 4 teaspoons borax in 250ml water. Slowly pour the contents of the first bowl into the second. Use a wooden spoon to roll the glue-based solution around in the borax solution 4 or 5 times. Lift out the glue mixture and knead for 2-3 minutes. Store in an airtight container or a self-sealing plastic storage bag.

WARNING: the mixture is not edible and children should avoid touching their eyes after handling it.

Borax

- **Clear a blocked drain** Before you use a caustic drain cleaner to clear a blocked kitchen or bathroom drain, try this much gentler approach. Use a funnel to insert 100g borax into the drain, then slowly pour in 400ml boiling water. Let the mixture set for 15 minutes, then flush with hot water. Repeat for stubborn clogs.

- **Eliminate urine odour on mattresses** If your child has an accident in bed, here's how to get rid of any lingering smell. Dampen the area, then rub in some borax. Let it dry, then vacuum up the powder.

- **Remove mildew from fabric** To remove mildew from upholstery and other fabrics, soak a sponge in a solution of 100g borax dissolved in 400ml hot water and rub it into the affected areas. Let it soak for several hours until the stain disappears, then rinse well. To remove mildew from clothing, soak it in a solution of 400ml borax in 2 litres water.

- **Get out rug stains** Remove stubborn stains from rugs and carpets. Thoroughly dampen the area, then rub in some borax. Let the area dry, then vacuum or blot it with a solution of equal parts vinegar and soapy water and let dry. Repeat if necessary. Don't forget to test the procedure first on an inconspicuous corner of the rug or on a carpet offcut before applying it to the stain.

- **Make your own dried flowers** Give homemade dried flowers a professional look. Mix 200g borax with 400g cornmeal. Place a 2cm coating of the mixture in the bottom of an airtight container, such as a large flat plastic food-storage container. Cut the stems off the flowers you want to dry, then lay them on top of the powder and lightly sprinkle more of the mixture on top of the flowers (be careful not to bend or crush the petals or other flower parts). Cover the container and leave it alone for 7-10 days. Then remove the flowers and brush off any excess powder with a soft brush.

- **Control smothering creepers** Is your garden being overrun by an invasive perennial weed such as bindweed? You may be able to conquer it with an application of borax. First, dissolve 230-280g borax in 120ml warm water. Then pour the solution into 10 litres warm water – this is enough to cover 90 square metres. Apply this treatment only once every two years. If you still have problems, consider switching to a standard herbicide. (See Take Care warning below about using borax in the garden.)

- **Keep away weeds and ants** Get rid of weeds that grow in the cracks of the concrete outside your house by sprinkling borax into all the crevices where you've seen weeds growing in the past. It will kill them off before they have a chance to take root. When applied around the foundations of your home, it will also keep ants and other insect intruders from entering your house. But be very careful when applying borax – it is toxic to plants. (See Take Care warning below.)

TAKE CARE

Borax, like its close relative, boric acid, has relatively low toxicity levels and is considered safe for general household use, but the powder can be harmful if ingested in sufficient quantities by young children or pets. Store it safely out of their reach.

Borox is toxic to plants, however. In the garden, be very careful when applying borax onto or near soil. It doesn't take much to leach into the ground to kill off nearby plants and prevent future growth.

Bread

- **Remove the scorched taste from rice** Place a slice of white bread on top of burned rice while it is still hot. Replace the pan lid and wait several minutes. When you remove the bread, the burned taste should be gone.

- **Soften up hard marshmallows** Place a couple of slices of fresh bread in the bag with the marshmallows and seal it shut (you may want to use a self-sealing plastic bag). Leave for a couple of days. When you reopen the bag, your marshmallows should be soft and taste fresh.

- **Soak up grease and stop flare-ups** One of the best ways to prevent a grease flare-up when grilling meat is to place a couple of slices of white bread in the drip pan to absorb the grease. It will also cut down on the amount of smoke that is produced.

- **Clean walls and wallpaper** You can remove most dirty or greasy fingerprints from painted walls by rubbing the area with a slice of white bread. Bread does a good job cleaning non-washable wallpaper as well. First cut off the crusts to minimise the chance of scratching the paper.

- **Pick up glass fragments** Picking up the large pieces of a broken glass or dish is usually easy enough, but gathering tiny slivers can be difficult and dangerous. The easiest way to make sure you don't miss any is to press a slice of bread over the area. Just be careful not to prick yourself when you throw the bread into the bin.

- **Dust oil paintings** You shouldn't try this with an original Renoir, or with any museum-quality painting, but you can clean off the everyday dust and grime that collects on the surface of an oil painting by gently rubbing over the surface with a piece of white bread.

Bubble wrap

- **Prevent condensation in the toilet cistern** If a toilet cistern 'sweats' in warm, humid weather, bubble wrap can help to prevent it. Lining the inside of the cistern with bubble wrap will keep the outside from getting cold and causing condensation when it comes in contact with warm, moist air. To line the cistern, shut off the water supply and flush to drain the cistern. Then wipe the inside walls clean and dry. Use silicone sealant to glue appropriate-sized pieces of bubble wrap to the major flat surfaces.

- **Protect patio plants** Keep outdoor container plants warm and protected from winter frost damage. Wrap each container with bubble wrap and use gaffer tape or string to hold the wrap in place. Make sure the wrap extends a couple of inches above the lip of the container. The added insulation will keep the soil warm all winter.

- **Keep cola cold** Wrap soft-drink cans with bubble wrap to keep drinks refreshingly cold on hot summer days. Do the same for packages of frozen or chilled picnic foods. Wrapping ice cream just before you leave for a picnic will help to keep it firm en route.

did you **KNOW?**

Inventors Alfred Fielding and Marc Chavannes initially came up with the idea of making a 'bubble wallpaper' when they began developing their product in the late 1950s. It wasn't long before they realised that their invention had far greater potential as packaging material and in 1960 they raised $85,000 (£50,000) and founded the Sealed Air Corporation.

Today Sealed Air is a top US company with $3.5 billion (£2 billion) in annual revenues. The company produces bubble-wrap cushioning in a multitude of sizes, colours and properties, along with other protective packaging materials such as padded Jiffy bags.

Bubble wrap

- **Protect produce in the fridge** Line the crisper drawer with bubble wrap to prevent bruises to fruit and other produce. Cleaning the fridge will be easier, too – when the lining gets dirty, just throw it away and replace it with fresh bubble wrap.

- **Add insulation to windows** Cut window-sized pieces of wide bubble wrap and gaffer-tape them to the inside of the windows for added warmth and savings on fuel bills in winter. Lower the blinds or draw curtains to make it less noticeable.

- **Make a bedtime buffer in winter** Keep cold air from creeping into your bed on a chilly night by placing a large sheet of bubble wrap between the bedspread or duvet and the top sheet. You'll be surprised at how effective it is in keeping warm air in and cold air out.

- **Cushion a toolbox** Reduce wear and tear on good-quality tools and extend their lives by lining your toolbox with bubble wrap. Use gaffer tape to hold it in place.

- **Cushion a work surface** When repairing delicate glass or china objects, cover the work surface with bubble wrap to help to prevent breakages.

- **Sleep on air while camping** Get a better night's sleep on a camping trip. Take a 2m roll of wide bubble wrap to use as a mat under a sleeping bag. If you don't have a sleeping bag, just fold a 3.6m-long piece of wide bubble wrap in half, bubble side out and gaffer-tape the edges. Then slip in and enjoy a restful night in your makeshift padded sleeping bag.

- **Cushion hard seats and benches** Take some bubble wrap out to sports events to soften hard stadium seats or benches. Or stretch a length along a picnic bench for more comfortable outdoor dining.

Buckets

- **Make a lobster pot** If you don't have a large stock pot you can cook lobsters in an old metal bucket. Make sure to use pot holders and tongs when cooking and removing the lobster. Let the bucket cool before handling it again.

- **Build a camp washing machine** Here's a clever way to wash clothes when camping. Make a hole in the lid of a large plastic bucket and insert a new toilet plunger. Put in clothes and laundry detergent. Snap on the lid and move the plunger up and down as an agitator. You can safely clean even delicate garments using this method.

- **Camp shower** A bucket perforated with holes on the bottom makes an excellent campsite shower. Hang it securely from a sturdy branch. Get someone to fill it using another bucket and then take a quick shower as the water comes out. If you want to shower in warm water, paint the outside of another bucket matt black. Fill it with water and leave it out in the sun all day.

- **Paint high** Avoid messy paint spills when painting on a scaffold tower or ladder. Put your paint can and brush into a large bucket and use hooks to hang the bucket and the brush. If the bucket is large enough, you'll even have room for your paint scraper, putty knife, rags or other painting tools you may need.

TIP finding big buckets

Ten to twenty litre plastic buckets are versatile, virtually indestructible and offer a host of handy uses. And you can usually get them for free. Ask nicely and your local fast-food restaurant or supermarket deli counter may be willing to give you the buckets that beans or coleslaw came in. Or check with neighbours doing home improvements. Don't forget to get the lids as well. Wash a bucket with water and household bleach, then let it dry in the sun for a day or two. Put some bicarbonate of soda inside and it should remove any lingering odours.

Buckets

- **Paint low** Use the lids from big plastic buckets as trays for 4 litre cans of paint. The lids act as platforms for the paint cans and are also large enough to hold a paintbrush as well.

- **Make stilts** Use two heavy-duty buckets (minus their handles) and a pair of old shoes to make your own mini-stilts. Drive screws through the shoe soles and into wood blocks inside the buckets to keep them rigid. Or punch holes in the bucket bottoms and tie or strap down the shoes.

- **Keep extension cords tangle-free** Cut or drill a hole near the bottom of a bucket, making sure it is large enough for the extension cord's plug end to pass through. Then coil the rest of the cord into the bucket. The cord will come out when pulled and is easy to coil back in. Plug the ends of the cord together when it's not in use. You can use the centre space to carry tools to the site where you're working.

- **Make a Christmas-tree stand** Partly fill a bucket with sand or gravel and insert the base of the tree in it. Then fill it the rest of the way and pour water on the sand or gravel to help keep the tree from drying out.

(KIDS' STUFF)
Making tom-toms

Add the beat of bucket tom-toms to make improvised music at a children's party. Cut plastic buckets to different lengths to create a distinct tone for each drum or use a mix of various-sized plastic and galvanised buckets. For more musical accompaniment, make a broom-handle string bass using a bucket as the sound box.

Butter

- **Swallow pills with ease** If you have difficulty getting pills to go down, try rolling them in a small amount of butter or margarine first. They should slide down more easily.

- **Soothe aching feet** Revitalise your feet by massaging them with butter, wrap in a damp, hot towel and sit for 10 minutes.

- **Remove sap from skin** Just rub butter onto your hands and the sap will wash straight off with soap and water.

- **Treat dry, brittle hair** Massage a small chunk of butter into your dry hair, cover it with a shower cap for 30 minutes, then shampoo and rinse thoroughly.

- **Keep mould off cheese** Give semi-hard cheeses a light coat of butter to keep them fresh and free from mould. Each time you use the cheese, coat the cut edge with butter before you rewrap it and put it back in the fridge.

- **Get rid of a fishy smell on your hands** Rub butter on your hands, wash with warm water and soap, and they will smell clean and fresh again.

did you **KNOW?**

Butter is the semi-solid material that results from churning cream – a process that is depicted on a Sumerian tablet from 2500 BC. A butter-filled churn was found in a 2,000-year-old Egyptian grave and butter was plentiful in King Tutankamun's day, when it was made from the milk of water buffaloes and camels. The Bible also contains many references to butter – as the product of cow's milk. Later, the Vikings are believed to have introduced butter to Normandy, a region now world-renowned for its butter.

Pure butter should contain at least 80 per cent milk fat. The remaining 20 per cent is composed of water and milk solids. It may be salted or unsalted. Salt adds flavour and also acts as a preservative for other foods. It takes 10kg of fresh cow's milk to make 500g of butter.

Butter

- **Cut sticky foods with ease** Rub butter on knife or scissor blades before cutting sticky foods like dates, figs or marshmallows. The butter will act as a lubricant and keep the food from sticking to the blades.

- **Remove an ink stain on a doll's face** You can undo the handy work of over-zealous, under-aged beauticians by rubbing butter on pen stains and leaving the doll face-up in the sun for a few days. Then wash the butter off with soap and water.

- **Emergency shaving cream** If you run out of shaving cream, try slathering some butter onto wet skin for a smooth, close shave.

- **Keep a leftover onion fresh** If a recipe calls for half an onion and you want to keep the remaining half fresh, rub butter on the cut surface and wrap the leftover onion in aluminium foil and put it in the fridge.

(KIDS' STUFF)
Making butter

Making butter is fun and easy, especially when there are several children to take turns churning. All you need is a jar, a marble and 200-400ml of thick whipping cream or double cream. Use the freshest cream possible and leave it out of the fridge until it reaches a temperature of about 15°C. Pour the cream into the jar, add the marble, close the lid and let the children take turns shaking (churning), about one shake per second. It may take anywhere from 5 to 30 minutes, but they will see the cream go through various stages from sloshy to coarse whipped cream. When the whipped cream suddenly seizes and collapses, fine-grained bits of butter will be visible in the liquid buttermilk. Before long a glob of yellowish butter will appear. Drain off the buttermilk, remove the marble and enjoy the taste of freshly made butter.

Candles

- **Unstick a drawer** If a drawer is sticking, remove it and rub a candle on the runners. The drawer should open more smoothly when you slip it back into place.

- **Weatherproof address labels** After addressing a package with a felt-tip pen, weatherproof the label by rubbing a white candle over the writing. It will survive rain, sleet and snow.

- **Make a squeaky door silent** Take the door off its hinges and rub a candle over the hinge surfaces that touch each other. The offending door should stop squeaking instantly.

- **Mend the ends of shoelaces** If the plastic or metal tips come off the ends of shoelaces, don't allow the laces to fray. Dip the end into melted candle wax and the lace will hold until you can buy a new pair.

- **Use a trick candle to ignite fires** Don't let a draught blow out the flame when you're trying to light a fire or barbecue. Start the fire with a trick puff-proof birthday candle, designed to relight after being blown out.

- **Make a secret drawing** Get a child to make an 'invisible' drawing with a white candle. Then let him or her cover it with a wash of watercolour paint to reveal the picture.

did you **KNOW?**

Beeswax, secreted by honeybees, was first used for candles in the Middle Ages. Before then, candles were made from tallow, a rendered animal fat that produced a smoky flame and acrid odours. Beeswax candles burned without smoke or smell but were too expensive for most people.

The growth of whaling in the late 1700s brought a major change to candle making as spermaceti – a waxy substance derived from sperm-whale oil – became available. The 19th century saw the advent of mass-produced candles and low-cost paraffin wax. Made from oil and coal shale, paraffin burned cleanly with no unpleasant odour.

Cans

- **Tuna can egg poacher** A shallow tuna can is the perfect size to use as an egg poacher. Remove the top and bottom of the can and the paper label. Place the metal ring in a frying pan of simmering water and crack an egg into it.

- **Feed the birds** For a basic bird feeder, wedge a small can filled with seeds between a couple of tree branches or posts.

- **Make a tool carrier** Are you fed up with fumbling around in your tool belt to find the tool you need? Use small empty fruit juice cans to transform the deep, wide pockets of a nail pouch into a convenient holder for wrenches, pliers and screwdrivers. Make sure to remove the bottom of each can as well as the top. Glue or tape the cylinders together to keep them from shifting around and slip them into the pouches to create dividers.

- **Make pigeonholes** Assemble half a dozen or more empty cans and paint them with brightly coloured enamel. After they are dry, glue the cans together and place them on their sides on a shelf. They can be used to store silverware, nails, office supplies or other odds and ends.

- **Store scissors safely** Use a punch-type can opener to pierce evenly spaced holes around the bottom of a large, clean can. Place the inverted can on a workbench or work table and slip the points of the scissors into the holes. This is also a good way to store screwdrivers.

- **Keep tables together** If you need more seating space for a large dinner party, you can lock card tables together by setting adjacent pairs of legs into empty cans to make up bigger tables.

- **Make light reflectors** It's easy to make reflectors for camping or garden lights. Just remove the bottom of a large empty can with a can opener and take off the label. Then use tin snips to cut the can in half lengthways to make two reflectors.

- **Make a quick floor patch** Nail can lids under wooden floorboards to plug knotty holes and keep rodents out.

- **Make a pair of child's stilts** Pierce a hole in opposite sides of the bottom of two identical large, sturdy cans. Knot thin rope or nylon cord through the holes to form handles – the length of the handles will depend on the height of the child, but they need to reach up as far as their hands. The child has only to step up onto the cans and pull up the handles and he or she is ready to walk tall.

- **Create decorative tea-light holders** Fill clean, empty cans of different sizes with water and freeze. Use a hammer and a large nail or an electric drill to pierce a pattern of holes in the sides of the cans, defrost the ice and insert small candles or tea-lights.

- **Make a miniature golf course** Remove both ends from a number of cans. Then arrange them so that the ball can pass through them, go up a ramp into them or ricochet off a board through them.

did you **KNOW?**

Cans are often described as 'hermetically sealed'. The word 'hermetic' comes from Hermes Trismegistus, a legendary alchemist who is reputed to have lived in the first three centuries AD and to have invented a magic seal to keep vessels airtight.

The hermetically sealed can was invented in 1810 by British merchant Peter Durand. His first cans were so thick they had to be hammered open! Two years later, Englishman Thomas Kensett set up America's first cannery on the New York waterfront to can oysters, meats, fruits and vegetables. He patented the process in 1825. In 1957, the first all-aluminium can appeared.

Cans

- **Organise your desk** If your desk is a mess, a few empty cans can be the start of a neat solution. Attach several tin cans of assorted sizes together in a group to make an office-supplies holder for your desk. Start by cleaning and drying the cans and removing any labels. Then spray paint them (or wrap them in felt). When the paint is dry, glue them together using a hot-glue gun. Your desk organiser is now ready to hold pens, pencils, paper clips, scissors and anything else you may need.

- **Make a fairground game** Arrange four or five cans of the same size in a row and tape them together using gaffer tape. Then add another two or three rows and tape them all together. You can either place the 'rack' vertically against the wall or on the floor. Gather some small balls or tiny bean bags (see page 41). Each 'player' has three balls per go. A point is scored for each ball that stays in the can.

- **Make a home ten-pin bowling set** Tape two clean, empty 400g cans together to make a skittle. You'll need ten skittles to make up a full set. Set up the skittles at the end of a hallway or in the garden. Use a tennis ball and see how many skittles you can hit at one go.

TIP gluing metals

When gluing cans and other metal pieces together, use a glue that adheres well to metal, such as polyvinyl chloride (PVC), liquid solder or epoxy. If the joint won't be subject to stress, you can use a hot-glue gun. Make sure to wash and dry the cans and to remove any labels first. Also let any paint dry thoroughly before gluing.

Cardboard boxes

- **Make a bed tray** Have breakfast in bed on a tray made from a cardboard box. Just remove the top flaps and cut arches from the two long sides to fit over your lap. Decorate the bottom of the box – which is now the top of your tray – with a wipeable adhesive plastic or some oilcloth.

- **Shield doors and furniture** Use cardboard shields to protect doors and furniture from stains when you polish knobs and handles. Cut out an appropriately sized shield and slide it over the items you are going to polish. This works best when you make shields that slip over the neck of knobs or knoblike handles. But you can also make shields for hinges and U-shaped handles.

- **Make an office in-box** Make an in or out-box for your desk. Cut the top and one large panel off a cereal box. Slice the narrow sides at an angle and cover with self-adhesive decorative paper.

- **Protect glassware or light bulbs** A good way to safely store crystal glassware is to put it in an empty wine or spirits carton with partitions. You can also use it for storing light bulbs, but make sure you sort the bulbs by wattage so that it is easy to find the right one when you need a replacement.

- **Make a magazine holder** Store a collection of magazines in holders made from empty detergent boxes. Remove the top, then cut the box at an angle, from the top of one side to the bottom third of the other. Cover the holders with self-adhesive decorative paper, colourful wrapping paper or attractive wallpaper.

- **Poster and artwork holder** A clean wine carton with its dividers intact is a great place to store rolled-up posters, drawings on paper and unmounted canvases. Just insert the items upright between the partitions.

Cardboard boxes

- **Store Christmas ornaments** When you take down a Christmas tree, wrap each ornament in newspaper or tissue paper and store it in an empty wine box with partitions. Each of the carton's segments will be able to hold several of the wrapped Christmas tree ornaments.

- **Create an impromptu sledge** Use a large, flat cardboard box to pull a small child over snow.

- **Organise children's sporting gear** Decorate an empty wine or spirits carton with partitions, and cut the top cut off. Use it to store tall items such as tennis rackets, cricket bats and fishing rods.

- **Make a play castle** Take a large empty appliance box and cut off the top flaps. Make battlements along the top by making a cut on either side of the section you want to remove. Fold the cut section forward and cut along the fold. To make a drawbridge, cut a large fold-down opening on one side. Attach the top of the drawbridge to the side walls with two ropes making holes for the rope and knotting it on the other side. Reinforce the walls with gaffer tape. Finally, cut out narrow window slits in the walls. The kids can paint stones and bricks on the sides to make castle 'walls'.

- **Make a puppet theatre** Stand a large cardboard box upside down. Remove one side so the puppeteer can get in. On the opposite side, cut out a hole for the stage. Add curtains.

did you **KNOW?**

Cardboard was first invented by the Chinese in the early 1500s. In 1871 a New Yorker named Albert Jones patented the idea of gluing a piece of corrugated paper between two pieces of flat cardboard to create a material rigid enough to use for shipping. But it wasn't until 1890 that another American, Robert Gair, invented the corrugated cardboard box. His boxes were pre-cut flat pieces manufactured in bulk that could be folded into cartons, exactly like the cardboard boxes that we use today.

Cardboard tubes...

...around the house

- **Extend the reach of a vacuum cleaner** If you can't reach a cobweb on the ceiling with an ordinary vacuum cleaner attachment, try using an empty wrapping-paper tube to extend the reach. Crush the end of the tube to create a crevice tool. Use gaffer tape to make the vacuum cleaner connection airtight.

- **Keep electrical cords tangle-free** Neatly fold the cord and pass it through a toilet-paper tube before plugging in. You can also use the tubes to store extension cords when they're not in use. Paper-towel tubes will also work. Just cut them in half before using them.

- **Make a fly and pest strip** Cover an empty paper-towel or toilet-paper roll with transparent tape, sticky side out, and hang up where it's needed.

- **Keep Christmas lights tidy** Make life easier by wrapping lights around a cardboard tube. Secure them with masking tape. Put small strands of lights or garlands inside cardboard tubes, and seal the ends of the tubes with masking tape.

- **Store fabric scraps** Roll up leftover fabric scraps tightly and insert them inside a toilet or paper-towel tube. For easy identification, tape or staple a sample of the fabric to the outside of the tube.

...around the house

- **Store string** To keep string ready to use, cut a notch into each end of a toilet-paper tube. Secure one end of the string in one notch, wrap the string tightly around the tube, and then secure the other end in the other notch.

- **Keep trousers crease-free** To stop creases forming from hanging trousers over a hanger, cut a paper-towel tube lengthways, fold it in half horizontally and place it over the hanger. Tape the sides of the cardboard together at the bottom to keep it from slipping. Now hang up your trousers.

- **Preserve children's artwork** If you want to save some of your children's artwork for posterity (or you don't want it to clutter up the house), simply roll up the artwork and place it inside a paper-towel tube. Label the outside with the child's name and date. The tubes are easy to store, and you can safely preserve the work of budding young artists. Use this method to hold and store documents, such as certificates and licences, too. With

precious or ancient documents you may want to wrap them in a layer of acid-free tissue paper before placing them in the tube.

- **Make boot trees** To keep the tops of long, flexible boots from flopping over and creasing when stored at the bottom of the wardrobe, insert cardboard poster tubes into them to help hold their shape.

TIP finding big cardboard tubes

Many carpet shops discard long, thick cardboard tubes. If you ask, they will probably be happy to provide you with one for free. Because the tubes are very solid and can be as much as 3.6m long, you may want to ask for them to cut it to the size you want before you take it away.

- **Store knitting needles** To keep knitting needles from bending and breaking, use a long cardboard tube from a pack of aluminium foil or cling film. Cover one end with sticky tape. Pinch the other end closed and secure it tightly with tape. Slide needles through the tape on the taped end to hold them in place.

...in the garden and great outdoors

- **Make a plant guard** To avoid scarring the trunk of a young tree when you are chopping weeds around it, cut a large cardboard postal tube in half lengthways using a sharp craft knife. Tie the two halves around the trunk while you work near the tree.

- **Start seedlings** Don't go to a garden centre to buy biodegradable starting pots for seedlings. Use the cardboard tubes from paper towels and toilet paper. Cut each toilet-paper tube into two pots, or each paper-towel tube into four. Fill a tray with the cylinders packed against each other so they won't tip when you water the seedlings. This will also prevent them from drying out too quickly. Now fill each pot with seed compost, gently pack it down and sow your seeds. When you plant the seedlings, make sure you break down the side of the roll and ensure all the cardboard is completely buried.

- **Make a sheath** Flatten a paper-towel tube and gaffer tape one end shut to make a perfect sheath for a picnic/camping knife. Use toilet-paper rolls for smaller cutlery.

- **Instant megaphone** Don't shout yourself hoarse when you're calling outside for a child or pet to come in. Give your vocal chords a rest by using a wide cardboard tube as a megaphone to amplify your voice.

C ...for children

- **Build a toy log cabin** Notch the ends of several long tubes with a craft knife and help your children to build log cabins, fences or huts with them. Use different-sized tubes for added versatility. For a bit of realism, get the children to paint or colour the tubes before construction begins.

- **Make a kazoo** Cut three small holes in the middle of a paper-towel tube. Then cover one end of the tube with greaseproof paper secured with a strong rubber band. Hum into the other end, while using your fingers to plug one, two or all three holes to vary the pitch.

- **Make a hamster toy** Entertain your children and their pet by placing a couple of paper-towel or toilet-paper tubes in their pet's cage. Hamsters love running and walking through them and they enjoy chewing on the cardboard, too. Replace them when the tubes start looking ragged.

- **Make 'exploding' crackers** Tie string 20cm long around a small gift, such as a sweet or tiny toy, leaving about 15cm spare. Place the gift in a toilet-paper tube so the string dangles out one end. Cover the tube with brightly coloured crêpe or tissue paper and twist the ends. When you pull the string, the gift will pop out.

did you **KNOW?**

It took nearly 500 years for toilet paper to make the transition from sheets to rolls. Toilet paper was first produced in China in 1391 for the exclusive use of the emperor, in sheets that measured a massive 60 x 90cm each. Toilet paper in rolls was first made in the USA in 1890 by the Scott Paper Company. Scott began making paper towels in 1907, thanks to a failed attempt to develop a new crêpe toilet tissue. This paper was so thick it couldn't be cut and rolled into toilet paper, so Scott made larger rolls, perforated into 33 x 45cm sheets, and sold them under the brand name Sani-Towels.

Carpet remnants

- **Muffle noisy appliances** Put a carpet offcut underneath the washing machine or spin dryer and, with any luck, it will be all you need to stop the machine from rattling.

- **Exercise in comfort** Cut a length of old carpet about a metre wide and as long as your height.

- **Make your own car mats** Just cut carpet remnants to fit the floor of your car.

- **Protect your knees** To make some kneepads to wear when gardening or washing the floor, cut two pieces of carpeting 25cm square and then cut two parallel slits in each. Run an old tie, scarf or strip of fabric through the slits and tie the pads to your knees.

- **Prevent scratched floors** Stop chairs and tables from scratching or making marks on wood or vinyl floors. Glue small circles of carpet remnants to the bottom of all chair and table legs.

- **Add traction** Keep a few good-sized carpet remnants in the car boot to add traction if you're stuck in snow or ice. Keep a piece with your spare tyre so that you won't have to kneel or lie on the ground when you have to look under the car or change a flat tyre.

- **Protect workshop tools** If you have a concrete floor in your workshop or garage, put down a few carpet remnants close to the workbench so that any tools that fall will be less likely to break.

- **Weatherproof a doghouse** Nail a carpet remnant over the entrance to your dog's shelter. In very cold areas, line the interior walls and the floor with small offcuts to add insulation.

- **Make a scratching post for your cat** Staple carpet scraps to a post or board and place it near your cat's favourite target. Nail a board to the bottom of the post to serve as a base.

Car wax

- **Stop CDs from skipping tracks** Before throwing away a scratched compact disc, try fixing it with car wax. Spread a cloth on a flat surface and place the CD on top of it, damaged side up. Then, holding the disc with one hand, use the other to wipe the polish into the scratched area with a soft cloth. Let it dry and buff using short, brisk strokes along the scratch, not across it. A cloth sold to wipe spectacles or camera lenses will work well. When you can no longer see the scratch, wash the disc with water and let it dry before playing again.

- **Keep bathroom mirrors fog-free** Apply a small amount of car wax to the mirror, let it dry and buff with a soft cloth. Next time you step out of the shower, you should be able to see your face in the mirror immediately. Rub the wax on other bathroom fixtures to prevent water spots.

- **Eliminate bathroom mildew** To get rid of grime and mildew in a shower, first clean the tiles or shower wall. Then rub on a layer of car wax and buff with a clean, dry cloth. You'll only need to reapply the wax about once a year. Don't wax the bath as it will become dangerously slippery.

- **Eradicate furniture stains** If an ugly white ring is disfiguring a wooden table and ordinary furniture polish doesn't work, try using a dab of car wax. Trace the ring with your finger to apply the wax. Let it dry and buff with a soft cloth.

- **Keep snow from sticking** Apply two thick coats of car wax to the work surface of a shovel before you begin shovelling snow. The snow won't stick to the shovel and the job will be far easier.

Castor oil

- **Soften cuticles** The high vitamin-E content of this thick oil can work wonders on brittle nails and ragged cuticles. Massage a small amount on your cuticles and nails each day and within three months you will have supple cuticles and healthy nails.

- **Soothe tired eyes** Before going to bed, rub odourless castor oil around your eyes. Rub some on your eyelashes, too, to keep them shiny. But be very careful not to get the oil in your eyes.

- **Lubricate kitchen scissors** Use castor oil to lubricate kitchen scissors and other utensils that touch food.

- **Repel moles** If moles are destroying your lawn, mix 100ml castor oil and 8 litres water and drench the molehill with it. It won't kill or hurt them, but they should depart.

- **Enjoy a massage** Castor oil is just the right consistency to use as a soothing massage oil. For a real treat, warm the oil on the hob or on half-power in the microwave.

- **Perk up ailing ferns** Give ferns a tonic made of 1 tablespoon castor oil and 1 tablespoon baby shampoo with a litre of lukewarm water. Give the fern about 3 tablespoons of the tonic, then add plain water. Your ferns should be perky by the time your tonic is finished.

- **Condition your hair** For a natural conditioner, mix 2 teaspoons castor oil with 1 teaspoon glycerine and an egg white. Massage it into wet hair, leave for several minutes and wash out.

did you **KNOW?**

Castor oil has hundreds of industrial uses. Large quantities are used in paints, varnishes, lipstick, hair tonic and shampoo. It is also converted into plastics, soap, waxes, hydraulic fluids and ink. And it is made into lubricants for jet engines and racing cars because it does not become stiff with cold or unduly thin with heat.

Cat litter

- **Make a mud mask** Mix two handfuls of fresh cat litter with enough warm water to make a thick paste. Smear the paste over your face, let it set for 20 minutes. Then rinse it clean with water. The clay in cat litter detoxifies your skin by absorbing dirt and oil from the pores. When your friends compliment you on your complexion and ask how you did it, smile and just tell them it's your little secret.

- **Trainer deodoriser** If your trainers reek, fill a couple of old cotton or wool socks with scented cat litter, tie them shut and place them in the shoes overnight.

- **Add traction on ice** Keep a bag of cat litter in the boot of the car. You can use it to add traction if you're stuck in ice or snow.

- **Prevent grease fires** Don't let a fire spoil a barbecue: pour a layer of cat litter into the bottom of the grill for trouble-free outdoor cooking.

- **Stop musty odours** Get rid of musty smells in a wardrobe or little-used room by placing a shallow box filled with cat litter in each musty cupboard or room. Cat litter works well as a deodorant because it's so effective at absorbing odours.

did you **KNOW?**

American salesman Ed Lowe might not have had the idea for cat litter if a neighbour hadn't asked him for some sand for her cats one day in 1947. Ed, who worked for his father's company selling industrial absorbents, suggested clay instead because it was more absorbent and would not leave tracks around the house. When she returned for more, he knew he had a winning idea. Soon he was crisscrossing the USA, selling bags of his new Kitty Litter from the back of his Chevy Coupe. By 1990 Edward Lowe Industries, Inc., was the nation's largest producer of cat litter with annual retail sales of more than $210 million (£125 million).

- **Preserve flowers** The fragrance and beauty of freshly cut flowers is so fleeting. You can't save the smell, but you can preserve their beauty by drying your flowers on a bed of cat litter in an airtight container for 7-10 days.

- **Remove a foul stench from bins** Rubbish bins don't have to smell disgusting. Sprinkle some cat litter into the bottom of each bin to keep it smelling fresh. Change the litter after a week or so, or if it becomes damp. If you have a baby in the house, you can use cat litter in the same way to freshen nappy buckets.

- **Repel moles** Moles may hate the smell of soiled cat litter even more than you do. Pour some down their tunnels and it will send them scurrying to find new homes.

- **Make grease spots disappear** Get rid of dirty grease and oil spots on a driveway or garage floor. Simply cover them with cat litter. If the spots are fresh, the litter will soak up most of the oil right away. To remove old stains, pour a little paint thinner on the stain before putting the cat litter on top. Wait for 12 hours and then sweep the floor or drive clean.

- **Freshen old books** Rejuvenate musty old books by sealing them overnight in a container filled with clean cat litter.

- **Keep tents must-free** Keep tents and sleeping bags smelling fresh and free of must when they are not in use. Pour some cat litter into an old sock, tie the end and store inside the bag or tent.

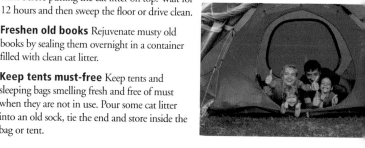

Chalk

- **Repel ants** If you draw a chalk line around the ants' home entry points, they will be repelled by the calcium carbonate in the chalk, which is made up of the ground-up and compressed shells of marine animals. Chalk dust will also repel snails and slugs.

- **Polish metal and marble** To make metal shine like new, put some chalk dust on a damp cloth and wipe. (Note: use a pestle and mortar to pulverise pieces of chalk.) Buff with a soft cloth for a shinier finish. Wipe marble clean with a damp soft cloth dipped in powdered chalk. Rinse with clear water and dry thoroughly.

- **Keep silver and jewellery from tarnishing** Put one or two pieces of chalk in the same drawer as your silver or jewellery. It will absorb moisture and slow tarnishing.

- **Remove grease spots from fabric** Rub chalk on a grease spot, then let it absorb the oil before you brush it off. If the stain lingers, rub the chalk in again before laundering. To clean dirty collars, mark the stains heavily with chalk before washing. The chalk will absorb the oils that are holding the stain in.

- **Reduce dampness in a wardrobe** Tie a dozen pieces of chalk together and hang them up in the damp wardrobe. The chalk will absorb moisture and help to prevent mildew. Replace with a fresh bundle every few months.

- **Hide ceiling marks** Temporarily cover up dried water or stain marks on the ceiling until you have time to paint or make a permanent repair. Rub a stick of white chalk over the mark until it lightens or disappears.

- **Keep tools rust-free** Eliminate moisture and prevent rust from invading a toolbox by placing a few pieces of chalk inside the box.

- **Stop a slipping screwdriver** Rub some chalk on the tip of the screwdriver before using and it won't slip nearly as much.

Charcoal briquettes

- **Keep books mould-free** Professional librarians use charcoal to get rid of musty odours on old books. You can do the same. If the bookcase has glass doors, it may provide a damp environment that can harbour must and mould. A couple of pieces of charcoal placed inside will help to keep the books dry and mould-free.

- **Make a dehumidifier** A humid wardrobe, attic or cellar can wreak havoc on your health as well as the condition of your clothes. Get rid of the humidity with several homemade dehumidifiers. Put some charcoal briquettes in a coffee can, punch a few holes in the lid and place in the humid areas. Replace the charcoal every few months.

- **Keep plant-rooting water fresh** Put a piece of charcoal in the water when you're rooting plant cuttings. The charcoal will keep the water fresh.

- **Banish bathroom moisture and odours** Hiding a few pieces of charcoal in the nooks and crannies of your bathroom is a great way to soak up moisture and cut down on any unpleasant odours. Remember to replace them every couple of months.

did you **KNOW?**

The first mass-produced charcoal briquettes were manufactured by the Ford Motor Company. They were made from waste wood that came from a Ford-owned sawmill in Kingsford, Michigan, USA, that had been built to provide wood for the bodies of Ford's popular 'Woody' station wagons. The charcoal was manufactured into briquettes and sold as Ford Charcoal Briquettes. Henry Ford II closed the sawmill in 1951 and sold the plant to a group of local businessmen, who formed the Kingsford Chemical Company. The company continues to make the charcoal briquettes that have now become a household name, despite relocating to Louisville, Kentucky, in 1961.

Cheesecloth

- **Make a homemade fishing net** Sew cheesecloth into a bag and glue or staple it to a hoop formed from a wire coat hanger and let your children use it as a little net when they are exploring.

- **Make a mini-mummy** For an inexpensive Halloween costume, wrap a child in cheesecloth (washed to remove the dressing) from head to toe and send him out with the ghosts and witches.

- **Convert a colander into a strainer** If you can't find a strainer when you need one, a colander lined with washed cheesecloth will work just as well.

- **Cut vacuuming time** To vacuum a drawer filled with small objects without having to remove the contents, cover the nozzle of the vacuum cleaner with cheesecloth, secured with a strong rubber band, and the vacuum will pick up only the dust.

- **Reduce waste when drying herbs** When drying fresh herbs, wrap them in washed cheesecloth to prevent seeds and smaller crumbly pieces from falling through.

- **Picnic food tent** Keep insects and dirt away from picnic food by wrapping a piece of cheesecloth around an old wire umbrella frame and placing it over the plates. Use a hacksaw to remove the umbrella handle and tack the cheesecloth to the umbrella ribs with a needle and thread.

- **Make instant festive curtains** Brighten a room with inexpensive, colourful cheesecloth curtains. Dye cheesecloth (available in bulk from fabric shops) in bright colours and cut it to the lengths and widths you need. Fold over the top, sides and bottom and hem. Attach clip-on curtain hooks.

- **Remove turkey stuffing with ease** To keep stuffing from sticking to the bird's insides, pack it in washed cheesecloth before you put it into the internal cavity. When the turkey is ready, pull out the cheesecloth and the stuffing will slide out with it.

Chest rub

- **Repel ticks and other insects** If you're going for a walk in the woods, smear chest rub on your legs and trousers before you leave the house. It will keep ticks (which spread Lyme disease) from biting and will also discourage gnats and mosquitoes.

- **Get rid of tough skin on your feet** Coat the hard skin with chest rub and then cover your feet with an adhesive bandage overnight. Repeat the procedure as needed. Most calluses will disappear after several days.

- **Soothe aching feet** Try applying a thick coat of chest rub and covering your feet with a pair of socks before going to bed at night. When you wake up, your sore, tired feet should be both moisturised and rejuvenated.

- **Stop insect-bite itch** Apply a generous coat of chest rub for immediate relief from itchy insect bites. Eucalyptus and menthol in the ointment soothe the itch.

- **Treat toenail fungus** Try applying a thick coat of chest rub to the affected nail several times a day. Many users and even some doctors swear that it works. If you don't see results after a few weeks, consult a doctor.

did you **KNOW?**

Lunsford Richardson, the pharmacist who created Vicks VapoRub in 1905, also originated America's first 'junk mail'. Richardson was working in his brother-in-law's pharmacy when he blended menthol and other ingredients into an ointment to clear sinuses and ease congestion. He called it Richardson's Croup and Pneumonia Cure Salve, but soon realised that he needed a more catchy name to sell it successfully. He changed the name to Vicks after his brother-in-law, Joshua Vick, and convinced the US Post Office to institute a new policy allowing him to send advertisements addressed only to 'Boxholder'. Sales of Vicks first surpassed a million dollars during the Spanish flu epidemic of 1918.

Chewing gum

- **Retrieve valuables** If you've just lost an earring or other small valuable down a drain, try retrieving it with a newly chewed piece of gum stuck to the bottom of a fishing weight. Dangle the gum from a string tied to the weight, let the object stick to it and reel it in.

- **Fill cracks** Fill a crack in a clay flowerpot or a dog bowl with pieces of chewed gum.

- **Use as makeshift window putty** Hold a loose pane of glass in place temporarily with a pad or two of freshly chewed gum.

- **Treat flatulence and heartburn** Settle stomach gases and relieve heartburn by chewing a stick of spearmint gum. The oils in the spearmint act as an anti-flatulent. Chewing stimulates the production of saliva, which neutralises stomach acid and corrects the flow of digestive juices. Spearmint also acts as a digestive aid.

- **Repair glasses** If one of the lenses on a pair of spectacles suddenly becomes loose, put a small piece of chewed gum in the corner of the lens to hold it in place until you can get the glasses properly repaired.

- **Lure a crab** Briefly chew a stick of gum so that it is soft but still hasn't lost its flavour, then attach it to a crab line. The crabs will be attracted to the gum.

did you **KNOW?**

Humans have been chewing gum for a long time. Ancient Greeks chewed mastic, a chewing gum made from the resin of the mastic tree. Ancient Mayans chewed chicle, the sap from the sapodilla tree. Native Americans chewed the sap from spruce trees, and passed the habit on to the Pilgrims. John B. Curtis produced the first commercial chewing gum in 1848 and called it State of Maine Pure Spruce Gum. Wrigley's gum was first launched in the UK in 1911.

Cling film

- **Treat a hangnail** You can get rid of a hangnail while you sleep. Before going to bed, apply hand cream to the affected area, wrap the fingertip with cling film and secure it in place with clear tape. The cling film will confine the moisture and soften the cuticle.

- **Protect computer keyboard** If you're off on holiday and won't be tapping a computer keyboard for a couple of weeks, cover the keyboard with cling film to keep out dust and grime during long periods of inactivity.

- **Enhance the effectiveness of a vapour rub** For pain in a knee and other sore spots, massage in some vapour rub and wrap the area with cling film. The cling film will increase the heating effect of the vapour rub. Test on a small area first to make sure your skin does not burn.

- **Keep ice cream smooth** Have you ever noticed how ice crystals often form on ice cream in the freezer once the container has been opened? The ice cream will stay smooth and free of the crystals if you completely re-wrap the container in cling film before you return it to the freezer.

- **Keep stored paint fresh** Leftover paint will stay fresh longer if you stretch a sheet of high-quality cling film over the top of the can before tightly replacing the lid.

TAKE CARE

When microwaving foods covered with cling film, always turn back a corner of the film or cut a slit in it to let steam escape. Never use cling film when microwaving foods with a high sugar content; they can become extremely hot and melt it. You can buy special kinds of cling film developed for use in the microwave.

Cling film

- **Treat psoriasis** Here is a method often recommended by dermatologists to treat individual psoriasis lesions. After applying a prescribed steroid cream, cover the area with a small piece of cling film and use adhesive tape to fix the cling film to the skin. It will enhance the effect of the steroid, seal in moisture and inhibit proliferation of the rash.

- **Repair a kite** Flying kites with children is a lot of fun, but it can be frustrating if the kite gets torn by a tree branch or fence. For a temporary fix that will keep the kite airborne for a while, cover the tear with cling film and fix it to the kite with clear tape.

- **Keep the top of the fridge clean** Make the next time you clean the top of your fridge the last time. After you've made it all clean and shiny, cover the top with overlapping sheets of cling film. Next time it's due for a clean, remove the old sheets, throw them away and replace with new layers of cling film.

did you **KNOW?**

Polyvinylidene chloride, the substance that is the basis of cling film, was accidentally discovered in 1933 by Ralph Wiley, a lab worker at the Dow Chemical Company. One day he came across a vial coated with a smelly, clear green film he couldn't scrub off. He called it eonite, after an indestructible material featured in the 'Little Orphan Annie' comic strip. Soon the material was being used by the US armed forces as a protective spray for fighter planes, while car makers used it to protect interior upholstery. Dow later found a way to dispense with the green colour and unpleasant smell and transformed it into a solid material, which was approved for food packaging after the Second World War and as a contact food wrap in 1956.

Clipboards

- **Makeshift trouser hanger** If you can't find a hanger for a pair of trousers, use a clipboard instead. Hang it up and clip the hems to the board to keep them crease-free overnight.

- **Keep recipes at eye level** When you are following a recipe clipped from a magazine or newspaper, it is hard to read and keep clean when the cutting is lying on the worktop. Instead, secure a clipboard to a wall cabinet at eye level. Attach the recipe of the day to the board and it will be more convenient to read and stay free of food splatters.

- **Hold place mats** Hang a clipboard inside a kitchen cabinet or pantry door and use the clamp as a convenient, space-saving way to store a set of place mats.

- **Keep sheet music in place** Flimsy pages of sheet music are susceptible to draughts and can sometimes spend more time on the floor than on the music stand. To eliminate the problem, attach the music sheets to a clipboard before placing it in the stand. The pages will remain upright and in place.

- **Aid road-trip navigation** Before starting out on a long drive, fold the map to the area you will be travelling in. Attach it to a clipboard and keep it close to hand so you can check your progress during rest stops along the way.

- **Organise grades of sandpaper** Most of the time, sandpaper is still good after the first or second time you use it. The trick is to find it again. Hang a clipboard on a hook on the workshop wall. Just clip still-usable sandpaper to the board when you are finished and the sandpaper will be handy next time you need it.

Clothes pegs

- **Fasten Christmas lights** Keep outdoor Christmas lights in place by fastening them securely with clip-on clothes pegs as you fix them to gutters, trees and bushes.

- **Keep snacks fresh** Use clip-on clothes pegs to reseal half-eaten bags of snacks, cereal, biscuits and seeds. The foods will stay fresh longer and you will have fewer spills in the cupboard.

- **Make a clothes-peg clipboard** Make a rack using traditional straight 'dolly' clothes pegs. Space several evenly across a piece of wood and screw them on with screws from the back of the board (pre-drill the holes so you don't split the clothes peg).

- **Organise the bottom of your wardrobe** Use clip-on clothes pegs to hold together pairs of shoes, boots or trainers. This works for gloves as well.

- **Keep gloves in shape** After washing wool gloves, insert a straight wooden 'dolly' clothes peg into each finger. The clothes pegs will help to keep the gloves in their proper shape.

- **Prevent the vacuum cord snapping back** If your vacuum cleaner suddenly stops, you've probably accidentally pulled out the plug and the cord may automatically retract and snap back into the machine. To avoid a similar annoyance in the future, simply clip a clothes peg to the cord at the length you want.

- **Make an instant bib** Make bibs for a child by using a clip-on clothes peg to hold a tea towel around the child's neck. It's much faster than tying on a bib.

- **Make clothes-peg puppets** Traditional straight 'dolly' clothes pegs without metal springs are ideal for making little dolls or puppets. Using the knob as a head, get children to stick on bits of wool for hair and scraps of cloth or coloured paper for clothes to give each its own personality. Draw faces on with felt-tip pens.

- **Hold a leaf bag open** If you've ever tried to fill a large bag with leaves all by yourself, only to see half the leaves fall to the ground because the bag won't stay open, here is a solution. Next time use a couple of clip-on clothes pegs to help. After you shake open the bag and spread it wide, use the clothes pegs to clip one side of the bag to a chain-link fence or other convenient site. The bag will stay fully open for easy filling.

- **Mark a bulb spot** When a flower that is supposed to bloom in the spring doesn't, push a straight clothes peg into the soil at the empty spot. In the autumn you will know exactly where to plant new bulbs to avoid gaps.

- **Grip a nail** Hammer the nail and not your fingers. Just remember to use a clip-on clothes peg to hold nails when hammering in hard-to-reach places.

- **Clamp thin objects** Use clip-on clothes pegs as clamps when you're gluing two thin objects together. Let the clothes peg hold them in place until the glue has set firmly.

- **Keep a paintbrush afloat** Keep a paintbrush from sinking into the solvent residue when you are soaking it. Clamp the brush to the container with a clothes peg.

did you **KNOW?**

Between 1852 and 1857, the Patent Office in the USA granted patents for 146 different kinds of clothes pegs. Today wooden clothes pegs are much less common – both traditional 'dolly' pegs and the spring-loaded kind. They have been largely overtaken by moulded plastic pegs. The most recent innovation in clothes-peg design is a peg that can sense whether rain is coming. It will then lock itself to prevent washing being hung on the line and drenched.

Coat hangers

- **Stop sealant ooze** To prevent sealant oozing from a tube once the job has been done, cut an 8cm piece of coat-hanger wire; shape one end into a hook and insert the other, straight end, into the tube. The ooze will stop and you'll keep the tube free of sealant. You should now be able to pull out the stopper easily as needed.

- **Secure a soldering iron** To keep a hot soldering iron safe on a workbench, make a holder for it. Bend a coat hanger in half to form a large V. Then bend each half in half so that the entire piece is shaped like an M and twist the hook to make it stand.

- **Extend your reach** If you can't reach something that has fallen behind the fridge, try straightening a wire coat hanger (except for the hook at the end), and use the hook to fish it out. You can also use a straightened hanger to clear a blockage in a vacuum cleaner hose or in the toilet.

- **Make a giant bubble wand** Shape a hanger into a hoop with a handle and dip it into a bucket with 1 part liquid dishwashing detergent in 2 parts water. Add a few drops of food colouring to make the bubbles more visible.

(**SCIENCE** FAIR)
Newton's Law

Here is a fun way to demonstrate Newton's first law of motion. Straighten a wire coat hanger and bend it into a large loopy M-shape with a small hook at each end. Holding the wire in the middle, attach a ball made of modelling clay to each of the hooks. Then place the low centre point of the M on top of your head. If you turn your head to the left or right, the inertia of the balls will be enough to keep them in place, demonstrating Newton's law that 'objects at rest tend to stay at rest'. With practice, you can turn all the way around and the balls will remain still.

- **Convert a window box into a mini-greenhouse** Bend three or four lengths of coat-hanger wire into U-shapes and place the ends into the soil. Punch small holes in a clear polythene dry-cleaning bag and wrap it around the box before putting it back in the window.

- **Make outdoor plant markers** Cut small rectangles from a plastic milk bottle or similar rigid, but easy-to-cut, plastic item. Write the name of the plant with an indelible marker. Cut short stakes from wire hangers. Make two small slits in each marker and pass the wire stakes through the slits. The signs will remain clear whatever the elements throw at them.

- **Make fairy wings** Use the wire from two or three wire coat hangers to make the structure for wings. Cover with a gauzy fabric, rolling it over the edges of the wire a few times before sewing it down or securing it with glue. Add a thin layer of glue and sprinkle with glitter. Add elastic armbands to keep the wings on the child's back.

- **Light a hard-to-reach pilot light** If a pilot light goes out inside your cooker or boiler, open up a wire hanger and tape the match to one end. Strike the match and use the hanger to reach the pilot light.

did you **KNOW?**

It was 1903, and when Albert J. Parkhouse, who worked at Timberlake Wire and Novelty Company in Jackson, Michigan, USA, went to hang his clothes on a coat hook in the staff cloakroom, they were all in use. Frustrated, he bent a piece of wire into two large rectangular hoops opposite each other, and twisted both ends at the centre into a hook. He hung his coat on it and went to work. The company were so impressed that they patented the design and made a fortune. But poor Albert never got a penny for inventing the wire coat hanger.

Coffee beans

- **Freshen your breath** If you've run out of peppermints and want to freshen your breath, just suck on a coffee bean for a while and your mouth should smell clean and fresh again.

- **Remove odour from hands** If your hands smell of garlic, fish or other strong-smelling foods, put some beans in your palms and rub well together. The oil released from the coffee beans will absorb the smell. Wash your hands with clean, soapy water.

Coffee cans

- **Bake a round loaf** Use small coffee cans to bake perfectly cylindrical loaves of bread. Clean and grease the tin well. For yeast breads use two cans and fill each only half full. Grease the inside of the lids and place them on the cans while the dough is rising. You will know it is time to bake when the rising dough pushes the lids off. Place the cans, without their lids, upright in the oven to bake.

- **Hold kitchen scraps** Line a coffee tin with a small plastic bag and keep it near the sink to hold kitchen scraps and peelings. Instead of walking back and forth to the bin, you'll only have to make one trip to the bin to dump all the scraps.

- **Create a bank or small-toy holder** Wash and dry a coffee can and file off any sharp edges. Paint on two coats of white acrylic paint, letting it dry between coats. Cut out a design from an old sheet to wrap around the can. Mix 4 tablespoons white glue with enough water to the consistency of paint. Paint on the glue mixture and gently press the fabric onto the can. Trim the bottom and tuck the top edges inside the can. Apply two coats of glue mixture over the fabric overlay to seal it, letting it dry between coats. For a bank, use a utility knife to cut a 3mm slit in the centre of the lid as the money slot.

- **Separate hamburgers** If you like to make hamburgers in bulk, before you put them in the freezer, stack them with a coffee-can lid between each and put them in a plastic bag. When they're are frozen you can peel off as many as you need.

- **Make a coffee-can bird feeder** To fashion a coffee can into a sturdy bird feeder, begin with a full can and open the top only halfway. (Note: pour the coffee into an airtight container.) Then open the bottom of the can halfway the same way. Carefully bend the cut ends down inside the can so the edges are not exposed to cut you or the birds. Punch a hole in the side of the can at both ends, where it will be the 'top' of the feeder, and put some wire through each end to make a hanger.

- **Keep toilet paper dry when camping** Bring a few empty coffee cans with you when you go camping. Use them to keep toilet paper dry in rainy weather or when you're carrying supplies in a boat.

- **Soak a paintbrush** An empty coffee can is perfect for briefly soaking a paintbrush in thinner before continuing a job the following day. Cut an X into the plastic lid with a craft knife and insert the brush handles so that the bristles clear the bottom of the can by about 12mm. If the tin has no lid, attach a stick to the brush handle with a rubber band and rest it across the top of the tin to keep the bristles off the bottom of the can.

- **Keep bits and pieces from getting washed by accident** Keep an empty coffee can nearby as you're going through children's pockets before putting in a load of washing. Use it to deposit gum and sweet wrappers, paper scraps and other assorted items that children like to stuff into their pockets. Keep another can handy for coins and notes.

- **Stop cupboard shelves from getting sticky** Put plastic coffee-can lids under bottles and jars of cooking oil, syrup and other sticky items.

Coffee cans

- **Make a dehumidifier** If your home suffers from damp, fill an empty coffee can with salt and leave it in a corner where it will be undisturbed. The salt will absorb moisture. Replace the salt at monthly intervals or as needed.

- **Store belts** If you have more belts than you have places to hang them up, roll them up and store them in a large, clean coffee can with a clear lid. Large coffee cans are just the right size to keep belts from creasing and a clear lid will let you find each belt easily. Decorate if the tin is on view.

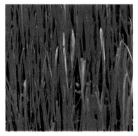

- **Make a spot lawn seeder** When it's time to re-seed bare spots on the lawn, for precise seeding make a spot seeder from an empty coffee can and a pair of plastic lids. Drill small holes in the bottom of the tin, just large enough to let grass seeds pass through. Put one lid over the bottom of the can, fill it with seeds, and cap it with the other lid. When you're ready to spread the seeds, remove the bottom lid. When you have finished, replace it to seal in any unused seed for safe storage.

- **Gauge rainfall or sprinkler coverage** Find out if your garden is getting enough water from the rain. Next time it starts to rain, place empty coffee cans in several places around the garden. When the rain stops, measure the depth of the water in the cans. If they measure at least 2cm, there's no need for additional watering. This is also a good way to test if a sprinkler is getting sufficient water to the areas it is supposed to cover.

- **Eliminate workshop clutter** If you want small items like screws, nuts and nails to be close to hand, but don't want them to take up workbench space, drill a hole near the top of a number of empty coffee cans so you can hang them on nails on the wall. Label the cans with masking tape so you will know what's inside.

Coffee filters

- **Line a frying basket** If you save cooking oil for re-use after deep-fat frying, line the basket with a basket-style coffee filter to remove smaller food remnants and other impurities.

- **Stop messy food from dripping** Serve wraps, deep-filled sandwiches, burgers, hot dogs, popcorn and other messy foods in cone or basket-style coffee filters.

- **Catch ice-cream drips** Just poke the choc-ice or ice-lolly stick through the centre of two basket-style coffee filters and the drips will fall into the paper.

- **Filter cork crumbs from wine** If you find a few floating cork crumbs, decant the wine through a coffee filter.

- **Make an instant funnel** Cut the end off a cone-style coffee filter to make an instant funnel. Keep a few in your car and use them to avoid spillage when you top up oil in the engine.

- **Keep cast iron rust-free** Prolong the life of good cast-iron cookware by putting a coffee filter in it when it's not in use. The filter will absorb moisture and prevent rusting.

- **Make an air freshener** Fill a coffee filter with bicarbonate of soda and tie it closed with a twist-tie to make an air freshener.

did you **KNOW?**

The coffee filter was invented in 1908 by a housewife from Dresden, Germany. Melitta Bentz was looking for a way to brew a perfect cup of coffee without the bitterness often caused by overbrewing. She decided to make a filtered coffee, pouring boiling water over ground coffee and filtering out the grounds. She experimented with different materials, until she found that the blotting paper that her son used at school worked best. She cut a round piece of blotting paper, put it in a metal cup, and the first Melitta coffee filter was born. Shortly after, Melitta and her husband, Hugo, launched the company that still bears her name.

Coffee grounds

- **Don't raise any dust** Before you clean the ashes out of a fireplace, sprinkle them with wet coffee grounds. They'll be easier to remove and the ash and dust won't pollute the atmosphere.

- **Deodorise a freezer** Get rid of the smell of spoiled food if a freezer breaks down or you have a power cut. Fill two bowls with used or fresh coffee grounds and put them in overnight. For a vanilla scent, add a few drops of essence to the grounds.

- **Keep bait worms alive** A cup of used coffee grounds will keep bait worms alive and wriggling all day long. Just mix the grounds into the soil in the bait box before you put in the worms. They like coffee almost as much as we do and the nutrients in the grounds will help them to live longer.

- **Fertilise plants** Coffee grounds are full of nutrients that acid-loving plants crave. Save them to fertilise rose bushes, azaleas, rhododendrons, evergreens and camellias. It's better to use grounds from a drip coffee maker than the boiled grounds from a percolator as the drip grounds are richer in nitrogen.

did you **KNOW?**

Ground coffee loses its flavour immediately unless it is specially packaged or brewed. While freshly roasted and ground coffee is often sealed in combination plastic-and-paper bags, vacuum-sealed cans keep coffee fresh for up to three years. The USA is the world's largest consumer of coffee, importing over a million kilograms each year. The typical coffee drinker has three cups of coffee per day. That translates into 170 million cups of coffee swallowed daily in the UK.

- **Keep cats out of the garden** Your neighbours' cats won't use your garden as a latrine again if you spread a pungent mixture of orange peel and used coffee grounds around your plants. The mix acts as a superb fertiliser, too.

- **Boost carrot harvest** To increase a carrot harvest, mix the seeds with freshly ground coffee before sowing. Not only does the extra bulk make the tiny seeds easier to sow, but the coffee aroma may repel cutworms and other pests. In addition, the grounds will add nutrients to the soil as they decompose around the plants. You might also like to add a few radish seeds to the mix before sowing. The radishes will sprout in a few days to mark the rows and when you cultivate the radishes, you will be thinning the carrot seedlings and cultivating the soil at the same time.

did you **KNOW?**

Coffee trees can reach a height of 6m, but growers keep them pruned to about 2m to simplify picking and encourage heavy berry production. The first visible sign of a coffee tree's maturity is the appearance of small white blossoms, which fill the air with a heady aroma reminiscent of jasmine and orange. The mature tree bears cherry-size oval berries, each containing two coffee beans with their flat sides set together. A mature coffee tree will produce 450g of coffee per growing season. It takes 2,000 hand-picked Arabica coffee berries or 4,000 beans to make 450g of roasted coffee.

Coins

- **Give carpet a lift** When you move a piece of furniture, you will see indentations in the carpet. To fluff it up again, hold a coin on its edge and scrape it against the flattened pile. If it doesn't pop back up, hold a steam iron 5cm above the affected spot. When the area is damp, try fluffing it again with the coin.

- **Make a rattle** Drop a few coins into an empty aluminium can, seal the top with gaffer tape and head for the stadium. Take the rattle with you when you walk the dog and use it as a training aid. When the dog is naughty, just shake the rattle.

- **Keep cut flowers fresh** Cut flowers will stay fresh longer if you add a copper coin and a cube of sugar to the vase water.

did you **KNOW?**

Coins were first produced around 700 BC by the Lydians, a people who lived in what is now Turkey. From there, their use spread to ancient Greece and Rome. The minting of coins in Britain began in the 1st century BC and the earliest coins were cast in moulds. Next, coins were struck using handheld tools, a technique that would be used for the next 1,500 years. Following the Roman Conquest, the coinage of Iron Age Britain was discontinued and Roman coins circulated in large numbers.

The first London mint began operating in AD 650. At first, it was a little precarious, but from the time of Alfred the Great (r.871-99) it became a continuous and important source of British coinage. At the end of 2008 there were 27,827 million coins in circulation in the UK.

- **Instant measure** If you need to measure something but you don't have a ruler, use a 2p piece. It measures exactly 2.5cm in diameter. Just line up a series of coins to measure the length of a small object.

- **Test tyre tread** Insert a one-penny piece into the tread. If you can't cover the top of the head inside the tread, it's time to replace the tyres. Check tyres regularly and you will avoid breaking the law by having the correct depth of tyre tread.

- **Decorate a hair slide** Use shiny 1p pieces to decorate a hair slide for a little girl. Gather enough pennies to complete the project and arrange them as you like on the hair slide and use a hot-glue gun to attach them. Allow 24 hours to dry.

- **Hang doors perfectly** Next time you hang a door, use coins to ensure proper clearance between the outside of the door and the inside of the frame. When the door is closed, the gap at the top should be the thickness of a 50p piece, and the gap at the sides should be that of a 5p piece. If you do it right, you will keep the door from binding and it won't let in draughts.

(**SCIENCE** FAIR)
Optical illusion

Scientists use optical illusions to show how the brain can be tricked. This simple experiment uses two coins, but you'll think you are seeing three. Hold two coins on top of each other between your thumb and index finger. Quickly slide the coins back and forth and you will see a third coin!

How does it work? Scientists say that everything we see is actually light reflected from objects. Our eyes use the light to create images on our retinas, the light-sensitive linings in our eyeballs. Because images don't disappear instantly, when something moves quickly you may see both an object and an after-image of it at the same time.

Colanders

- **Prevent grease splashes** Stop grease spitting all over the top of the cooker when you are frying by inverting a large metal colander over the frying pan. The holes will let heat escape but the colander will trap the splashes.

  WARNING: the metal colander will be hot so wear an oven glove when you remove it.

- **Heat a pasta bowl** Does your pasta get cold too quickly? To keep it warm for longer, heat the bowl first. Place a colander in the bowl, pour the pasta and water into the colander, and let the hot water stand in the bowl for a few seconds to heat it. Pour out the water, add the pasta and sauce, and it will be ready to serve.

- **Keep berries and grapes fresh** Do you find that berries and grapes often go mouldy before you have had a chance to enjoy them? To keep them fresh for longer, store them in a colander, not a closed plastic container, in the fridge. The cold air will circulate through the holes in the colander, keeping them fresh for days.

- **Keep bath toys tidy** Don't let the bathroom that your children use look like another messy toy box. After each bath, collect your child's small playthings into a large colander and store it in the bath. The water will drain from the toys, keeping them ready for next time, and the bathroom will stay tidy.

- **Use as a beach toy** Don't spend money on expensive beach toys for budding diggers and archaeologists. A simple inexpensive plastic colander is perfect for digging on the beach or in a sandpit.

Cold cream

- **Erase temporary tattoos** Children love temporary tattoos, but removing them can be a painful chore. To make removal easier, loosen the tattoo by rubbing cold cream on it and then gently rub it off with a flannel.

- **Remove stickers** Are your windows or your bumper covered with tatty, partly peeling stickers? Rub cold cream on the stickers and let it soak in. Once it does, you should be able to peel them off with ease.

- **Make face paint** This is a safe, easy recipe for party face paint. Mix 1 teaspoon cornflour, ½ teaspoon water, ½ teaspoon cold cream and 2 drops food colouring (depending on the character) together. Use a small paintbrush to paint designs on your child's face. It can be removed with soap and water.

did you KNOW?

Cold cream is cold because it is made with a lot of water that evaporates and cools your warm face. Cold cream is one of the oldest of all facial ointments.

It was invented by the Greek physician Galen in AD 157. It's not known exactly why Galen created his mixture, but experts suggest that ancient medicine was based on treating with opposites. And Galen might have been seeking a cure for a hot and dry skin condition like eczema or psoriasis. But the women of ancient Greece soon discovered the soothing white cream was superb for removing make-up, which remains the primary use for cold cream to this day.

Compact discs

- **Use as festive ornaments** Decorate a Christmas tree in style by hanging CDs, shiny side out, to create a flickering array of lights, or paint and decorate the label side to create inexpensive personalised ornaments. For variety, cut some of the CDs into stars and other shapes with sharp scissors. Drill a 6mm hole through each CD shape and thread a ribbon through to hang.

- **Make artwork in a child's room** Old CDs make inexpensive and quirky wall decorations for a teenager's room. Attach the CDs with drawing pins and use them to create a border at the ceiling or halfway up the wall. Or let your child use them to frame his or her favourite posters.

- **Make artistic bowls** Create a decorative bowl by placing a CD in the oven on a low heat over a metal bowl until the CD softens. Wearing protective gloves, gently bend the CD into the shape you want. Seal the hole by gluing the bottom edge to another surface, such as a flat dish, using epoxy or PVC glue. Note: but don't be tempted to use the bowl to hold food – not even snacks like crisps and nuts.

- **Make a decorative sun catcher** Glue two CDs together, shiny side out, and wrap wool or coloured string through the hole, then hang them in a window. The prism will make a beautiful light show.

- **Use as garden/driveway reflectors** Drill small holes into a CD and screw it onto a gate post or wooden stake and push it into the ground. Install several to light a night-time path.

- **Use as a template for a perfect circle** If you need to draw a perfect circle, don't trace around a cup or use a cumbersome compass. Every CD provides two circle sizes – you can trace around the inner hole or the outer circumference.

- **Create a spinning top** Turn an old CD into a fun toy. With a knife, make two slits across from each other in the CD hole. Force a 1p piece halfway through the hole and then spin the CD on its edge.

- **Make a CD clock** Turn a disc into a funky clock. Paint and design one side of the CD and let it dry. Write (using a permanent marker) or use stickers to create the numbers around its edge. Attach a digital clock mechanism – available from craft shops – onto the back of the CD.

- **Cover with felt and use as coasters** CDs can help to prevent unsightly stains from cups left on a table. Cut a round piece of felt to fit over the CD and glue it onto the label side of the CD so that the shiny side is facing upwards when you use the coaster.

TIP CD repair

Before throwing away or recycling a scratched CD, try to repair it. First, clean it thoroughly with a lint-free cloth or mild soap and a little water. Hold the CD by the edge to keep from getting fingerprints on it. Polish it from the middle to the edge, but not in a circular motion. If your CD still skips, try fixing it with a little nongel toothpaste. Dab some toothpaste on the end of your finger and rub it lightly onto the entire CD. Use a damp paper towel to remove the toothpaste and dry it with a fresh paper towel. The fine abrasive in the toothpaste may smooth out the scratch. You might also want to try car wax on a scratch (see page 82).

Cooking-oil spray

- **Prevent rice and pasta from sticking** Most cooks know that a little cooking oil in boiling water will keep rice or pasta from sticking together when you drain it. If you run out of cooking oil, however, a quick squirt of cooking-oil spray will also do the job.

- **Cure door squeak** Have you heard a door squeak just once too often? Put some nonstick cooking-oil spray on the hinge. Wipe up any drips with some paper towels.

- **Prevent tomato sauce stains** Are you fed up with indelible tomato sauce stains on plastic containers? To prevent them, apply a light coating of nonstick cooking-oil spray to the inside of the container before you pour in the tomato sauce.

- **De-bug your car** When insects crash into your car at speed they can really stick. Give the grille a squirt of nonstick cooking-oil spray so you can just wipe away any insect debris.

- **Keep car wheels clean** The fine black coating that collects on the wheels of the car and is so hard to clean is brake dust – produced every time you apply the brakes and the pads wear against the brake disks or cylinders. The next time you invest the elbow grease to get your wheels shiny, give them a light coating of cooking-oil spray first. The brake dust should wipe right off.

- **Grating cheese** Put less elbow grease into grating cheese by using a little nonstick cooking-oil spray on the cheese grater for smoother grating. The spray also makes it easier and quicker to clean the grater.

- **Prevent snow sticking** Shovelling snow is hard enough, but it can be more difficult when the snow sticks to the shovel. Spray the shovel with nonstick cooking-oil spray before shovelling and the snow will slide right off.

- **Remove paint and grease** Use cooking-oil spray to remove paint and grease from your hands. Work it in well and rinse. Wash again with soap and water.

- **Lubricate a bicycle chain** Do you have a creaky bike chain but no lubricating oil to hand? Give it a shot of nonstick cooking-oil spray. Don't use too much – the chain shouldn't look wet. Wipe off the excess with a clean rag.

- **Quick casting** Take some cooking-oil spray when you go fishing. Spray it on the fishing line and the line will cast more easily and go further.

- **Prevent grass from sticking** Mowing the lawn should be easy, but cleaning stuck grass from the mower is tedious. Prevent grass from sticking by spraying the blades and underside with cooking oil before mowing.

- **Dry nail polish** If you need nail polish to dry in a hurry, spray it with a coat of cooking-oil spray and let it dry. The spray is also an excellent moisturiser for the dry skin on your hands.

did you **KNOW?**

The first patent for a nonstick cooking-oil spray was issued in 1957 to Arthur Meyerhoff and his partner, Leon Rubin, who began marketing PAM (Product of Arthur Meyerhoff) All Natural Cooking Spray in 1959. After appearing on local Chicago TV cookery shows in the early 1960s, the product developed a loyal following and it quickly became a household name – and was copied all over the world.

Corks

- **Create a fishing float** Push a staple into the top of the cork, then pull the staple out just a little way so you can slide the fishing line through it to attach it.

- **Prevent pottery and chair scratches** Handmade pottery often has a rough base that can scratch furniture. To protect table tops, cut thin slices of cork and glue them to the bottom of ceramic objects. You can do the same for the bottom of chair legs to minimise noise and prevent scratches on floors.

- **Picture-perfect frames** To keep picture frames straight, cut some small flat pieces of cork, all of the same thickness, and glue them to the back of the frame. The cork will grip the wall and stop the sliding. It will also prevent the frame from making any marks on the wall.

- **Block sun glare** In the past, cricketers and American baseball players would burn cork and rub it under their eyes to reduce glare from the sun and stadium lights. These days, they use commercial products, but cork still works just as well.

- **Create craft stamps** Carve the end of a cork into any shape or design you want. Use it with ink from a stamp pad to decorate note cards. Or let the children dip carved corks in paint to make stamps and artwork.

did you **KNOW?**

Cork, the bark of the cork oak, has been used to seal wine bottles and other vessels for more than 400 years. The bark has a unique honeycomb cell structure. Each cell is sealed, filled with air and not connected to any other cell. This makes it waterproof and a poor conductor of heat and vibration. Plus, cork contains suberin, a natural waxy substance that makes it impermeable to liquids and gases and prevents the cork from rotting. It is still used for most sparkling wine and champagne, but synthetic corks are frequently used in other wines.

- **Create a cool bead curtain** Drill a hole through a number of corks and string them onto a cord along with some beads and other decorations. Make as many strings as you need and tie them onto a curtain rod.

- **Fasten earrings** When you lose the back of an earring, slice a small piece of cork about the size of the earring backing and push it on. An eraser cut off the end of a pencil will also work.

- **Use to make face paint** To create an authentic pirate moustache and stubble, char the end of a piece of cork by holding it over a candle. Let it cool a little, then rub it on the child's face.

- **Mass-produce sowing holes** Quickly sow seeds in straight rows of evenly spaced holes. Mark out the spacing you need on a board. Drill screws through the holes, using screws that will protrude about 2cm through the board. Now twist wine corks onto the screws. Just press the board, corks down, into the garden bed and you have made instant seed holes.

TAKE CARE

To open a bottle of wine, use a traditional corkscrew that twists into the stopper. Peel the top of the plastic to expose the cork. Insert the corkscrew into the centre. Twist the corkscrew straight down and then pull the cork straight out using an even pressure.

Never use a corkscrew to open a bottle of champagne or sparkling wine. Pushing down into a bottle of champagne against the pressure of the carbonation can actually make it explode. If possible, wait a day before opening and let the carbonation settle a little. Wrap the cork in a towel and twist the bottle, not the cork, slowly.

Cornflour

- **Dry shampoo** If the dog needs a bath, but you just don't have time, rub cornflour into his coat and brush it out. The dry bath will fluff up and freshen his coat.

- **Soak up furniture polish residue** If you've finished polishing the furniture, but there's still polish left on the surface, sprinkle some cornflour lightly onto the furniture. Wipe up the oil and cornflour, then buff the surface.

- **Remove ink stains from carpet** Mix a little milk with cornflour to make a paste. Apply the paste to the ink stain. Allow it to dry on the carpet for a few hours, then brush off the dried residue and vacuum it up.

- **Give carpets a fresh scent** Before vacuuming a room, sprinkle a little cornflour onto the carpet. Wait about half an hour and then vacuum as usual.

- **Make your own paste** The next time the children want to get creative with paper and paste, save money by making the paste yourself. Mix 3 teaspoons cornflour for every 4 teaspoons cold water. Stir until you reach a paste consistency. This is especially good for applying with fingers or a wooden ice-lolly stick. If you add food colouring, the paste can be used for painting objects.

- **Make finger paints** Mix together 50g cornflour and 400ml cold water. Bring to a boil and continue boiling until the mixture becomes thick. Pour your product into several small containers and add food colouring to each container to make a collection of homemade finger paints.

- **Clean stuffed animals** Rub a little cornflour onto the toy, wait about 5 minutes, and then brush it clean. Or place the stuffed animal (or a few small ones) into a bag. Sprinkle cornflour into the bag, close it and shake. Brush their fur to remove grime and remaining cornflour.

- **Untangle knots** Sprinkle a stubborn knot with a little cornflour and it will then be easy to work the segments apart.

- **Lift a scorch mark from clothing** Wet the scorched area and cover it with cornflour. Let the cornflour dry, then brush it away along with the scorch mark.

- **Remove grease splashes from walls** This is a handy remedy for unsightly grease spots. Sprinkle cornflour onto a soft cloth. Rub the grease spot gently until it disappears.

- **Get rid of bloodstains** With blood, the quicker you act, the better the result. Whether it's on clothing or table linens, you can remove or reduce a bloodstain with this method. Make a paste of cornflour mixed with cold water. Cover the spot with the paste and rub it gently into the fabric. Now put the cloth in a sunny place to dry. Once dry, brush off the remaining residue. If the stain has not gone completely, repeat the process.

- **Polish silver** Make a simple paste by mixing cornflour with water. Use a damp cloth to apply this to your silverware. Let it dry, then rub it off with cheesecloth or another soft cloth to reveal the shine.

- **Say good riddance to cockroaches** Make a mixture of 50 per cent plaster of Paris and 50 per cent cornflour. Spread this into crevices wherever cockroaches appear.

- **Make windows sparkle** Create a streak-free window-cleaning solution by mixing 2 tablespoons cornflour with 100ml ammonia and 100ml white vinegar in a bucket containing 3-4 litres warm water. Mix the milky concoction well and put the solution in a trigger-spray bottle. Spray on the windows, then wipe with a warm-water rinse. Now rub with a dry paper towel or lint-free cloth for crystal clear, streakless windows.

Cream of tartar

- **Make play clay** This fun dough is like the famous commercial stuff. Mix 2 tablespoons cream of tartar, 200ml salt, 800g plain flour and 1-2 tablespoons cooking oil. Stir well with a wooden spoon, then slowly stir while adding 800ml water. Cook the mixture over a medium heat, stirring occasionally until it thickens. It is ready when it forms a ball that is not sticky. Work in food colouring. Let it cool. It dries out more quickly than the commercial variety, so store in an airtight container in the fridge.

- **Bath scrubber** Fill a small, shallow cup or dish with cream of tartar and add hydrogen peroxide, drop by drop, until you have a thick paste. Apply to the stain and let it dry. When you remove the dried paste, you will find that the stain is gone too.

- **Brighten discoloured aluminium pots** Make a mixture of 2 tablespoons cream of tartar dissolved into 1 litre water. Bring the mixture to a boil inside the pot and boil for 10 minutes.

Curtain rings

- **Hold your hammer** Sometimes you need three hands when you're doing household repair jobs. Attach a sturdy metal shower-curtain ring to your belt and slip your hammer through it. Now you can climb a ladder or otherwise work with both hands and just grab the hammer when needed.

- **Get hooked** If you don't want to carry a backpack, lash a few items to your belt loop with the help of a curtain ring. Attach shoes or boots to your sleeping bag with a metal curtain ring, while gloves and cutlery can dangle from a metal shower-curtain ring or a brass key ring.

- **Keep track of mini-mittens** Drive a nail into the hall wall or the back of a door. Give your child a curtain ring and tell them to use it to clip his mittens together and hang them on the nail.

Dental floss

- **Remove a stuck ring** Wrap the length of your finger from the ring to the nail tightly with dental floss. You should be able to slide the ring off over the floss 'corset'.

- **Lift biscuits off a baking tray** Use dental floss to remove biscuits from a baking tray. Hold a length of dental floss taut and slide it neatly between the bottom of the biscuit and the tray.

- **Slice cake and cheese** Use dental floss to cut cakes, especially delicate and sticky ones that tend to adhere to a knife. Just hold a length of the floss taut over the cake and then slice away, moving it slightly side to side as you cut through the cake. You can also use dental floss to cut small blocks of cheese cleanly – like an old-fashioned cheesewire.

- **Make hardwearing repairs to outdoor items**
  Because dental floss is strong and resilient but fine, it is an ideal replacement for thread when you are repairing items such as an umbrella, tent or backpack, which can get hard wear. Sew up the small holes with floss. To fix larger rips, sew back and forth over the holes until you have covered the space with a floss 'darn'.

- **Separate photos** Sometimes photographs get stuck to each other and it seems the only way to separate them is to ruin them. Try working a length of dental floss between the pictures to gently prise them apart.

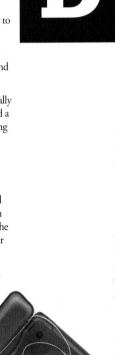

- **Extra-strong string for hanging things**
  Dental floss is remarkably strong. Use it instead of string or wire to hang pictures, mobiles or wind chimes securely. Use it with a needle to thread papers you want to hold together or as a mini-clothesline for items you want to display.

Denture tablets

- **Re-ignite a diamond's sparkle** Drop a denture tablet into a glass of water, followed by your diamond jewellery. Let it sit for a few minutes. Remove and rinse thoroughly.

- **Banish mineral deposits on glass** Fresh flowers often leave a persistent ring on glass vases. To remove it, fill the vase with water and drop in a denture tablet. When the fizzing has stopped, the mineral deposits will be gone. Use the same method to clean Thermos flasks, cruets, glasses and decanters.

- **Clean the toilet** Drop a denture tablet in the porcelain toilet bowl. Wait about 20 minutes and flush.

- **Clean enamel cookware** Fill the pan with warm water and drop in a tablet or two, depending on its size. Once the fizzing has stopped, your cookware will be clean.

- **Clean a coffee maker** Hard water leaves mineral deposits in the tank of an electric coffee maker that makes it slower and affects the taste. Drop two denture tablets in the tank and fill with water. Run the coffee maker. Discard the first pot and follow with one or two rinse cycles with clean water for a full bacterial clean-out.

- **Unblock a drain** If a drain is sluggish, drop a couple of tablets into the drain and run water until the problem clears. For a more stubborn blockage, drop 3 tablets down the sink, follow that with 200ml white vinegar, then wait a few minutes. Now run hot water into the drain until the blockage has gone.

did you **KNOW?**

Bleaching agents are a common component of denture-cleaning tablets, providing the chemical action that helps the tablets to remove plaque and to whiten and bleach away stains. This is what makes them surprisingly useful for cleaning toilets, coffee makers, jewellery and enamel cookware, among other things.

Disposable nappies

- **Keep a plant watered longer** Before potting a plant, place a clean disposable nappy in the bottom of the flowerpot, absorbent side up. It will absorb water that would otherwise drain out the bottom and will keep the plant from drying out too fast. You'll also cut back on how often you have to water the plant.

- **Make a heating pad** Soothe your aching neck, back or shoulder. Use a disposable nappy's high level of absorbency to your advantage by creating a soft, pliable heating pad. Moisten a disposable nappy and place it in the microwave on medium-high setting for about 2 minutes. Check that it is not too hot for comfort and then apply to your sore joint.

- **Pad a package** If want to post a fragile item, but don't have any protective wrapping, wrap the item in disposable nappies or insert them as padding before sealing the package. Nappies cost more than ordinary protective packaging wrap, but at least you will have sent the package out quickly and you can be assured your gift will arrive in one piece.

- **Make a crash pad for delicate items** Line a large flat-bottomed shopping bag with a couple of disposable nappies and keep it in your car. You can use it to transport glass jars and bottles or delicate fruit on a shopping trip.

did you **KNOW?**

It took a mother to invent disposable nappies. Looking for an alternative to messy cloth nappies, Marion Donovan first created a plastic covering for nappies. She made her prototype from a shower curtain and later parachute fabric. Manufacturers weren't interested, but when she created her own company and released the product in 1949 at Saks Fifth Avenue in New York City, it was an instant success. Donovan soon added disposable absorbent material to create the first disposable nappy and, in 1951, sold her company for $1 million (£600,000).

Earrings

- **Use as a bulletin-board tack** Lend a little personal style to a bulletin board. Use cheap pierced earrings that have lost their other halves to tack up pictures, notes, souvenirs and clippings.

- **Create a brooch** If you have a batch of single pierced earrings collecting dust, snip off the stems with wire cutters and use your creativity. Arrange the earrings on a piece of coloured card and secure them with a glue gun. Add a pin backing to make a new brooch. Use the same method to jazz up a plain picture frame.

- **Decorate a Christmas tree** Scatter clip-on earrings around the boughs of the Christmas tree as an eye-catching accent to larger tree decorations. Or use them as the main adornment on a small tree or wreath.

- **Make a magnet** Give your fridge some glitz. Use wire cutters to cut the stem off an orphan earring and glue it to a magnet.

- **Clip your scarf** If you've lost a favourite clip earring wear the survivor by using it to secure a scarf. Just tie the scarf as desired, then clip it with the earring.

- **Make an instant button.** If you're dressed to go out and you discover a button missing, just dip into your collection of clip-on earrings. Clip the earring onto the button side of the garment to create a new 'button', then button as usual using the buttonhole. If you have time, move the top button to replace the lost one and then use the earring at the top of the garment.

did you **KNOW?**

People have been wearing earrings for nearly 5,000 years. According to historians who have studied jewellery, they were probably introduced in western Asia in about 3000 BC. The oldest earrings were discovered in Iraq and date from 2500 BC.

Egg cartons

- **Make ice** If you are making lots of ice for a party, use the bottom halves of clean polystyrene egg cartons as auxiliary ice trays.

- **Use for storing and organising** With six or a dozen handy compartments, egg cartons are brilliant for storing and organising small items such as coins, buttons, safety pins or small nuts and screws on a workbench.

- **Protect Christmas ornaments** Keep small, delicate Christmas ornaments from being crushed by packing them in handy, stackable egg cartons.

- **Start a fire** Fill a cardboard egg carton with briquettes (and a bit of leftover candle wax if it's handy). Place on the barbecue and light. Egg cartons can also be filled with small bits of wood and paper and used as a fire starter in a fireplace.

- **Start seedlings** An egg carton can become the perfect nursery for seeds. Use a cardboard egg carton, not a polystyrene one. Fill each cell in the carton with soil and plant a few seeds in each one. Once the seeds have sprouted, divide the carton into individual cells and plant, cardboard cells and all.

- **Reinforce a bin bag** If you have ever pulled a plastic rubbish bag out of the kitchen bin only to have something horrible drip on the floor, put an opened empty egg carton at the bottom of the bin bag to prevent tears and punctures.

- **Post homemade goodies** to distant parts. Here is a great way to brighten the day of a faraway friend or loved one. Cover an egg carton with bright wrapping paper. Line the individual cells with sweet wrappers or coloured tissue paper. Nestle homemade treats inside each. Include the carton in your next package or birthday gift and rest assured that the treats will arrive intact.

- **Golf-ball caddy** Keep an egg carton in a golf bag. It is a great way to keep golf balls clean, organised and ready for teeing off.

Eggs

- **Make a facial** For a little pampering, head to the refrigerator for an egg. If you have dry skin that needs moisturising, separate the egg and beat the yolk. Those with oily skin should use the egg white, to which a bit of lemon or honey can be added. For normal skin, use the entire egg. Apply the beaten egg, relax and wait 30 minutes, then rinse. Your skin should be soft, fresh and clean.

- **Use as glue** If you have run out of white glue, egg whites can act as a glue substitute for gluing pieces of paper or light cardboard together.

- **Add to compost** Eggshells are a great addition to your compost because they are rich in calcium, a nutrient that is beneficial to plants. Crushing them thoroughly before you put them in your compost heap will help them to break down faster.

- **Water your plants** After boiling eggs, don't pour the water down the drain. Instead, let it cool, then water plants with the nutrient-filled water.

- **Start seeds** You can plant seeds in eggshells. Remove the top quarter of the eggshell and remove the egg. Make a pinhole in the bottom of the each shell. Place the eggshells in an egg carton and fill each one with soil, leaving 1.5cm space at the top. Press in 2 or 3 seeds into the soil. They will draw extra nutrients from the eggshells. Once the seedlings are about 7.5cm tall, transplant them into the garden. Remove the shell before you put them in the ground. Then crush the eggshells and put them on the compost heap or mix them with soil in the garden.

Electrical tape

● **Make a lint lifter** To lift lint and pet hair off clothing and upholstery, you don't need a special lint remover. Simply wrap your hand with electrical tape, sticky side out, and rub it against the surface of the material.

● **Cover casters** Prevent wheeled furniture from leaving unsightly black marks on a wood or vinyl floor by wrapping caster wheels with electrical tape.

● **Clean a comb** Remove the dirt that builds up between the teeth of a comb, by pressing a strip of electrical tape along the comb's length. Lift it off, then dip the comb in a solution of alcohol and water, or ammonia and water, to sterilise it.

● **Organise tubes of glue and caulk** If an untidy pile of glue and caulk tubes is cluttering a workbench, cut a strip of electrical or gaffer tape several centimetres long and fold it over the bottom of each tube, leaving a flap at the end. Punch a hole in the flap with a paper-hole punch and hang the tube on a nail or hook. You'll free up space on the bench and be able to find the right tube quickly.

● **Safely remove glass from a broken window** Removing a broken pane of glass can be dangerous as there is always the possibility that a sharp fragment will fall out and cut you. To prevent this, crisscross both sides of the broken pane with electrical tape before removing a sash or hinged window. Don't forget to wear heavy-duty leather gloves when you pull the glass shards out of the frame.

● **Reinforce book binding** Electrical tape is perfect for repairing broken book binding. Using coloured tape of a suitable shade (matching or contrasting the cover so that it looks appealing), run the tape down the length of the spine and cut shorter pieces to run perpendicular to that if you need extra reinforcement.

Electrical tape

- **Cover a book** Use electrical tape in any colour to create a durable book cover for a textbook or a paperback that you want to read on the beach. Make a pattern for the cover on a sheet of newspaper; fit the pattern to your book, then cover the pattern, one row at a time, with electrical tape, overlapping the rows. The resulting removable cover will be waterproof and sturdy.

- **Wrap Christmas presents** For a novel way to wrap a special gift, don't bother with the paper; go straight for the tape. Press electrical tape directly onto the gift box. Make designs or cover in stripes and then add decorative touches by cutting shapes, letters and motifs from tape to attach to the 'wrapped' surface.

- **Repair a rear light** If someone has backed into your car and smashed the rear light, this is a quick fix that will last until you have time to get it repaired. Depending on where the cracks lie, use yellow or red electrical tape to hold the remaining parts of the rear-light cover together.

- **Repair outdoor cushions** Don't let a little rip in the cushion that go with your garden furniture get any worse. Repair the tear with closely matched coloured electrical tape and it will hold up for several seasons.

- **Make bicycle streamers** Add streamers to the handlebars of child's bicycle. Make them using electrical tape in various colours. Cut the tape into strips about 1cm wide by 25cm long. Fold each strip in half, sticky sides together. Once you have about half a dozen for each side, stick them into the end of the handlebar and secure them with lengths of electrical tape. Make sure that the child will still be able to get a good grip on the handlebars.

Emery boards

- **Sand deep crevices** When refinishing an elaborate piece of wood such as turned table legs or chair spindles, you can use emery boards to gently smooth any hard-to-reach crevices before applying stain or finish. These filelike nail sanders are easy to handle and provide a choice of two sanding grades.

- **Remove dirt from an eraser** To clean a dirty eraser on the end of a pencil, take an emery board and rub lightly over the eraser until the dirt is filed off.

- **Prepare seeds for planting** Use an emery board to remove the hard coating on seeds before you plant them. This will speed sprouting and help the seeds to absorb moisture more effectively.

- **Revitalise suede** If a favourite pair of suede shoes have become stained and tired, an emery board can revive them. Rub the stain lightly with an emery board, and then hold the shoe over the steam from a kettle or pan of boiling water to remove the stain. This technique will work for suede clothing, too.

did you **KNOW?**

Emery boards were first introduced in around 1910. The emery coating is a natural mixture of corundum and magnetite – diamonds are the only minerals harder than corundum. Sapphires and rubies are also varieties of corundum. Not surprisingly perhaps, a manicurist's magazine urged women to 'treat their nails like jewels, not tools'. These days, emery boards come adorned with bright designs, give off scents or may even be shaped as hearts and stars.

Envelopes

- **Shred old receipts faster** The best way to get rid of receipts that may have your credit card number or other personal information on them is to shred them. But feeding each tiny receipt into a shredder can be tedious. Instead, place all the old receipts into a few old envelopes and shred the envelopes.

- **Make a small funnel** It is much cheaper to buy spices in bulk and transfer them to smaller, handier bottles for use in the kitchen. To make the job of transferring them much easier, make a couple of disposable funnels from an envelope. Seal the envelope, cut it in half diagonally and snip off one corner on each half to make two funnels for pouring spices into smaller jars.

- **Sort and store sandpaper** Stop sheets of sandpaper from curling up into useless tubes and keep them organised by storing them in A5 card-backed envelopes. Use one envelope for each type of grit and write the grit grade on the envelopes.

- **Make file folders** Don't let papers get disorganised just because you have run out of file folders. Cut the short ends off a light card-backed A4 envelope. Cut a 2cm wide strip lengthwise off the top of one side. The other edge will become the place where you label your file.

- **Make bookmarks** Recycle envelopes by making them into useful bookmarks of different sizes. Cut off the gummed flap and one end of the envelope. Then slip the remainder over the corner of the page where you have stopped reading to make a quick placeholder that won't damage your book. You could hand a batch to the children to decorate to make their own set or to give as a homemade gift.

Epsom salts

- **Clean bathroom tiles** Clean grubby grout with some Epsom salts. Mix it in equal parts with washing-up liquid, then dab it onto the offending area and start scrubbing. The Epsom salts work with the detergent to dissolve the grime.

- **Frost your windows for Christmas** If you are dreaming of a white Christmas, but the weather won't cooperate, you can make your windows look frosty. Mix Epsom salts with some stale beer until the salts stop dissolving. Apply the mixture to the windows with a sponge. For a realistic look, sweep the sponge in an arc at the bottom corners. When the mixture dries, the windows will look frosted.

- **Get rid of foxes** Are urban foxes raiding your rubbish bin, strewing mess around the front of the house? A few tablespoons of Epsom salts spread around bins should deter them as they won't like the taste. Reapply after it rains.

- **Deter slugs** Are you tired of going out into the garden only to find the patio and lawn crawling with slimy slugs? Sprinkle Epsom salts where they glide and they will soon find another spot to gather in.

- **Fertilise tomatoes and other plants** Every week, for each 30cm of the height of a tomato plant, add one tablespoon of Epsom salts to the soil and the tomatoes will flourish. Epsom salts are also a good fertiliser for houseplants, roses, gardenias and other flowers and trees.

- **Make the grass greener** Use Epsom salts to add extra brightness to a lawn and add needed magnesium and iron to your soil. Add 2 tablespoons to 4 litres of water. Spread on the lawn and then water with plain water to make sure it has thoroughly soaked into the grass.

Epsom salts

- **Regenerate a car battery** If a car battery is starting to sound as if it won't turn over, and you are worried that you'll be stuck the next time you try to start your car, give the battery a little more life with this potion. Dissolve about 30g of Epsom salts in warm water and add it to each battery cell.

- **Get rid of blackheads** This works. Mix a teaspoon of Epsom salts and 3 drops iodine in 100ml boiling water. When the mixture cools enough to stick your finger in it, apply it to the blackhead with a cotton wool ball or bud. Repeat this three or four times, reheating the solution if necessary. Gently remove the blackhead and then dab the area with an alcohol-based astringent

(KIDS' STUFF)
Two fun winter projects

Here are two fun winter-inspired projects using Epsom salts.

Make snowflakes by folding a piece of blue paper several times and snipping shapes into the resulting square of paper. Unfold your snowflake. Brush one side with a thick mixture of water and Epsom salts. After it dries, turn it over and brush the other side. When it's finished, you'll have a frosty-looking snowflake that you can hang in the window.

To make a snowy scene, use crayons to draw a picture on stiff paper. Mix equal parts of Epsom salts and boiling water. Leave it to cool; then use a wide artist's paintbrush to paint over the whole picture. When it dries, 'snow' crystals will appear.

Fabric softener

- **End clinging dust on the TV** Does dust fly back onto the television screen and other plastic surfaces, as soon as they have been cleaned? To eliminate the static that attracts dust, simply dampen a duster with a little fabric softener straight from the bottle and dust as usual.

- **Remove old wallpaper** Removing old wallpaper is easy if you use fabric softener. Just stir 1 capful liquid softener into a litre of water and sponge the solution onto the wallpaper. Let it soak in for 20 minutes, then scrape the paper from the wall. If the wallpaper has a water-resistant coating, score it with a wire-bristle brush before treating with the fabric softener solution.

- **Abolish carpet shock** To eliminate static shock when you walk across a carpet, spray the carpet with a fabric softener solution. Dilute 200ml softener with 2.5 litres water; fill a spray bottle and lightly squirt onto the carpet. Take care not to saturate it and damage the carpet backing. Spray in the evening and let the carpet dry overnight before walking on it. The effect should last for several weeks.

- **Remove hair-spray residue** Dried-on hair spray can be tough to remove from walls and mirrors, but even a build-up of residue is no match for a solution of 1 part liquid fabric softener to 2 parts water. Stir to blend, pour into a spray bottle, squirt the surface and polish it with a dry cloth.

- **Clean now, not later** Clean glass tables, shower doors and other hard surfaces, and repel dust with liquid fabric softener. Mix 1 part softener into 4 parts water and store in a spray bottle, such as an empty window-cleaning liquid bottle. Apply a little solution to a clean cloth, wipe the surface and then polish with a dry cloth.

Fabric softener

- **Float away baked-on grime** Don't scrub. Instead, soak burned-on foods from casseroles with liquid fabric softener. Fill the casserole with water, add a squirt of liquid fabric softener and soak for an hour or until the residue wipes easily away.

- **Keep paintbrushes pliable** After using a paintbrush, clean the bristles thoroughly and rinse them in an old can full of water with a drop of liquid fabric softener mixed in. After rinsing, wipe the bristles dry and store the brush as usual.

- **Remove hard-water stains** Hard-water stains on windows can be difficult to remove. To speed up the process, dab full-strength liquid fabric softener onto the stains and let it soak for 10 minutes. Then wipe the softener and stain off the glass with a damp cloth and rinse.

- **Make your own fabric softener sheets** Fabric softener sheets are convenient to use, but they're much more expensive than liquid softeners. You can make your own dryer sheets and save money. Just moisten an old facecloth with 1 teaspoon liquid softener and put it into the tumble drier with your next load.

did you **KNOW?**

How does fabric softener reduce cling as well as soften clothes? The secret is in the electrical charges. Positively charged chemical lubricants in the fabric softener are attracted to negative charges in the clothes, softening the fabric. The softened fabrics create less friction and less static, as they rub against each other in the dryer and because fabric softener attracts moisture, the slightly damp surface of the fabrics makes them electrical conductors. As a result, the electrical charges travel through them instead of staying on the surface to cause static cling and sparks as you pull the clothing from the drier.

Fabric-softener sheets

- **Freshen up your car** Tuck a new fabric-softener sheet under each car seat to counteract musty odours and cigarette smells.

- **Freshen drawers** For a fresh fragrance, tuck a new fabric-softener sheet under existing drawer liners, or tape one to the back of each drawer.

- **Deodorise trainers, gym bags and waste-paper baskets** Tuck a new fabric-softener sheet into each trainer and leave overnight to neutralise odours. Leave a fabric-softener sheet at the bottom of a gym bag until your nose lets you know it's time to renew it, or place a used fabric-conditioner sheet in the bottom of laundry baskets and waste-paper baskets to counteract odours.

- **Use as an inconspicuous air freshener** Tuck a few sheets of unused, tumble-dryer fabric softener into wardrobes, chest of drawers and cupboards. If you put a sheet in a suitcase before storing, it will smell great the next time you use it.

- **Pick up pet hair** A used fabric-softener sheet will suck pet hair off a fabric-covered sofa with a couple of swipes.

- **Do away with dog odour** Wipe your wet, smelly friend with a used fabric-softener sheet and he should smell as fresh as a daisy.

- **Wipe soap scum from shower screens** You will find that a used fabric-softener sheet is very effective in removing soap scum.

TAKE CARE

People with allergies or chemical sensitivities may develop rashes or skin irritations when they come into contact with laundry treated with some commercial fabric softeners or fabric-softener sheets. If you are sensitive to softeners, you can still soften your laundry by substituting 50ml white vinegar or adding the same amount of your favourite hair conditioner to the washing machine's last rinse cycle. It will give you noticeably softer, fresher-smelling laundry.

Fabric-softener sheets

- **Lift burned-on casserole residue** Fill the dish with hot water and place three or four used softener sheets in the dish. Soak overnight, remove the sheets, and you will have no trouble washing away the residue. Rinse it well afterwards.

- **Repel dust from electrical appliances** Because television and PC screens are electrically charged, they actually attract dust, making dusting them a never-ending chore. If you dust them with used fabric-softener sheets, designed to reduce static cling, the dust won't resettle for several days.

- **Buff chrome to a brilliant shine** After chrome is cleaned, it can still look streaky and dull, but you can easily buff up the shine with a used fabric-softener sheet.

- **Keep dust off blinds** Wipe blinds down with a used fabric-softener sheet to repel dust. Repeat whenever the effect wears off.

- **Do away with static cling** You'll never be embarrassed by static cling again if you keep a used fabric-softener sheet in your handbag or dresser drawer. When faced with static, dampen the sheet and rub it over tights to put an end to clinging skirts.

- **Remove sawdust before painting** Get rid of all traces of sawdust on a woodworking project before you paint or varnish it, by rubbing with an unused fabric-softener sheet; it will attract sawdust and hold it like a magnet.

- **Renew grubby stuffed toys** Wash fake-fur stuffed animals in the washing machine on a delicates programme. Put the stuffed animals into the tumble dryer with a pair of old tennis shoes and a fabric-softener sheet and they will come out fluffy and silky soft.

- **Abolish tangled sewing thread** After threading a needle, insert it into an unused fabric-softener sheet and pull all of the thread through to give it a nonstick coating.

Flour

- **Repel ants with flour** Sprinkle a line of flour along the backs of your pantry and kitchen-cabinet shelves and anywhere else that you see ants entering the house. Repelled by the flour, the ants won't cross over the line.

- **Make modelling clay** Keep children busy with some homemade modelling clay – they can even help you to make it. Knead together 600g flour, 50g salt, 200ml water, 1 tablespoon vegetable oil and 1 or 2 drops food colouring. If the mixture is sticky, add more flour; if it's too stiff, add more water. When the 'clay' is of a workable consistency, it can be stored until needed in a self-sealing plastic bag.

- **Safe paste for children's crafts** Look no further than your kitchen for an inexpensive, nontoxic paste that is ideal for children's paper-craft projects, such as papier-mâché and pasting items into a scrap book. To make the paste, add 600ml cold water to a saucepan and blend in 200g flour. Stirring constantly, bring the mixture to a boil. Reduce heat and simmer, stirring until smooth and thick. Cool and pour into a plastic squeeze bottle to use. The paste will keep for weeks in the refrigerator, and can be easily cleaned up with soap and water.

did you **KNOW?**

Have you ever wondered why the word 'flour' is pronounced exactly like the word 'flower'? Flour is actually derived from the French word for flower, which is *fleur*. The French use the word to describe the most desirable, or floury (flowery) and protein-rich, part of a grain after processing removes the hull. And because much of our food terminology comes from the French, we still bake and make sauces with the flower of grains, such as wheat, which we call flour.

Flour

● **Polish brass and copper** Don't buy special cleaners for brass and silver. You can make your own far cheaper. Combine equal parts of flour, salt and vinegar, and mix into a paste. Spread the paste onto the metal, let it dry and then buff it off with a clean, dry cloth.

● **Bring back the lustre to a dull sink** To buff a stainless-steel sink back to a warm shine, sprinkle flour over it and rub lightly with a soft, dry cloth. Then rinse the sink and polish again to restore its shine.

● **Freshen playing cards**
After a few games, cards may accumulate a greasy patina, but you can restore them with some flour in a paper bag. Drop the cards into the bag with enough flour to cover, shake vigorously and remove the cards. The flour will absorb the oils and it can be easily knocked off the cards by giving them a thorough shuffle.

Flowerpots

- **Container for baking bread** Take a new, clean, medium-sized clay flowerpot, soak it in water for about 20 minutes and then lightly grease the inside with butter. Place bread dough, prepared in the usual way, in the pot and bake. The clay pot will give the bread a crusty exterior while keeping the inside moist.

- **Unfurl wool without knots** The sweater you're knitting will take forever if you're constantly stopping to pull out tangles in the wool. To prevent this, place the ball of wool under an upturned flowerpot and thread the end through the draining hole. Set it next to where you are sitting for relaxed, tangle-free knitting.

- **Create an aquarium fish cave** Some fish love to lurk in shadowy corners of their tanks, keeping themselves safe from imagined predators. Place a mini-flowerpot on its side on the aquarium floor to create a cave for shy fish.

- **Help container plants to root** When planting a number of shallow-rooted plants in a deep container, one easy solution is to find another smaller flowerpot that will fit upside down in the base of the deeper pot and occupy a lot of that space. After you insert it, fill around it with soil before putting in your plants.

- **Keep soil in a flowerpot** Soil from a houseplant won't slip away when it's watered if you place broken clay flowerpot shards in the bottom of the pot. The water will drain out, not the soil.

did you **KNOW?**

For thousands of years people have been putting plants into pots to transport native plants to a new land or to bring exotic plants home. In 1495 BC, Egyptian queen Hatshepsut sent workers to Somalia to bring back incense trees in pots. And in 1787 Captain Bligh reportedly had more than 1,000 breadfruit plants in clay pots aboard the HMS *Bounty*. The plants were destined for the West Indies, where they were to be grown as food for the islands' slave population.

Foldback clips

- **Strengthen your grip** Does a weak grip or arthritis make it hard for you to open jars and do other tasks with your hands? A large foldback clip can help to boost your grip. Squeeze the folded-back wings of the clip, hold for a count of five and relax. Do this a dozen or so times with each hand a few times a day. It will strengthen your grip and release tension, too.

- **Mount a picture** Here is a stylish way to mount and hang a picture so that it has a clean frameless look. Sandwich the picture between a sheet of glass or clear plastic and piece of hardboard or stiff cardboard. Then use tiny binder clips along the edges to clamp the pieces together. Use two or three clips on each side. After the clips are in place, remove the clip handles at the front. Tie picture wire to the rear handles to hang the picture.

- **Keep your place** A medium-sized foldback clip makes an ideal bookmark. If you don't want to leave impression marks on the pages, tape a soft material like felt or even just some adhesive tape, to the inside jaws of the clip before using.

- **Make a money clip** To keep paper money in a neat bundle in your pocket or purse, stack the notes, fold them in half and put a small foldback clip over the fold.

- **Keep passport handy** If you are at an airport and you know you will be asked to show your passport and tickets a number of times, instead of fishing in your bag, use a foldback clip to firmly and conveniently attach your passport and other travel documents to your belt. You can also use a small binder clip to secure your office ID to your belt or a breast pocket if you need to keep it to hand.

Freezers

- **Eliminate unpopped popcorn** Eliminate stale popcorn that won't pop by keeping the unpopped supply in the freezer.

- **Remove wax from candlesticks** Place the candlesticks in the freezer and then pick off any accumulated wax drippings.
  WARNING: don't do this if the candlesticks are made from more than one type of metal. The metals may expand and contract at different rates and damage the candlesticks.

- **Unstick photos** If water has dripped onto a batch of photographs, causing them to stick together, place them in the freezer for about 20 minutes. Then use a butter knife to separate them. If they don't come free, place them back in the freezer. This works for envelopes and stamps, too.

- **Extend candle life** Place candles in the freezer for at least 2 hours before burning. They will last longer.

- **Remove odours** If you place a musty book or a smelly plastic container in the freezer overnight, it will be fresh by morning.

TIP freezer tactics

Here are some ways to get the most out of your freezer or your refrigerator's freezer compartment:
- To prevent food from spoiling, keep the freezer at –18°C. To check the temperature, place a freezer thermometer (sold at hardware stores) between two frozen food containers.
- A full freezer runs the compressor less often and stays colder longer, which is worth remembering the next time there's a power cut.
- The shelves on a freezer door are a little warmer than the freezer interior, making them ideal for storing items such as bread and coffee.
- When defrosting the freezer, place a large towel or sheet on the bottom. Water will drip onto it, making cleaning up much easier.
- The next time you defrost the freezer, apply a thin coat of petroleum jelly to the walls to keep any frost from sticking.

Fruit baskets

- **Fashion a string dispenser or screwdriver holder** If you don't want to have to untangle knots every time you need a piece of string, twine or wool, make a dispenser with two fruit baskets. Place the ball inside one fruit basket. Feed the cord through the top of a second, inverted basket, then tie the two baskets together with twist ties. You can mount an inverted fruit basket on your workshop wall to hold and organise screwdrivers, which will fit neatly between the slats.

- **Use as a dishwasher basket** If the smaller items you place in the dishwasher (such as baby bottle caps, food-processor accessories and jar lids) won't stay put, try putting them in a fruit basket. Place the items inside one basket, then cover with a second basket. Fasten them together with a thick rubber band and place on the dishwasher's upper rack. Because the baskets are perforated, water will be sieved through them when the machine is running.

- **Use as a colander** If you need a small colander to wash individual servings of fruits and vegetables or to drain off a child's portion of hot macaroni shells, use an empty fruit basket. It makes an excellent mini-colander.

- **Arrange flowers** Droopy or lopsided flower arrangements are not elegant. That's why professionals use a substance known as oasis to keep cut flowers in place. For an alternative stabiliser, insert an inverted fruit basket into a vase (trim the basket to fit). It should keep flower stalks standing tall.

- **Organise pills and medicines** A clean fruit basket is ideal for organising vitamins and medicine bottles. If you're taking several medicines, it is a convenient way to place them all – or pre-packaged individual doses – in one, easy-to-remember location. You can also use baskets to organise medicines in your cupboard or medicine cabinet according to expiry dates or uses.

- **Protect seedlings** Help young plants to thrive in the garden by placing inverted fruit baskets over them. The baskets will let water, sunlight and air in, but keep rabbits, rats and squirrels out. Make sure the basket is buried below ground level and tightly secured (placing a few large stones around it may suffice).

- **Make a bulb cage** Squirrels and other rodents view freshly planted flower bulbs as nothing more than tasty morsels and easy pickings. But you can put a damper on their meal by planting bulbs in fruit baskets. Be sure to place the basket at the correct depth, then insert the bulb and cover with soil.

- **Build mini-hanging planters** Make little hanging baskets for small-scale plants such as violas, or to highlight your favourite annuals. Fill a series of berry baskets with sphagnum moss mixed with a bit of potting compost, plant your desired combination of plants and suspend them from a balcony or outside a back door with a length of monofilament fishing line.

(KIDS' STUFF)
Baskets for craft projects

Fruit baskets can be useful for all sorts of children's crafts. For example, you can cut apart the panels and carve out geometric shapes for them to use as stencils. You can also turn one into an Easter basket by adding some fake grass and a (preferably pink) pipe cleaner for a handle. Or use one as a multiple bubble maker; simply dip it in some water mixed with washing-up liquid and wave it through the air to create swarms of bubbles. Lastly, let children decorate the baskets with ribbons, stiff paper or lightweight card and use them to store their own little trinkets and toys.

Funnels

● **Separate eggs** To make an exceptional egg separater, use a funnel. Simply crack the egg into the funnel. The white will slide out of the spout into another container, while the yolk stays put. Just be careful not to break the yolk when you're cracking the egg.

● **Make a string dispenser** Don't get tied up in knots over tangled string. Nail a large funnel to the wall, with the stem pointing down. Place a ball of string in the funnel and thread the end down through the funnel's stem. You will have an instant knot-free string dispenser.

● **Make a kids' telephone** Use two small plastic funnels to make a durable string telephone for your children. For each funnel, tie a button to one end of a length of kite string and thread it through the large end of the funnel. Tie another button at the bottom of the spout to keep the string in place and let the children start talking to each other on their free telephone.

Gaffer tape see page 143

Garden hose

- **Capture earwigs** Cut a piece of hose into 30cm lengths, making sure the inside is completely dry. Place the hose segments down where you have seen earwigs crawling around and leave them overnight. By the morning the hoses should be filled with the earwigs and they can be transferred far away from their favourite meal.

- **Unclog a drainpipe** When leaves and debris clog up your drainpipe and guttering, use a garden hose to get things flowing again. Push the hose up the pipe and poke it through the blockage. You won't even have to turn the hose on, because the water in the gutters will flush out the blockage.

- **Stabilise a tree** A short length of old garden hose is a good way to tie a young tree to its stake. The hose is flexible enough to bend when the tree does, but strong enough to keep the tree tied to its stake until it can stand on its own. Nor will the hose damage the bark of the young tree as it grows.

TIP buying a hose

Bear these points in mind when going to buy a new hose – it's one of the most important outdoor tools:
- To determine how long a hose you need, measure the distance from the tap to the furthest point in the garden. Add a couple of metres to allow for watering around corners; this will help you to avoid the annoying kinks that cut water pressure.
- Vinyl and rubber hoses are generally sturdier and more weather resistant than those made of cheaper forms of plastic. If a hose flattens when you step on it, it is not up to gardening duties.
- Buy a hose with a lifetime warranty; only good-quality hoses will have one.

Garden hose

- **Cover the chains on a child's swing** Put a length of old hose over each chain to protect little hands from getting pinched or twisted. If you have access to one end of the chains, just slip the chain through the hose. Otherwise, slit the hose down the middle and slip it over the chains of the swing. Close the slit hose with a few wraps of gaffer tape.

- **Make a paint can grip** Slit a length of hose down the middle and encase the handle of the paint can to make it easier and more comfortable to carry.

- **Make a sander for curves** To sand a tight concave surface – for example, a piece of cove moulding – take a 25cm length of garden hose, split it open lengthways and insert one edge of a piece of sandpaper. Wrap the sandpaper around the hose, cut it to fit and insert the other end in the slit. Firmly close the slit with a piece of gaffer tape and you should be able to get at the most awkward bend.

- **Create a template for a new garden design** Use a garden hose to create a template for curves, circles and other free-form elements of your design. Using the line of the hose, you should be able to mark the edges of new curved beds, patios or pathway features and get a smooth, elegant line to follow.

- **Protect handsaw and ice-skate blades** Keep a handsaw blade sharp and safe by protecting it with a length of garden hose. Cut a piece of hose to the right length, slit it along its length and slip it over the teeth. This is also a good way to protect the blades of ice skates and cooking knives when you're in transit.

Gaffer tape...

...around the house

- **Temporarily hem your jeans** Thick denim jeans can be difficult to sew through. Make a temporary hem with gaffer tape. The new hem will last through a few washes.

- **Remove lint on clothing** To remove pet hairs, wrap one hand with a length of gaffer tape, sticky side out. Then roll the sticky tape against the article of clothing in a rocking motion until every last hair has been picked up. Don't wipe, since that may affect the nap of the fabric.

- **Make a DIY bandage** Here's how to protect a bad scrape until you can get a proper dressing. Fold tissue paper or paper towel to cover the wound and cover it with a piece of gaffer tape. It will keep the wound clean until you can treat it properly.

- **Keep a secret car key** You will never get locked out of your car again if you fix an extra key to the undercarriage of your car with gaffer tape.

- **Catch flies and other insects** If you are plagued by swarms of flies and midges, take a roll of gaffer tape and tear off a few 30cm strips. Hang them from the ceiling to use as flypaper. You should soon get rid of the flies and you can roll up the tape and throw it away.

...around the house

- **Repair a vacuum-cleaner hose** If a vacuum-cleaner hose has cracked and developed a leak, you don't need to buy a whole new machine. Repair the broken hose with gaffer tape and your vacuum cleaner should last until the motor wears out.

- **Reuse a vacuum-cleaner bag** Save money by using a vacuum-cleaner bag twice. After the bag is full the first time, don't empty it the usual way through the hole in front. Take out the bag and cut a slit down the middle of the back. After you have emptied the bag into a bin, hold the cut edges together, fold them closed and seal them securely with gaffer tape. Take care not to overfill during the second use.

- **Replace a shower-curtain eyelet** Make sure the curtain is dry, then cut a rectangular piece of tape in a matching colour and fold it from front to back over the torn hole. Slit the tape with a craft knife, razor blade or scissors, and push the shower-curtain ring back in place.

- **Reinforce book binding** Gaffer tape is perfect for repairing a broken book binding. Run the tape down the length of the spine and cut shorter pieces to run perpendicular to that if you need extra reinforcement.

did you KNOW?

In the USA, gaffer tape is known as duct tape. But it really did start being known as duck tape. In the Second World War, the US military needed a flexible, durable, waterproof tape. Permacell, a division of Johnson & Johnson, devised a strong, flexible green tape based on its own medical tape that was easy to rip into useful strips. It was used for everything from sealing ammunition cases to repairing windscreens. GIs nicknamed it duck tape because it was waterproof, like a duck's back.

After the war, the tape, now available in silver, was used for joining heating and air-conditioning ductwork and became known as duct tape. In the UK it is known as gaffer tape after the electrician in charge of lighting on a film or television set.

...sport and the great outdoors

- **Tighten cricket pads** Use gaffer tape to attach pads firmly in place. Put on all the necessary equipment, including socks. Split the gaffer tape to the width appropriate for your size – children might need narrower strips than adults – and start wrapping around the pads to keep them tight to your legs.

- **Add life to a hockey stick** If you have a hockey stick that is showing its age, breathe a little more life into it by wrapping the bottom with gaffer tape. Replace the tape as often as needed.

- **Extend the life of a skateboarder's shoes** Anyone who performs skateboard jumps wears out their shoes quickly because jumping involves sliding the toe or side of the foot along the board. Protect feet and prolong the life of shoes by putting a layer or two of gaffer tape on the area that scrapes along the board.

- **Repair ski gloves** Gaffer tape is the perfect solution for ripped ski gloves because it is waterproof, incredibly adhesive, strong and can easily be torn into strips of any width. Make the repair lengthways or around the fingers.

- **Repair a tent or ski wear** If you discover a small tear in your tent, cover the hole with gaffer tape and mirror the patch on the inside. You can use the same technique to repair nylon ski wear.

- **Make a pool patch** Gaffer tape can repair a hole in a swimming-pool liner well enough to stand up to water for at least a season. Be sure to cover the area thoroughly.

- **Stay afloat** You can repair a small hole in a canoe with gaffer tape. Pull the canoe out of the water, dry the area around the hole, and apply a gaffer tape patch to the outside of the canoe to make a watertight repair.

G

...sport and the great outdoors

- **Waterproof footwear** Make a waterproof pair of shoes by covering an old pair of canvas shoes or trainers with gaffer tape, overlapping the edges of each row. Make a small cut in the tape as you go around corners, to overlap edges effectively.

- **Protect yourself from ticks** When you are hiking, protect your ankles by wrapping gaffer tape around your trouser cuffs to keep ticks out. You can also do this if you don't have bicycle clips.

- **Create a clothesline** When you don't have a clothesline or any rope, twist a long piece of gaffer tape into a rope and bind it between trees. It makes a skipping rope as well or a basic rope sturdy enough to lash two items together.

- **Protect your gas-barbecue hose** Protect the the rubber hose that connects the gas bottle to an outdoor barbecue from mice and squirrels by wrapping it in gaffer tape.

- **Make a shoelace** To make a temporary shoelace, cut a piece of tape that's as long as you need and twice the width. Fold in half along its length, sticky side in, then thread the lace as normal.

- **Extra insulation** Make winter boots a little bit warmer by taping the insoles with gaffer tape, silver side up. The shiny tape will reflect the warmth of your feet back into the boots.

- **Hang Christmas lights** Use gaffer tape to hang outdoor lights and removing them will be much easier. Tear the tape into thin strips. At intervals, wrap the strips around the Christmas lights' wire and tape the strand to the gutter or wherever you hang them.

...for children

- **Make fancy-dress costumes** Use classic silver gaffer tape to make a costume for the Tin Man from *The Wizard of Oz* or a robot. Make a basic costume from flat-bottomed paper bags, with openings in the back so it can be put on and taken off easily. Cover this pattern with rows of gaffer tape. For the legs, cover an old pair of trousers, giving your child an easy way to remove the outfit for toilet breaks. Gaffer tape and electrical tape come in several colours, so you can easily add 'go faster' strips and other special robot markings.

- **Make a toy sword** Make toy swords for the junior pirates and swordsmen by sketching a child-size sword onto a piece of cardboard. Use two pieces if you don't have one thick enough. Be sure to make a handle that the child's hand can fit around comfortably once it has been increased in thickness by several layers of gaffer tape. Wrap the entire blade shape in silver gaffer tape. Wrap the handle in black tape.

- **Make play rings and bracelets** Make rings by tearing gaffer tape into strips about 1cm wide, then folding the strips in half lengthways, sticky sides together. Add more strips over the first one until the ring is thick enough to stand on its own. Adjust the size with scissors and tape the ends closed. To make a stone for the ring, cover a small item such as a pebble and attach. Make a bracelet by winding gaffer tape around a stiff paper pattern.

- **Make hand puppets** Use a small, strong paper bag as the base for the body of the puppet. Cover the bag with overlapping rows of gaffer tape. Make armholes through which fingers can poke out. Crumple a piece of paper into a ball and wrap with gaffer tape to create a head. Stick on buttons or beads to make the eyes and mouth and strands of wool or shredded paper for the hair. Stick the head to the body.

Gloves

- **Dust delicate knick-knacks** To dust a collection of glass animals or other delicate items, put on some fabric gloves, the softer the better, and rub each item carefully using your fingers.

- **Dust a chandelier** If a chandelier has become a haven for spiders' webs and dust, try this infallible dusting tip. Soak some old fabric gloves in window-cleaning fluid. Slip them on and wipe off the lighting fixture for sparkling crystals in no time.

- **Grip a stubborn jar lid** If the lid on a jar of jam or chutney won't come loose, put on some rubber gloves and you'll instantly have a better grip to unscrew the top.

- **Paper-sorting finger** Cut off the index finger piece from an old rubber glove and you have an ideal sheath for your finger the next time you have to quickly sort through a thick pile of papers.

- **Make strong rubber bands** To make some extra-strong rubber bands, cut up a pair of old rubber gloves. Make horizontal cuts in the finger sections to produce small rubber bands and in the body of the glove for large ones.

- **Latex surgical gloves for extra insulation** If your hands get cold when you are doing work in the garden, cleaning the car or other outdoor activities, even when you are wearing gloves or mittens, try slipping on a pair of latex surgical gloves underneath your usual mittens or gloves. The rubber is a superb insulator, so your hands should stay toasty warm and dry, too.

- **Remove cat hair** Here's a quick and easy way to remove cat hair from upholstery. Put on a rubber glove and dampen it. When you rub it against fabric, the cat hair will stick to the glove. If you are worried about getting the upholstery slightly damp, test the wet glove in an inconspicuous area first.

Glycerine

- **Make your own soap** Homemade soap is a great gift and easy to make. Cut the glycerine, which is usually sold in blocks, into 5cm cubes. Using a microwave set at half-power, heat several cubes in a glass container for 30 seconds at a time, checking and stirring as needed, until the glycerine melts. Add a few drops of coloured dye or a scent at this point, if you wish. Pour the melted glycerine into soap or sweet moulds. If you don't have any moulds, fill the bottom 2cm of a polystyrene cup. Let it harden for 30 minutes.

- **Clean a freezer spill** Spilled sticky foods frozen to the bottom of the freezer don't have a chance against glycerine. Remove the spill and wipe it clean with a rag dabbed with glycerine, which is an effective natural solvent.

- **Remove tar stains** A difficult tar or mustard stain can be shifted using glycerine. Rub a little glycerine into the spot and leave it for about an hour. Then, with paper towels, gently remove the spot using a blot-and-lift motion. You may need to do this several times.

- **Make new liquid soap** If you have tiny leftover slivers of soap, add a bit of glycerine and crush them together with some warm water. Pour the mixture into a pump bottle to make liquid soap on the cheap.

did you **KNOW?**

Glycerine is a clear, colourless thick paste that is a by-product of the soap-making process. Commercial soap-makers remove the glycerine when they make soap so that they can use it in more profitable lotions and creams. Glycerine works well in lotions because it is essentially a moisturising material that dissolves in alcohol or water. It is used to make nitroglycerine and sweets, and to preserve fruit and laboratory specimens. You can purchase glycerine online at www.aromantic.co.uk

Greaseproof paper

- **Fail-safe cake decorating** Here's a way to make piping icing sugar onto cake much easier. Cut a piece of greaseproof paper the same size as your cake, using the cake tin as a guide. Pipe the name and the message (or pattern) onto the paper and freeze it. After half an hour it should be easy to handle. Loosen the icing and slide it off onto the cake using a spatula. You'll be amazed at the professional results you can achieve.

- **Funnel spices into jars** Roll a piece of greaseproof paper into a funnel shape and pour spices into the jars without spilling a single peppercorn. Use a couple of layers to funnel liquids into jars. Offset the papers so the seams in the layers don't line up and let any drips of liquid through.

- **Make cleaning the kitchen quicker and easier**
  Greaseproof paper can be used to help keep all kinds of kitchen surfaces clean.

  - Line vegetable and meat containers with a layer of greaseproof paper. When it needs replacing, throw it away or, if it's not stained with meat juices, compost it.

  - If your kitchen cabinets don't extend to the ceiling, a layer of greaseproof paper on top will catch dust and grease particles. Every month or two, just fold up the paper, discard it and put a fresh layer down.

  - If you're worried about meat juices seeping into a chopping board, cover it with three layers of greaseproof paper before slicing raw meat and throw the paper out as soon as you've finished.

- **Uncork bottles with ease** If you keep a bottle of cooking wine in the kitchen, wrap some greaseproof paper around the cork before re-inserting it. It'll be easier to remove the next time and the paper will help to keep crumbly little bits of cork from getting into the wine.

- **Keep cast iron rust-free** To prevent rust from forming on cast iron between uses, rub a sheet of greasepaper over a grill pan or Dutch oven after washing and while it's still warm. Then place the sheet between the pot and the lid to store.

- **Store delicate fabrics** Antique lace and other fabric heirlooms may decay quickly if not stored with care. A sheet of greaseproof paper between each item will help to block extraneous light and prevent transfer of dyes without trapping moisture.

- **Keep candles from staining table linen** If you keep matching coloured candles alongside your table linen, wrap them in greaseproof paper to make sure that no colour is transferred to the cloth.

- **Protect surfaces from glue** Woodworkers know that there is enough glue in a wood joint if some squeezes out when they clamp the joint. They also know that excess glue will be difficult to remove if it drips on a workbench or, worse, bonds the clamping blocks to the project. To prevent this, cover the bench with strips of greaseproof paper and put pieces of greaseproof paper between the clamping blocks and the project. The glue won't adhere to, or soak through, the paper.

(KIDS' STUFF)
Homemade stained glass

All children enjoy making homemade 'stained-glass' artworks that take only minutes to produce. First, make crayon shavings using a vegetable peeler. Keep each colour separate. Put a paper towel or bag on the worktop. Place a sheet of greaseproof paper on top, sprinkle it with crayon shavings and cover with another layer of greaseproof paper and a paper towel. Press it for a few minutes using a warm iron and remove the paper towel layers. Cut your new see-through artwork into sun-catching medallions or colourful bookmarks using craft scissors to create a decorative edge.

Hair conditioner

- **Clean and shine your houseplants** If your houseplants need a good dusting, put a bit of hair conditioner onto a soft cloth and rub the plant leaves to remove dust and shine the leaves.

- **Smooth-sliding shower curtain** Are you tired of yanking on a shower curtain? Instead of closing smoothly, does it stutter along the curtain rod, letting the showerhead spray water onto the floor? Rub the rod with hair conditioner and the curtain should glide across it.

- **Shine stainless steel** Don't buy expensive polishes specifically designed for stainless steel: apply hair conditioner to taps, golf clubs, chrome fixtures or anything else that needs a shine. Rub it off thoroughly with a soft cloth and you will be impressed with the bright gleam.

- **Clean silk garments** Do you dare ignore the 'dry clean only' label in a silk shirt? Here's a low-cost alternative. Fill the sink with water (warm water for whites and cold water for colours). Add a tablespoon of hair conditioner. Immerse the shirt in the water and let it sit for a few minutes. Then pull it out, rinse and hang it up to dry. The conditioner will help to keep the shirt feeling silky smooth.

did you **KNOW?**

Hair conditioner has been around for about 50 years. While researching ways to help burn victims during the Second World War, Swiss chemists developed a compound that improved the health of hair. In the 1950s, other scientists developing fabric softeners found that the same material was also good for softening hair.

Despite our efforts to keep hair healthy, we still lose on average between 50 and 100 strands a day. For most of us, thankfully, there are still many more strands left. Interestingly, people with blonde hair have an average of 140,000 strands of hair, brown-haired people, 100,000, and those with red hair, 90,000.

- **Protect your shoes in foul weather** Keep salt and chemicals off your shoes in winter by lathering heavy-duty shoes or boots with hair conditioner to protect them from winter's harsh elements. It's a good leather conditioner as well.

- **Lubricate a zipper** When a zip on a jacket sticks, it is tempting to tug and pull until it finally zips up. A dab of hair conditioner rubbed along the teeth of the zip can help you to avoid this bother next time.

- **Take off make-up** Why buy expensive make-up removers when there is a perfectly good substitute in the bathroom already? A dab of hair conditioner quickly and easily removes make-up for far less money than name-brand make-up removers.

- **Unstick a ring** If Grandma's antique ring has just got stuck on your middle finger, slick the finger with a little hair conditioner. The ring should slide right off.

- **Smooth post-shave legs** After you shave your legs, they may feel rough and irritated. Rub on hair conditioner; it acts like a lotion and will smooth and soften your just-shaved legs.

- **Prevent rust on tools** Every good do-it-yourselfer knows how important it is to take care of the tools in a toolbox. One way to condition them and keep rust from invading is to rub them down with hair conditioner.

- **Oil skateboard wheels** Do your child's skateboard wheels squeak? Or are well-used in-line and roller skates getting a bit sticky? Rub hair conditioner on the axles of the wheels and the wheels should be running smoothly in no time.

Hairspray

- **Protect children's artwork** To keep a child's priceless work of art at its very best before you put it on the pinboard or fridge door, preserve it with hairspray to help it to last longer. This works especially well on unstable chalk or pastel pictures as it stops them from getting smudged so easily.

- **Exterminate flies and other insects** Get rid of the bluebottle that has been bobbing and weaving around your house for two days with a squirt of hairspray. Make sure the hairspray is water-soluble so that if any spray hits the walls you will be able to wipe it clean. It works on wasps, mosquitoes and other flying insects as well.

- **Remove lipstick from fabric** If a passionate embrace has left lipstick on your collar, apply hairspray to the lipstick stain and let it sit for a few minutes. Wipe off the hairspray and the stain should come off with it. Then wash the shirt in the usual way.

- **Reduce runs in tights and stockings** Runs in tights or stockings often start at the toes. Head off a running disaster by spraying hairspray on the toes of a new pair of tights. The spray strengthens the threads and makes them last longer.

- **Preserve a Christmas wreath** When you buy a festive wreath it is fresh, green and lush looking. A week later, it is starting to shed needles and look a little dry. To make the wreath last longer, take a can of hairspray and squirt it all over as soon as you get the fresh wreath home. The hairspray traps the moisture in the needles.

- **Preserve your shoes' shine** After you've lovingly polished your shoes to give them a fresh-from-the-box look, lightly spray them with hairspray. The shoe polish won't rub off so easily with this added protection.

- **Keep curtains dirt-free** Have you just bought new curtains or had the old ones cleaned and want to keep the as-new look for a while? The trick is to apply several coats of hairspray, letting each coat dry thoroughly before the next one.

- **Remove ink marks on garments** If a toddler has just gone mad with a ballpoint pen on white upholstery or a new shirt, squirt the stain with hairspray and the pen marks should come straight off.

- **Extend the life of cut flowers** Postpone the wilting of a beautiful bouquet of cut flowers with a squirt of hairspray. Stand 30cm away from the bouquet and give the flowers a quick spray on the undersides of the leaves and petals.

- **Keep recipe cards splatter-free** Don't let spaghetti sauce bubbling on the hob splatter a favourite recipe card. A coating of hairspray will prevent the card from being ruined by kitchen eruptions. With the added protection, spills will wipe off easily.

did you **KNOW?**

Here are some great moments in hairspray history:
- A Norwegian inventor developed the technology that became the aerosol can in the early 1900s.
- L'Oréal introduced its hairspray, called Elnett, in 1960. The next year Alberto VO5 introduced its version.
- In 1964 hairspray surpassed lipstick as women's most popular cosmetic aid – possibly due to the fashion at the time for enormous beehive hairstyles.

Hydrogen peroxide

- **Remove stains of unknown origin** Mix a teaspoon of 3 per cent hydrogen peroxide with a little cream of tartar or a dab of nongel toothpaste. Rub the paste on the stain with a soft cloth. Rinse. The stain, whatever it was, should be gone.
    WARNING: be sure the fabric is colourfast before you try this.

- **Remove wine stains** Dab a little hydrogen peroxide on the wine stain – it will come off easily.

- **Remove grass stains** Mix a few drops of ammonia with just 1 teaspoon of 3 per cent hydrogen peroxide. Rub on the stain. As soon as it disappears, rinse and launder.

- **Remove mildew** Bring out some tough ammunition to combat mildew: a bottle of 3 per cent hydrogen peroxide. Pour the peroxide directly onto the offending area. Wipe it clean and the mildew should be gone for good.

- **Remove bloodstains** This works only on fresh bloodstains. Apply 3 per cent hydrogen peroxide directly to the stain, rinse with fresh water and launder as usual.

- **Sterilise a chopping board** To kill the germs on a chopping board, especially after preparing chicken or other meat, use a paper towel to wipe the board down with vinegar, then use another paper towel to wipe it with hydrogen peroxide. Ordinary 3 per cent hydrogen peroxide is fine.

TAKE CARE

Hydrogen peroxide is considered corrosive – even in a relatively weak 3 per cent solution. Don't put it in your eyes or around your nose. Don't swallow it or try to set it on fire either. Use gloves when handling it.

Ice-cream scoops

● **Scoop meatballs and biscuit dough** To make meatballs that are the same size every time, try using an ice-cream scoop to measure out perfect spheres. This method works well for biscuits, too.

● **Make butter balls** For an attractive way to present butter at a dinner party, scoop out large globes of butter to serve to guests with their bread. A smaller scoop, or melon baller, will create individual-size balls of butter.

● **Create special sandcastles** Take an ice-cream scoop the next time you visit the beach. The children will have a fun tool for making sandcastles; the scoop allows them to make interesting rounded shapes with the sand.

● **Plant seeds** If you're out in the garden about to start putting seeds into a plot of earth, use an ice-cream scoop to make equal-sized planting holes for the seeds for a future harvest.

● **Repot a houseplant** An ice-cream scoop is the perfect way to add soil to the new pot without making a mess.

did you **KNOW?**

Spade, dipper, spatula or spoon – the styles of ice-cream scoop you can buy are almost as varied as the flavours of ice cream you will use them for. One website lists 168 choices of scoops. Did you know that:

● A scoop introduced during the Depression of the 1930s, called the slicer, helped US ice-cream parlour owners to scoop out the same amount every time and not give away any extra.

● Many ways have been developed to help the ice cream plop out of a scoop. Some scoops split apart; others have a wire scraper to nudge it out. Still others have antifreeze in the handle or a button on the back to make the ice cream pop out.

● Some ice-cream scoops, also called moulds, can imprint symbols on the ice cream.

Ice cubes

- **Make creamy salad dressing** Here's how to make homemade salad dressing as smooth and even as the bottled variety. Put all the dressing ingredients in a jar with a lid, then add a single ice cube. Close the lid and shake vigorously. Spoon out the ice cube and serve. Your guests will be impressed by how creamy your salad dressing is.

- **Stop sauces from curdling** If you've made eggs Benedict for a posh Sunday brunch, but the butter and egg yolks mixed with lemon juice for the hollandaise sauce have curdled, place an ice cube in the saucepan, stir and the sauce should turn back into a silky masterpiece.

- **De-fat soup and stews** To quickly remove as much fat as possible from homemade soup or stew, fill a metal ladle with ice cubes and skim the bottom of the ladle over the top of the liquid in the soup pot. Fat will collect on the ladle.

did you **KNOW?**

Here are some cold, hard facts about ice cubes:
- To make clear ice cubes, use distilled water and boil it first. It's the air in the water that causes ice cubes to turn cloudy.
- A Canadian company sells fake ice cubes that glow and blink in your drink.
- They never use real ice cubes when photographing cool drinks for adverts, because they don't last under hot studio lights. The cubes are actually made of plastic or glass.

- **Water hanging plants and Christmas trees** If you struggle to reach hanging plants when you're watering, ice cubes can help. Just place several cubes into the pots. The ice will melt and water the plants and it also does it without causing a sudden downpour. This is also a good way to water a Christmas tree, whose base may be hard to reach with a watering can.

- **Reheat rice** Do you find that leftover rice dries out and becomes tough when it is reheated in the microwave? Try this solution: put an ice cube on top of the rice when you put it in the microwave. The ice cube will melt as the rice reheats, giving the rice much-needed moisture to keep it soft.

- **Help iron out creases** If a shirt is full of creases, turn on the iron and wrap an ice cube in a soft cloth. Rub the cube over the crease just before you iron and the shirt will smooth out.

- **Remove dents in carpeting** If you've recently rearranged furniture in the living room, you know that heavy pieces can leave ugly dents in the carpet. Use ice cubes to remove them. Put an ice cube, for example, on the spot where a chair leg stood. Let it melt, then brush up the dent.

- **Smooth sealant seams** When you're putting sealant around the bath, it oftens adheres to your finger as you try to smooth it and you know that if you don't do something about it, the finished job will look awful. You can solve the problem by running an ice cube along the sealant line. This forms the sealant into a nice even bead and it will never stick to the ice cube.

Ice cubes

- **Unstick a sluggish waste disposal** If your waste disposal is not working at its best because of grease build-up (not a blockage), ice cubes may help. Throw some down the disposal and grind them up. The grease should cling to the ice, making the disposal residue-free.

- **Mask the taste of medicine** No matter what flavour is used in children's medicine, they may still turn up their noses at the taste. Get them to suck on an ice cube before taking the medicine. It will numb the taste buds and allow the medicine to go down, without any additional spoonful of sugar.

- **Prevent a burn blistering** Stop a burn from turning into a mass of blisters by applying an ice cube directly to the burn.

- **Pluck a splinter** Removing a splinter from the hand of a screaming, squirming toddler is one of the most difficult jobs a parent can face. Before you start jabbing with a needle, grab an ice cube and numb the area. This should make splinter removal much quicker and more painless.

- **Cool water for pets** Imagine what it's like to wear a fur coat in the middle of summer. Rabbits, hamsters, mice, rats and gerbils will love your thoughtfulness if you place a few cubes in their water dish to cool down. This is also a good tip for the cat, who's spent the hot morning lounging on your bed, or the dog, who's just come in thirsty after a long romp in the park.

- **Remove gum from clothing** You can get rid of stuck-on chewing gum on a child's trousers with an ice cube. Rub the ice on the gum to harden it, then scrape it off with a spoon.

Ice-cube trays

- **Freeze extra eggs** Did you know that you can freeze eggs for future baking projects? Medium eggs are just the right size to freeze in plastic ice-cube trays with one egg in each cell, with no spillover. After they are frozen, put them into a self-sealing plastic bag. Defrost as many as you need when the time comes.

- **A painter's palette** Your child, a budding Picasso or Rembrandt, needs a paint palette for mixing colours. A plastic ice-cube tray provides the perfect sturdy container for holding and mixing small amounts of paints and watercolours.

- **Organise a workbench** An ice-cube tray can help you to organise and store small parts that you may need at one time or another, for example, screws, nails, bolts and other diminutive items of hardware.

- **Freeze foods in handy cubes** An ice-cube tray is a great way to freeze small amounts of many different kinds of food for later use. The idea is to freeze the food in the tray's cells, pop out the frozen cubes and put them in a labelled self-sealing plastic bag for future use. Turn the page for some more ideas:

(KIDS' STUFF)
Ice cool jewellery

This is a great summer project. Collect a number of small objects from around the house, including buttons, beads and tiny toys. Then get an ice-cube tray and place one or more of the items in each tray cube. Fill the tray with water. Cut a length of wool (long enough to make a comfortable necklace, bracelet or anklet). Lay the wool in the ice-cube tray, making sure it touches every cube and is fully submerged. Freeze. When frozen, pop out and tie on the 'jewellery'. The children will cool off while they see how long their creation takes to melt.

Ice-cube trays

● If garden or windowsill pots are brimming with basil, but your family can't eat pesto as quickly as you make it, make a big batch of pesto (without the cheese) and freeze it in ice-cube trays. Later, defrost as many cubes as you need, add cheese and mix with pasta.

● There's only so much mashed swede, carrot or squash that a growing baby will eat at one sitting. Freeze the rest in ice-cube trays for future baby ready-meals.

● If a recipe calls for 100g chopped celery, but you have an entire head of celery and no plans to use it soon, chop it all, place in an ice-cube tray, add a little water and freeze. The next time you need chopped celery, it's at your fingertips. This also works well for onions, carrots or any other vegetable that you use in soups and stews.

● If there's a bit of chicken soup left in the bottom of the pan – too little for another meal, but too much to throw it out – freeze the leftovers. The next time you make soup or another dish that needs seasoning, use a cube or two.

● If you are cooking homemade broth, make an extra-large batch and freeze the excess in ice-cube trays. You'll have broth cubes to add instant flavour to future quick-cook dishes. You can do the same with a leftover half-can of broth.

● Are you always throwing out leftover parsley? Just chop it up, put it in an ice-cube tray with a little water and freeze for future use. This also works with other fresh herbs.

● Here's what to do with a half-drunk bottle of red or white wine. Freeze the wine into cubes that can be used later in pasta sauce, casseroles or stews.

Ice-lolly sticks

- **Emergency splint for a finger** If someone seems to have a broken finger and you're on the way to casualty, use an ice-lolly stick as a temporary splint. Gently tape it on with adhesive tape to help to stabilise the finger until it can be set.

- **Teach letters to future artists and writers** Ice-lolly sticks are good for spreading finger-paint. Or, for a fun way to help youngsters to practise writing letters, let them use lolly sticks to write letters into a pile of shaving cream.

- **Skewer kids' food** It is often more fun to eat food if you get to play with it first, as the parents of many picky eaters know. Skewer bites of sausage, chicken, melon, cherry tomatoes and similar. Or give children a stick so that they can skewer their own.

- **Label your plantings** If you've planted parsley, sage, rosemary or thyme in the garden, remember its location by using ice-lolly sticks as plant labels. Just write on the stick using indelible marker.

- **Keep track of paint colours** After you've painted a room, dip an ice-lolly stick in the can. Let it dry. Write the name of the paint and the room where it was used on the stick. These guides can also help a home decorator pick out fabrics and decorative items to go with a newly painted room.

(KIDS' STUFF)
Make a bookmark

You need an ice-lolly stick, paint, coloured felt, glue and a marker pen. Paint the ice-lolly stick in a bright colour. When it's dry, write a reading slogan on one side such as 'I love to read' or 'I'll hold the page'. Then cut a shape out of the felt, such as a heart, flower, cat or a dog. Glue it to the top of the lolly stick and you have a bookmark.

Ice scrapers

- **Remove splattered paint** If you've just painted the bathroom and left paint splatters all over an acrylic bath, use an ice scraper to remove them without scratching the bath surface. Use ice scrapers to remove paint specks from other non-metallic surfaces too.

- **Smooth wood filler** Do you have small gouges in a wooden floor that you want to get rid of? Once you've packed wood filler into a hole, an ice scraper is the perfect tool to smooth and level it.

- **Scrape out your freezer** A windscreen isn't the only place where ice and frost build up. If the frost is building up in your freezer and you want to delay the defrosting chore for a while, head out to the car and borrow the ice scraper.

- **Remove wax from skis** Every experienced skier knows that old wax build-up on skis can slow you down. An ice scraper can swiftly and neatly take off the old wax and prepare the skis for the next coat.

- **Clean up bread dough** No matter how much flour you put on your work surface, some of the sticky bread dough always seems to stick to it. A clean ice scraper is just the tool for skimming sticky dough off the work surface. A plastic scraper can also substitute for a spatula for nonstick pans, but take care not to let it rest on the edge of a hot pan or it will melt.

Jar lids

- **Make safety reflectors** Is it difficult to manoeuvre in your drive when it's dark? With scrap wood and jar lids you can make inexpensive reflectors to guide drivers. Spray the lids with reflective paint, screw them to the sides of scrap-wood stakes and drive the stakes into the ground at places where you need guidance.

- **Cut biscuits** Lids with deep rims or preserving jar bands (the part with the cut-out centre) can be used to make impromptu biscuit cutters. Dip the bottom edge of the lid in flour to keep it from sticking when you press it into the dough. Avoid lids with rims that are rolled inwards; the dough can get stuck inside and be hard to extract.

- **Make coasters to protect furniture** Drips from drinking glasses and hot coffee mugs can really ruin furniture finishes. The simple solution is to keep plenty of coasters on hand. Glue rounds of felt or cork to both sides of a jar lid (especially flat preserving jar lids, which shouldn't be reused anyway), and keep a stack wherever cups and glasses accumulate in the house.

- **Saucers for potted plants** Lids with a rim are perfect for catching excess water under small potted plants. Unlike ceramic saucers, if they get encrusted with minerals, you won't mind throwing them out.

(KIDS' STUFF)
What's on the fridge?

For a stimulating craft project, set out a variety of fun materials – paints, glue, fabrics, family photos, googly eyes, glitter, pompoms or even just paper and markers – and let your child decorate several jar lids.

Glue some strong magnets from a hardware shop on the backs using a glue gun and put them on the fridge.

Jars

- **Stamp out biscuits** Any clean, empty wide-mouthed jar will be just about the right size for cutting biscuits out of any rolled dough.

- **Make a piggy bank** Encourage a child to save by making a money bank. Take the metal lid off the jar, place it on a flat work surface like a chopping board and tap a screwdriver with a hammer to carefully punch a slot hole in the centre. Smooth the rough edges underneath the slot with the hammer or a rasp. Let your child personalise the mini-bank with paints or collage.

- **Bring along baby's treats** Dry cereal can be a nutritious snack for a baby. Pack individual servings in clean, dry baby-food jars. If they get spilled, the mess is minimal.

- **Make baby-food portions** Take advantage of the fact that baby-food jars are already the perfect size for baby's portions. Clean them thoroughly before reusing and fill them with anything from puréed carrots to vanilla pudding. Attach a spoon with a rubber band and you have a perfect portable meal for your little one.

- **Collect insects** Help children to observe nature at close quarters by gently collecting insects in clear jars. Punch a few small airholes in the lids for ventilation. Don't make the holes too large, or your insects will escape. Don't forget to carefully let the creatures go after you've admired them.

- **Use to quickly dry out gloves or mittens** If you've taken a break from working outside, help your gloves or mittens dry out during lunch by pulling each one over the bottom of an empty jar. Then stand the jar upside down on a radiator or hot-air vent. Warm air will fill the jar and radiate out to dry damp clothing in an instant.

- **Waterproof camping storage** When you are boating or camping, keeping things like matches and paper money dry can be a challenge. Store items that you don't want to get wet in clear jars with screw tops. Even if you are backpacking, plastic jars with screw tops are light enough not to weigh you down, plus they provide more protection for crushable items than a resealable plastic bag.

- **Create workshop storage** Don't let various bits of hardware in your workshop get mixed up. Keep all your nails, screws, nuts and bolts organised by size and type by screwing jar lids to the underside of a wooden or melamine shelf. (Make sure the screw does not poke through the top of the shelf.) Then put each type of hardware in its own jar, and screw each jar onto its lid. By using clear jars, you can find what you need at a glance. This idea also works well for storing seeds in a potting shed.

(SCIENCE FAIR)
Make a biosphere

Turn a large wide-mouthed jar into a miniature biosphere. Clean the jar and lid, then place a handful of pebbles and charcoal chips in the bottom. Add several trowelfuls of slightly damp, sterilised potting compost. Select a few plants that require similar conditions (such as ferns and mosses, which both like moderate light and moisture). Add a few colourful stones, seashells or a piece of driftwood. Add water to make the atmosphere humid. Tighten the lid and place the jar in dim light for two days. Then display in bright light but not direct sunlight. You shouldn't need to add water – it cycles from the plants to the soil and back again. It's important to use sterilised soil to avoid introducing any unwanted organisms. The charcoal chips will filter the water as it recycles.

Ketchup

- **Get rid of chlorine green** If chlorine from swimming pools is turning your blonde hair green or just giving your hair an unwanted scent, eliminate the problem with a ketchup shampoo. To avoid making a mess, do it in the shower. Massage ketchup generously into your hair and leave it for 15 minutes, then wash it out, using baby shampoo. The odour and colour should be gone.

- **Make copper pots gleam** When copper pots and pans, or decorative moulds, become dull and tarnished, you can brighten them with ketchup. It's cheaper than commercial tarnish removers and completely safe to apply without gloves. Coat the copper surface with a thin layer of ketchup. Let it sit for 5 to 30 minutes. Acids in the ketchup will react with the tarnish and remove it. Rinse the pan and dry immediately.

- **Keep silver jewellery sparkling** Let ketchup do the work of shining tarnished silver. If a ring, bracelet or earring has a smooth surface, soak it in a small bowl of ketchup for a few minutes. If it has a tooled or detailed surface, use an old toothbrush to work ketchup into the crevices. To avoid damaging the silver, don't leave the ketchup on any longer than necessary. Rinse the piece of jewellery clean, dry it and it will be ready to wear.

did you **KNOW?**

Ketchup originated in the Far East as a salty fish sauce. The word 'ketchup' (also spelled catsup) probably comes from Chinese or Malay. Brought to the West, it had been transformed by the 1700s into a huge variety of sauces with both vegetable and meat-based ingredients. To this day, you can still find banana ketchup, mushroom ketchup and other variants. Tomato ketchup is a relative newcomer, first sold in 1837, but it is now a favourite accompaniment for dishes ranging from fish and chips to a full English breakfast.

Keys

- **Weigh down curtains** If you need to keep curtains hanging straight, just slip a few old keys in the hems. If you are worried about them falling out, tack them in place with a few stitches going through the holes in the keys. You can also keep cords for blinds from tangling by using keys as weights on their bottoms.

- **Create an instant plumb bob** If you are getting ready to hang wallpaper and you need to draw a perfectly vertical line on the wall to get you started, take a length of cord or string and tie a key or two to one end. You've made a plumb bob that will give you a true vertical line. You can do the same using a pair of scissors too.

- **Make fishing sinkers** Old unused keys make great weights for a fishing line. Since they already have a hole in them, attaching them to the line is easy. Whenever you come across an unidentified key, set it aside to use in your tackle box.

Ladders

- **Set it down and plant it** A rickety unsafe straight ladder, or the front part of a stepladder, can be used lying down to make a shallow planter with ready-made sections that look appealing filled with annuals, herbs or salad greens.

  WARNING: after a couple of years of contact with soil, a wooden ladder will decompose, so once you've decided to use it like this, it can't be used again.

- **Create a garden focal point** If you have some old, unreliable, straight wooden ladders, use them to create a decorative garden archway. Cut two sections to the desired height and position them opposite one another along a path. Screw the legs of each one to two strong posts sunk deeply into the soil. Cut a third ladder section to fit across the top of the two others and tie it to them using young willow twigs or heavy jute twine. Let climbing plants clamber up and over it or festoon the archway with fun and fanciful objects, such as old tools. It also works well as the entrance to an enclosed area.

- **Make a temporary table** Create a makeshift table by placing a straight ladder across two trestles. Top it with plywood and cover it with a tablecloth. The ladder will be strong enough to support your buffet, as well as any guests who might lean on it.

- **Make a pot rack** Accessorise a country kitchen with a pot rack made from a sawn-off section of a wooden straight ladder with thin, round rungs. Sand the cut ends smooth; then tie two pieces of sturdy rope to the rungs at either end. To suspend a pot rack, screw four large metal eye hooks into the ceiling joists; then tie the ropes to them. Leave the rack unfinished if you want a rustic look or paint or stain it to match your decor. Hang S-hooks from the rungs to hold kitchenware.

super item **30 uses!**
Lemons...

...around the house

- **Polish chrome** Get rid of mineral deposits and polish chrome taps and other tarnished chrome by rubbing lemon rind over the chrome. Rinse well and dry with a soft cloth.

- **Get rid of tough stains on marble** Cut a lemon in half, dip the exposed flesh into some table salt and rub it vigorously on the stain. You will be amazed how well it works.

- **Deodorise a humidifier** Pour 3 or 4 teaspoons lemon juice into the water tank. The lemon will remove the 'off' odour and replace it with a lemon fragrance. Repeat every couple of weeks.

- **Clean tarnished brass, copper or stainless steel** Make a paste of lemon juice and salt (or bicarbonate of soda or cream of tartar) and coat the affected area. Leave on for 5 minutes. Wash in warm water, rinse and polish dry. Use the same mixture to clean metal kitchen sinks too. Apply the paste, scrub gently and rinse.

- **Make invisible ink** All children need to send secret messages is lemon juice to use as ink, a cotton bud to write with and some white paper. When the 'ink' is dry, get them to hold the paper up to bright sunlight or a light bulb. The heat will cause the writing to darken to a pale brown and the message can be read. Make sure they don't overdo the heating and ignite the paper.

...in the kitchen

- **Keep insects out of the kitchen** Squirt lemon juice on the thresholds of doors and windowsills and squeeze it into any holes or cracks where ants are getting in. Then scatter small slices of lemon peel around the outdoor entrance. Lemons are also effective against cockroaches and fleas. Simply mix the juice of four lemons (along with the rinds) with 2 litres water and wash the floor with it; then watch the fleas and cockroaches flee from a smell they hate.

- **Make soggy lettuce crisp** With the help of a little lemon juice you can revive a wilting lettuce. Add the juice of half a lemon to a bowl of cold water. Put the lettuce in it and refrigerate for 1 hour. Dry the leaves completely before putting them into salads or sandwiches.

- **Keep rice from sticking** Add a teaspoon of lemon juice to the boiling water when cooking rice. When it is done, leave to cool for a few minutes, then fluff with a fork before serving.

- **Prevent vegetables and fruit from turning brown** Potatoes and cauliflower sometimes turn brown when boiling. Squeeze a teaspoon of fresh lemon juice into the cooking water to make them stay white. Sprinkle a liberal amount of fresh lemon juice over guacamole to keep it fresh and green. Make fruit salad hours in advance as well. Just squeeze some lemon juice onto apple slices and they will stay snowy white.

TIP before you squeeze

To get the most juice out of fresh lemons, bring them to room temperature and roll them under your palm against the kitchen worktop before squeezing. This will break down the connective tissue and juice-cell walls, allowing the lemon to release more liquid when you squeeze it.

- **Freshen the fridge** Remove refrigerator odours by dabbing some lemon juice onto a cotton-wool ball or sponge and leaving it in the fridge for several hours. Throw out anything that is 'off'.

- **Refresh a chopping board** Chopping boards can retain the odour of the many different foods that come into contact with it. To get rid of the smell and help to sterilise the board, rub it all over with the cut side of half a lemon or wash it in undiluted juice straight from the bottle.

- **Clean your microwave** Is the inside of the microwave caked with bits of hardened food? Just mix 3 tablespoons lemon juice into 300ml water in a microwave-safe bowl. Microwave on High for 5-10 minutes, allowing the steam to condense on the inside walls and the roof of the oven. Then just wipe away the softened food with a dishcloth.

- **Deodorise the waste disposal** If a clogged waste disposal is beginning to make your sink smell unpleasant, save leftover lemon and orange peels and push them down the drain. To keep it smelling fresh, repeat once a month.

(SCIENCE FAIR)
Make a battery

You can turn a lemon into a battery. It won't start your car, but you will be able to feel the current with your tongue. Roll the lemon on a flat surface to 'activate' the juices. Then cut two small slices in the lemon about 1.25cm apart. Place a 1p piece into one slot and a 5p into the other. Now touch your tongue to the 1p and the 5p at the same time. You'll feel a slight electric tingle. Here's how it works: the acid in the lemon reacts differently with each of the two metals. One coin contains positive electric charges, while the other contains negative charges. The charges create current. Your tongue conducts the charges, causing a small amount of electricity to flow.

L ...in the laundry

- **Bleach delicate fabrics** Household chlorine bleach can cause the iron in water to precipitate out into fabric, leaving more stains. For a mild, stain-free bleach, soak delicates in a mixture of lemon juice and bicarbonate of soda for at least 30 minutes before washing.

- **Remove unsightly perspiration stains** You can remove unsightly stains from under the arms of light-coloured shirts and blouses simply by scrubbing them with a mixture of equal parts lemon juice (or white vinegar) and water.

- **Boost laundry detergent** To remove rust and mineral discoloration from white cotton T-shirts and briefs, pour 200ml lemon juice into the washing machine during the wash cycle. The natural bleaching action of the juice will zap the stains and leave the clothes smelling fresh.

- **Rid clothes of mildew** If you have unpacked clothes you have stored for the season only to discover that some are stained with mildew, get rid of it by making a paste of lemon juice and salt and rubbing it on the affected area, then dry the clothes in sunlight. Repeat the process until the stain is gone. This works well for rust stains on clothes too.

- **Whiten clothes** Diluted or straight, lemon juice is a safe and effective fabric whitener when added to washing water. Clothes will also come out smelling lemon-fresh.

did you **KNOW?**

A lemon tree isn't very pretty and its flower isn't sweet either. The tree's straggly branches bear little resemblance to an orange tree's dense foliage and its purplish flowers lack the pleasant fragrance of orange blossoms. The fruit of the lemon is sour, thanks to its high citric-acid content. But sailors have been sucking on vitamin C-rich lemons for hundreds of years to prevent scurvy. To this day, the British Navy requires ships to carry enough lemons so that every sailor can have one ounce of juice daily.

...in the medicine cabinet

- **Lighten age spots** Before buying special creams to lighten liver spots and freckles, apply lemon juice directly to the area, let it sit for 15 minutes and then rinse clean. Lemon juice is a safe and effective skin-lightening agent.

- **Create blonde highlights** For blonde highlights worthy of the finest beauty salon, add 50ml lemon juice to 150ml water and rinse your hair with the mixture. Then sit in the sun until your hair dries. Lemon juice is a natural bleach. Don't forget to put on plenty of sunscreen before you sit out in the sun and to condition your hair thoroughly afterwards. To maximise the effect, repeat once daily for up to a week.

- **Clean and whiten nails** Pamper your fingernails. Add the juice of ½ lemon to 200ml warm water and soak your fingertips in the mixture for 5 minutes. After pushing back the cuticles, rub some lemon peel back and forth against the nail.

- **Freshen your breath** Rinse your mouth with lemon juice and swallow it for longer-lasting fresh breath. The citric acid in the juice alters the pH level in your mouth, killing the bacteria that cause bad breath. Rinse thoroughly after a few minutes, because long-term exposure to the citric acid can harm tooth enamel.

- **Remove berry stains** It is great fun picking your own berries, but your fingers often get stained with juice that won't come off with soap and water. Try washing your hands with undiluted lemon juice. Wait a few minutes and wash with warm, soapy water. Repeat if necessary until the stain is completely gone.

- **Cleanse your face** Clean and exfoliate your face by washing it with lemon juice. You can also dab lemon juice on blackheads to draw them out during the day. Your skin should improve after several days of treatment.

L ...in the medicine cabinet

- **Soften dry, scaly elbows** It is bad enough that your elbows feel dry and itchy, but they look terrible, too. Your elbows will look and feel better after a few special treatments. Mix bicarbonate of soda and lemon juice to make an abrasive paste. Then rub the paste into your elbows for a smoothing exfoliating treatment.

- **Soothe nettle rash** You won't need an ocean of calamine lotion the next time you or a child falls foul of a patch of stinging nettles. Just apply full-strength lemon juice directly onto the affected area to soothe itching and alleviate the rash.

- **Treat flaky dandruff** If itchy, scaly dandruff has you scratching your head, just massage 2 tablespoons lemon juice into your scalp and rinse with water. Then stir 1 teaspoon lemon juice into 200ml water and rinse your hair with it. Repeat this daily until the dandruff disappears. Your scalp should stop itching and your hair will smell lemon-fresh.

- **Disinfect cuts and scrapes** Stop bleeding and disinfect minor cuts and scrapes by pouring a few drops of lemon juice directly onto the cut or apply the juice with a cotton-wool ball and hold firmly in place for 1 minute.

- **Relieve rough hands and sore feet** You don't have to take extreme measures to soothe your extremities. If you have rough hands or sore feet, rinse them in a mixture of equal parts of lemon juice and water, then massage with olive oil and dab dry with a soft cloth.

- **Remove warts** If you have tried countless remedies to get rid of warts, and nothing seems to work, try this. Apply a dab of lemon juice directly onto the wart, using a cotton bud. Repeat for several days until the acids in the lemon juice dissolve the wart completely.

Lighter fluid

- **Wipe away rust** Rust marks on stainless steel will come off in an instant. Just pour a little lighter fluid onto a clean rag and rub the rust away. Use another rag to wipe away any remaining fluid.

- **Get gum out of hair** Gum in hair is a pain to remove. Here is an easy solution that really works. Apply a few drops of lighter fluid directly to the sticky area, wait a few seconds and comb or wipe away the gum. The solvents in the fluid break down the gum, making it easy to remove from many surfaces besides hair. Wash your hair immediately.
  WARNING: stay away from naked flames.

- **Remove labels with ease** Lighter fluid will remove labels and adhesives from almost any surface. Use a little of it to quickly and easily remove the tape from new appliances or to take stickers off book covers. Wipe away any residue.

- **Remove crayon marks** Have children left their mark with crayon art on walls? Dab some lighter fluid on a clean rag and wipe till the marks vanish.

- **Remove heel marks from floors** You don't have to scrub to remove black heel marks on the kitchen floor. Just pour a little lighter fluid on a paper towel and the marks will wipe straight off.

TAKE CARE

Lighter fluid is inexpensive, easy to find (look for a small bottle or can) and has many surprising uses. But it is highly flammable and can be hazardous to your health if inhaled or ingested. Always use it in a well-ventilated area. Do not smoke around it or use it near an open flame.

Lip balm

- **Remove a stuck ring** Simply coat the finger with a little lip balm and gently wriggle the ring loose.

- **Groom wild eyebrows** Use lip balm as a styling wax for grooming unruly eyebrows, moustaches and other wild hairs. You can also use petroleum jelly.

- **Stop shaving cuts from bleeding** Just dab a bit of lip balm directly onto the nick and the bleeding from most shaving cuts will quickly stop.

- **Lubricate a zip** Rub a small amount of lip balm up and down the teeth of a sticky or stuck zip. Then zip and unzip it a few times. It will act as a lubricant to make the zip work smoothly.

- **Simplify carpentry** Rub some lip balm over nails and screws that are being drilled or pounded into wood. The lip balm will help them slide in more easily.

- **Keep a light bulb from sticking** Outdoor light bulbs, which are exposed to the elements, often get stuck in place and become hard to remove. Before screwing a light bulb into an outdoor socket, coat the threads on the bulb with lip balm. This will prevent sticking and make removal easier.

- **Lubricate tracks for sliding things** Apply lip balm to the tracks of drawers and windows, or to the ridges on a medicine cabinet, to make opening and shutting easier.

TIP the best time to use lip balm

During the dry winter months you may be tempted to apply a layer of lip balm before you put on your lipstick. Beauty experts say this is not a good idea because the lip balm may interfere with the adherence of the lipstick. Instead of using lip balm during the day, experts recommend that you switch to a moisturising lipstick. You can save the lip balm for moisturising your lips before you go to bed.

Magazines

- **No-cost gift wrap** Cut out colourful pages and use them to make no-cost wrapping paper for small gifts.

- **Keep wet boots in shape** Roll up a couple of old magazines and use them as boot trees inside a pair of damp knee-length boots. They will help the boots maintain their shape as they dry.

- **Use in children's craft projects** Let the children go through magazines to find pictures and words to use in collages. Suggest a theme to get them started.

- **Line drawers** Pages from magazines with heavy coated paper make excellent drawer liners. Place the page inside the drawer and press around the edges to define where to trim with scissors.

Magnets

- **Prevent a frozen car lock** Put fridge magnets over the outside locks of the car overnight and they will prevent the locks from freezing.

- **Keep a desk drawer neat** Place a magnet in an office desk drawer to keep the paper clips together.

- **Keep your broom handy** Use a screw to attach a magnet about halfway down your broom handle. Then store the broom attached to the side of your refrigerator.

did you **KNOW?**

The ancient Chinese and Greeks discovered that certain rare stones, called lodestones, seemed to magically attract bits of iron and always pointed in the same direction when allowed to swing freely. Man-made magnets come in many shapes and sizes, but every magnet has a north pole and a south pole. If you break a magnet into pieces, each piece, no matter how small, will have a north and south pole.

Margarine tubs

- **Organise odds and ends** Do you have loose drawing pins all over the house? Odd bolts and nails in a broken cup? Stray ping-pong balls under the sofa? These are just some of the items waiting to be organised into spare plastic margarine tubs. Get a board game started more quickly by storing the loose pieces in a tub until the next time. If you've sorted out all the sky pieces for a puzzle, keep them separate and safe in their own tub. With or without their lids, a few clean margarine tubs can do wonders for a junk drawer in need of organising.

- **Make a baby-footprint paperweight**
  Make an enduring impression of a baby's foot, using quick-drying modelling clay. A wide range of colours are available. Put enough clay in a margarine tub to hold a good impression. Put a thin layer of petroleum jelly on the baby's foot and press it firmly into the clay. Let the clay dry as directed, then flex the tub away from the edges until the clay comes free. Years from now you will be able to show Johnny that his size 13s were once smaller than the palm of your hand! You can also preserve a pet's paw print the same way.

- **Use as a paint container** If you want to touch up little spots here and there in the living room, but don't want to lug around a large pot of paint, pour a little paint into a margarine tub to carry as you make your inspection. Hold it in a nest of paper towels to catch any possible drips. Tubs with lids are also perfect for storing a little bit of leftover paint for future touch-ups.

- **Make easy moulds for jelly desserts** Use a large margarine tub as the mould for a jelly or mousse. For individual dessert moulds, use the smaller tubs and put a surprise chocolate button, sprinkles or mini-marshmallow on the top, which will show through from the bottom when the mould is inverted. The soft, flexible tubs are easy to squeeze when you want to release the dessert.

- **Make low-cost freezer storage** Reuse clean, sturdy margarine and other plastic containers to freeze measured portions of soups and stocks and to break up leftovers into single servings. A 1kg container, for example, stores the perfect amount of sauce for 500g of pasta. Note: before freezing, let the food cool just enough to reduce condensation.

- **Bring fast food for baby** If you need to take home-cooked baby food on a journey, use a disposable margarine tub to make a container that won't break in your baby bag. It's also a handy food bowl and, if you don't need to reuse it, you won't have to wrap it up and bring it home for cleaning.

- **Make a piggy bank** Use a tall tub as a homemade money bank. Cut out a piece of paper to wrap around the side, tape it in place and encourage your child to decorate it with flair. Cut a slit in the top and start saving spare change.

- **Create seed starters** Take a margarine tub, poke a few holes in the bottom, add moistened seed compost and sow the seeds following the packet instructions. Use permanent marker on the side of the tub to help you to remember what you've sown, and use the tub's lid as a drip saucer. Small tubs are space savers as well as money savers, especially if you want to start only one or two of each type of plant.

Margarine tubs

- **Vary a child's lunch box** As a break from the usual sandwich, put some fruit salad, rice or pasta salad or other interesting fare into one or two recycled margarine tubs for your child's lunch. The tubs are easy to open and will prevent the food from getting crushed. Tape some plastic cutlery to the lid so your child won't have to use their fingers to eat.

- **Make individual ice-cream portions** Small margarine tubs are just the right size for a quick ice-cream snack. When it comes back from the supermarket, ice cream is the perfect consistency to portion out into the tubs. You won't have to spend ages getting out bowls, finding a scoop and waiting for the ice cream to soften up enough to dish out. Just go to the freezer and get out the tubs.

- **Travel light with your pet** Lightweight, disposable margarine tubs make perfect pet food containers and double as food and water bowls. And dog biscuits don't get crushed if you put them in a plastic tub. If your pet is staying at a friend's house while you're away, make things easier for the petsitter by putting one serving into each container, to be used and discarded as needed.

Masking tape

- **Label foods and school supplies** Use inexpensive masking tape to mark food containers and freezer bags. You can also use it to conveniently mark children's schoolbooks and supplies.

- **Fix a broken umbrella rib** Use a piece of masking tape and a length of wire cut from a coat hanger to make a 'splint'.

- **Keep a paint can neat** To prevent paint from filling the groove at the top of a paint tin, simply cover the rim of the tin with masking tape.

- **Make a road for toy cars** Make a highway for toy cars by taping two strips of masking tape to a floor or table top. Add a handmade cardboard stop sign or two and the cars can get going. Guiding a toy car along the taped roadway is more than just fun for small children, it also helps them to gain motor control of their fingers for skills they will need later, such as writing.

- **Hang party streamers** Use masking tape instead of transparent tape to put up streamers and balloons for your next party. The masking tape won't leave a residue on the wall like transparent tape does. But remove the masking tape within a day or two. If you wait too long, it may take paint off the wall when you remove it.

did you **KNOW?**

In 1923, when Richard Drew joined manufacturer 3M as an engineer, they made only sandpaper. Drew was testing one of the company's sandpapers at a local mechanic's when he noticed that workers found it difficult to make clean dividing lines on two-colour paint jobs. This inspired Drew to look for a solution, despite direct orders from 3M's president to devote his attention solely to sandpaper. Luckily for 3M, he didn't listen. In 1925, Drew invented the first masking tape, a 5cm wide tan-coloured paper with a pressure-sensitive adhesive backing. Five years later, he invented Scotch cellophane tape.

Mayonnaise

- **Strengthen your fingernails** To condition your fingernails, plunge them into a bowl of mayonnaise every so often. Keep them immersed for about 5 minutes, then wash with warm water.

- **Relieve sunburn pain** Treat dry, sunburned skin by smoothing mayonnaise liberally over the affected area. The mayonnaise will relieve the pain and moisturise the skin.
  WARNING: apply to a small area first to ensure you are not allergic to any of the ingredients.

- **Remove dead skin** Soften and remove dead skin from elbows and feet. Rub mayonnaise over the dry, rough tissue, leave it on for 10 minutes and wipe it away with a damp cloth.

- **Make plant leaves shiny** Professional florists use this trick to keep houseplant leaves shiny and clean. Just rub a little mayonnaise on the leaves with a paper towel and they will stay bright and shiny for weeks and, if you are lucky, months.

- **Remove crayon marks from wooden furniture** Rub some mayonnaise on the crayon marks and let it soak in for several minutes. Then wipe the surface clean with a damp cloth. You can clean piano keys in the same way.

- **Remove bumper stickers** The easiest way to remove a sticker is to rub some mayonnaise over it. Leave it for several minutes and wipe it off. The mayonnaise will dissolve the glue.

- **Clean piano keys** If the keys on a piano are starting to yellow, apply a little mayonnaise with a soft cloth. Wait a few minutes, wipe with a damp cloth and buff. The piano keys will look like new.

Milk

- **Make frozen fish taste fresh** If you want fish from the freezer to taste as if it's been freshly caught, try this trick. Place the frozen fish in a bath of milk until it thaws. The milk will make it taste fresher.

- **Boost the flavour of corn on the cob** This will make corn on the cob taste sweeter and fresher. Add 50g powdered milk to a pan of boiling water before you put in the corn.

- **Soothe sunburn and insect bites** If your skin is suffering from too much sun or if itchy insect bites are driving you mad, try using a little milk paste for soothing relief. Mix one part powdered milk with two parts water and add a pinch or two of salt. Dab it on the burn or bite. The enzymes in the milk powder will help to neutralise the insect-bite venom and relieve the pain of sunburn.

- **Impromptu make-up remover** If you run out of make-up remover, use powdered milk instead. Just mix 3 tablespoons powdered milk with 80ml warm water in a jar and shake well. Add more water or powder as necessary to achieve the consistency of heavy cream. Now you are ready to apply your makeshift make-up remover with a facecloth. When you have finished, wipe it off and rinse thoroughly with water.

- **Soften skin** You've heard of Cleopatra bathing in asses' milk. Milk acts as a natural skin softener so toss 100g or so of powdered milk into the tub as it fills and treat yourself to a luxurious milk bath.

- **Give yourself a facial** Give yourself a luxurious facial at home. Make a mask by mixing 50g powdered milk with enough water to form a thick paste. Thoroughly coat your face with the mixture, let it dry completely, then rinse with warm water. Your face will feel fresh and rejuvenated.

Milk

- **Clean and soften dirty hands** If a heavy stint in the garden has left you with stained and gritty hands that ordinary soap won't budge, make a paste of oatmeal and milk and rub it vigorously on your hands. The stains will be gone and the oatmeal-and-milk mixture will soften and soothe your skin.

- **Polish silverware** Tarnished silverware will look like new with a little help from some sour milk. If you don't have any sour milk, you can make some by adding vinegar to fresh milk. Then simply soak the silver in the milk for half an hour to loosen the tarnish, wash in warm, soapy water and buff gently with a soft cloth.

- **Clean patent leather** Make patent-leather bags or shoes look like new again. Just dab on a little milk, let it dry and buff with a soft cloth.

- **Remove ink stains from clothes** To remove ink stains from coloured clothes, an overnight milk bath will often do the trick. Just soak the affected garment in milk overnight and launder as usual the next day.

- **Repair cracked china** Before you throw out a cracked plate from your grandmother's old china set, try mending it with milk. Place the plate in a pan, cover it with milk (fresh or reconstituted powdered milk) and bring to the boil. As soon as it starts to boil, lower the heat and simmer for about 45 minutes. The protein in the milk will miraculously meld most fine cracks.

Milk cartons

- **Make ice blocks for parties** Keep drinks cold at a barbecue or party with ice blocks made from empty milk cartons. Just rinse out the old cartons, fill them with water and put them in the freezer. Peel away the container when you're ready to put the blocks in the punch bowl; but if you intend to use them as cooler blocks, leave the container in place.

- **Make a lacy candle** Use this easy method to make a delicate, lacy candle. Coat the inside of a milk carton with cooking spray, put a taper candle in the middle, anchoring it with a base of melted wax, then fill it with ice cubes. Pour in hot wax; when the wax cools, peel off the carton. The melting ice will leave beautiful, lacy voids in the wax.

- **Instant kids' bowling alley** Make an indoor bowling alley with ninepins made from empty milk and juice cartons. Just rinse the cartons (use whatever sizes you like) and let them dry. Then take two same-sized cartons and slide one upside down into the other, squeezing it a little to make it fit. Once you've made ten, set the ninepins up at the end of the hall and let the children use a tennis ball to roll for strikes and spares.

did you **KNOW?**

John Van Wormer, a toy-factory owner, didn't cry over spilt milk when he dropped a bottle on the floor one morning in 1915. Instead, he was inspired to patent a paper-based milk carton that he named Pure-Pak. It took him ten years to perfect a machine that coated the paper with wax and sealed the carton with animal glues. The early waxy containers were slow to catch on with sceptical consumers and bore little resemblance to today's milk cartons, but now some 30 billion Pure-Pak cartons are sold annually.

Milk cartons

- **Make seed starters** Milk cartons are the perfect size to use for seed starters. Cut off the top half of a carton, punch holes in the bottom, fill with potting compost and sow the seeds according to instructions on the packet.

- **Make vegetable-garden collars** Use empty milk cartons to discourage slugs and snails from attacking young tomato plants. Cut off the tops and bottoms of the containers and when the ground is soft, push them into the ground around the tomatoes when you are planting them out.

- **Collect food scraps for compost** Keep an empty milk carton handy near the kitchen sink and use it to collect food scraps for the compost heap.

- **Disposable paint holder** If you have a small painting job to complete and you don't want to lug a heavy can around, an empty milk carton can help. Cut off the top of the carton and pour in the amount of paint you need. When you have finished painting, throw the carton into the bin.

- **Feed birds in winter** To make an attractive winter treat for feathered garden visitors, combine melted suet and birdseed in an empty milk carton. Suet is beef fat; you can get it from a butcher or buy it in blocks. To render it, chop or grind the fat and heat it over a low flame until it melts. Then strain it through washed cheesecloth into the carton. Insert a loop of string into the mixture while it is still soft. After it hardens, tear away the carton and tie your new mass of bird food to a branch. Only use this feed in cool or cold weather. Once the temperature gets above about 20°C, the suet will turn rancid and melt.

Mothballs

- **Rinse woollens for storage** To give woollens even more protection, don't just use mothballs, dissolve a few mothballs in the final rinse when you wash them prior to seasonal storage.

- **Kill bugs on potted plants** Put the plant in a clear plastic bag such as a cleaning bag, add a few mothballs and seal for a week. When you take it out, it will be insect-free.

- **Repel mice from garage or shed** Place a few mothballs around the garage and the mice will seek alternative accommodation. To keep mice out of a potting shed, put the mothballs around the base of wrapped or covered plants.

- **Keep animals out of your garden** Scatter old mothballs around the garden and flowerbeds to deter cats, dogs, rats, mice and squirrels. Most animals hate the smell.

- **Keep insects at bay** Add mothballs to boxes stored in the attic and silverfish and other insects will stay away.

  WARNING: keep mothballs well out of the reach of pets and small children as they can be harmful if swallowed.

(**SCIENCE** FAIR)
Mothball dance

Make mothballs dance and give children a basic science lesson too. Fill a glass jar about two-thirds full of water. Add about 50-75ml vinegar and 2 teaspoons bicarbonate of soda. Stir gently, then throw in a few mothballs and watch them bounce up and down. The vinegar and bicarbonate of soda create carbon-dioxide bubbles, which cling to the irregular surfaces of the mothballs. When enough bubbles have accumulated to lift the weight of a mothball, it rises to the surface of the water. There, some of the bubbles escape into the air and the mothball sinks to the bottom of the jar to start the cycle again. The effect will last longer if the container is sealed.

Mouthwash

● **Cleanse your face** An antiseptic mouthwash makes a wonderful astringent for cleansing your face. Check the ingredients to make sure it does not contain sugar, then use as follows. Wash your face with warm, soapy water and rinse. Dab a cotton-wool ball with mouthwash and gently wipe your face as you would with any astringent. You should feel a pleasant, tingling sensation. Rinse with warm water followed by a splash of cold water. Your face will look and feel clean and refreshed.

● **Treat athlete's foot** A sugarless antiseptic mouthwash may be all you need to treat mild cases of athlete's foot or a toenail fungus. Use a cotton-wool ball soaked in mouthwash to apply to the affected area several times a day. It will sting a bit but athlete's foot should respond after a few days. Toenail fungus may take up to several months. If you do not see a response by then, make an appointment with a dermatologist or chiropodist.

● **Cure underarm odour** Regular deodorants mask unpleasant underarm odours with a heavy perfume smell but may do little to attack the cause of the problem. To get rid of the bacteria that cause perspiration odour, dampen a cotton-wool ball with a sugarless, alcohol-based mouthwash and swab your armpits. If you've just shaved your armpits, wait a day before trying this.

● **Give sports socks a power wash** Smelly sports socks are often full of bacteria and fungi that may not all come out in the wash, unless you add a cup of alcohol-based, sugarless mouthwash during the wash cycle.

● **Disinfect a cut** When you need to clean out a small cut or wound, use an alcohol-based mouthwash to disinfect the skin. Remember that before it was adopted as a mouthwash, the mixture was successfully used as an antiseptic to prevent infections after surgery.

- **Get rid of dandruff** To treat a bad case of dandruff, wash your hair with your usual shampoo, then rinse with an alcohol-based mouthwash. You can follow with an ordinary conditioner.

- **Clean a computer-monitor screen** If you've run out of glass cleaner, a strong, alcohol-based mouthwash will work as well as, or better than, glass cleaner on a computer monitor or TV screen. Apply with a damp, soft cloth and buff dry. Remember to use only on glass screens, not liquid crystal displays as the alcohol can damage the material used in LCDs.

- **Clean the toilet** If you've run out of toilet cleaner, try pouring 50ml alcohol-based mouthwash into the bowl. Let it stand in the water for half an hour, then scrub with a toilet brush before flushing. The mouthwash will disinfect germs and leave the toilet bowl sparkling and clean.

TIP make your own mouthwash

Freshen your breath with your own alcohol-free mouthwash. Place 30 whole cloves and/or 85g fresh rosemary in a 500ml jar and pour in 400ml boiling water. Cover the jar tightly and let it steep overnight before straining. If you need a mouthwash immediately, dissolve ½ teaspoon bicarbonate of soda in 100ml warm water.

Mustard

- **Soothe an aching back** Take a bath in yellow mustard to relieve an aching back or arthritis pain. Simply pour a 200ml jar of powdered mustard into the hot water as the tub fills. Mix well and soak yourself for 15 minutes. If you don't have time for a bath, you can rub some mustard directly onto the affected areas. Use only mild yellow mustard and make sure to apply it to a small test area first. Undiluted mustard may irritate your skin.

- **Relax stiff muscles** Next time you take a bath in Epsom salts, throw in a few tablespoons of yellow mustard as well. The mustard will enhance the soothing effects of the Epsom salts and also help to relax stiff, sore muscles.

- **Relieve congestion** Rub your chest with prepared mustard, soak a cloth in hot water, squeeze and place over the mustard.

- **Make a face mask** Pat your face with mild yellow mustard for a bracing facial that will soothe and stimulate your skin. Test it on a small area to make sure it does not irritate.

- **Remove the odour from bottles** If you've collected some attractive bottles, but after washing they still smell like the substance they originally held, you can kill the smell with mustard. After washing, just put a little mustard in the bottle, fill with warm water and shake it up. Rinse well, and the smell will be gone.

did you **KNOW?**

Ancient Romans brought mustard back from Egypt and used the seeds to flavour unfermented grape juice, called 'must'. This is believed to be how the mustard plant got its name. The Romans also made a paste from the ground seeds for medicinal purposes and may have used it as a condiment. The mustard we use today was first prepared in Dijon, France, in the 13th century. Dijon-style mustard is made from darker seeds than yellow or English mustard.

Nail varnish see page 199

Nail-varnish remover

- **Remove stains from china** Rub the soiled areas with nail-varnish remover and clean off the spots with a cotton bud.

- **Eliminate ink stains** Use nail-varnish remover to remove nonwater-soluble ink stains from skin. Take a cotton-wool ball and wipe the affected areas with the solution. Once the ink stains are gone, wash skin with soap and water.

- **Rub paint off windows** Working in a well-ventilated area, dab nail-varnish remover onto the painted areas of the window in small sections. Leave it for a few minutes before rubbing it off with a cloth. To finish, wipe again with a damp cloth.

- **Clean computer keyboards** You can keep a computer keyboard clean with nail-varnish remover and an old toothbrush. Simply moisten the brush with remover and lightly rub the keys.

- **Unhinge superglue** Superglue will stick tenaciously to just about anything, including your skin. Trying to peel it off your fingers can actually cause skin damage. Instead, soak a cotton-wool ball with acetone-based nail-varnish remover and hold it on the skin until the glue dissolves.

- **Clean patent shoes** Scuff marks can show up badly on patent shoes. To remove the marks, rub them lightly but briskly with a soft cloth or paper towel dipped in nail-varnish remover. Afterwards, remove any residue with a damp cloth.

- **Keep watches clean** Get rid of scratches on the face of a watch with nail-varnish remover. If the face is made from unbreakable plastic, rub the remover over the scratches until they diminish or disappear.

Nail-varnish remover

- **Dilute correction fluid** To thin correction fluid or old nail varnish, dilute it with nail-varnish remover. Pour just a few drops into the bottle and then shake. Add a little more varnish remover to the solution, if needed, to attain the desired consistency.

- **Prepare brass for re-lacquering** Old or damaged lacquer coatings on brass can be safely removed with nail-varnish remover. Take a soft cloth and pour a small amount of remover on it. Rub the brass object until the old lacquer has been lifted. Your brass item will be ready to be polished or professionally re-lacquered.

- **Remove stickers from glass** Wipe with acetone-based nail-varnish remover to remove both the sticker and the gluey residue left behind.

- **Dissolve melted plastic** If you've ever come too close to a hot, metal toaster with a plastic bag of bread or rolls you will know that the resulting mess can be a real cleaning challenge. Eliminate the sticky mess with nail-varnish remover. First unplug the toaster and wait for it to cool. Then pour a little nail-varnish remover onto a soft cloth and gently rub over the damaged areas. Once the melted plastic has gone, wipe with a damp cloth and dry with a paper towel to finish. The same solution works for melted plastic on curling irons or hair straighteners.

TAKE CARE

Too-frequent use of nail-varnish remover containing acetone (check the label) can cause dry skin and brittle nails. All nail-varnish removers are flammable and potentially hazardous if inhaled for a long time; use them in a well-ventilated area away from flames. And work carefully; they can damage some synthetic fabrics, wood finishes and plastics.

Newspaper

- **Protect glassware when moving** Use several sheets of soaking-wet newspaper to wrap up fragile and glass items. Let them dry thoroughly before packing. The newspaper will harden and form a protective cast around the glass that will dramatically improve its chances of surviving the move without breaking.

- **Line a waste-disposal unit** Putting a few layers of newspapers at the bottom of a waste-disposal unit will not only soak up the unpleasant odours caused by rotting foods, it will also protect the unit against damage caused by any sharp objects that manage to squeeze through.

- **Dry wet shoes** If your shoes get soaked after walking through the rain or slogging through the snow, stuff them with dry, balled-up newspaper to prevent any long-term damage. Place the shoes on their sides at room temperature so the moisture can be thoroughly absorbed. If the shoes are extremely wet you may need to replace the stuffing a few times.

- **Store sweaters and blankets** Don't treat moths to a fine meal of woollen sweaters and blankets. When putting them into storage, wrap wool garments in a few sheets of newspaper (be sure to tape up the corners). It will keep away the moths and keep out dust and dirt.

- **Make an impromptu ironing board** If you always pack a travel iron, it's easy to make your own travel ironing board. Fill a pillowcase with four or five newspapers, keeping the stack level. Place it on a flat surface or the floor before starting to iron.

- **Deodorise containers and luggage** To freshen a plastic container, wooden box, trunk or suitcase with a persistent, unpleasant odour, stuff it with a few sheets of crumpled newspaper and seal it closed for three or four days.

Newspaper

- **Unscrew a broken light bulb** To remove a broken light bulb, make a pad of several sheets of newspaper, press the paper over the bulb and turn it anticlockwise. (Note: make sure you're wearing protective gloves and that the power is off.) The bulb should loosen up enough to remove from the socket. Wrap it in the paper and throw it in the dustbin.

- **Slow-ripen tomatoes in autumn** If frost is expected and you still have some tomatoes on the vine, pick them and wrap individually in a couple of sheets of newspaper. Store them in airtight containers inside a dark cabinet or cupboard at room temperature. Check each one every three to four days; they will all eventually ripen to perfection.

- **Roll your own fireplace logs** Bolster a supply of logs by making a few of your own out of old newspapers. Just lay out a number of sheets end to end, roll them up as tightly as you can, tie up the ends with string or wire and wet them in a solution of slightly soapy water. Although it will take a while, let them dry thoroughly, standing on end, before using. Note: do not use newspaper logs in a wood-burning stove unless the manufacturer specifies that it is safe.

- **Add to compost** Adding moderate amounts of wet, shredded newsprint, printed in black ink only, to the compost heap is a good and relatively safe way to reduce the smell and to give earthworms a tasty treat.

- **Use as mulch** Newspaper makes excellent mulch for vegetables and flowers. It is superb at retaining moisture and does an equally fine job at fighting off and suffocating weeds. Just lay down several sheets of newspaper. Then cover the paper with about 8cm of wood mulch so it doesn't blow away. Don't use glossy paper and coloured newsprint for mulching (or composting); coloured inks may contain lead or harmful dyes that can leach into the ground. To check the content of your newsprint, contact the newspaper and ask about the inks they use; many papers now use only safe vegetable-based inks.

- **Farewell, earwigs** If your garden is under siege from earwigs, get rid of them by making your own environmentally friendly traps. Tightly roll up a wet newspaper, and put a rubber band around it to keep it from unravelling. Place the 'trap' in the area where you've seen the insects and leave it overnight. Repeat until your traps are free from earwigs.

- **Protect outdoor taps for winter** To prevent damage from ice and cold temperatures, make sure you shut off the valve to each tap and drain off any excess water. Then insulate each tap by wrapping it with a few sheets of newspaper covered with a plastic bag (keep the bag in place with gaffer tape or a few rubber bands).

- **Protect windows when painting** Don't bother buying thick masking tape when painting around windows. Simply dampen several long strips of newspaper and place them on the glass alongside the wood you're painting. The newspaper will easily adhere to the surface and keep the paint off the glass or frames, and it is much easier to remove than tape.

did you **KNOW?**

Newspapers were first published frequently and on a regular basis in the early 17th century. The German newspaper *Relation* was first published in 1605 while the UK's oldest surviving paper is the *London Gazette*, founded in 1665 and still published as a court journal. In 1785, John Walter founded the *Daily Universal Register,* which became *The Times* on 1 January 1788 and is Britain's oldest surviving newspaper with continuous daily publication. The oldest Sunday newspaper is *The Observer*, founded in 1791.

Newspaper

- **Put traction under your wheels** Unless you have a four-wheel drive vehicle, it's always a good idea to keep a small stack of newspapers in the boot of the car during the winter months to prevent getting stranded on a patch of ice or slush. Placing several sheets of newspaper under each rear wheel will often provide the traction you need to enable you to get your car back on the road.

- **Clean and polish windows** Instead of using absorbent paper towels to dry off just-washed windows, try using crumpled-up newspaper instead. Many people reckon that newspaper dries and polishes windows better than paper towels. And it's cheaper, too.

- **Pick up broken glass shards** If you break a large glass bowl or vase, a safe way to get up the small shards of glass that remain after you've removed the large pieces is to blot the area with wet newspapers. The tiny fragments will stick to the paper, which makes for easy disposal. Then carefully drop the newspaper into the rubbish bin.

did you **KNOW?**

What we call newsprint – the type of paper used by newspapers around the world – was invented around 1838 by a Canadian teenager called Charles Fenerty. After hearing frequent complaints from local paper mills about maintaining adequate supplies of rags to make rag paper, Fenerty hit upon the idea of making paper from spruce pulp. Unfortunately, Fenerty didn't go public with his discovery until 1844. By then, a consortium of European investors had already patented a process for creating paper solely from wood fibre.

...around the house

- **Make buttons glow in the dark** If you have trouble in a dim light seeing buttons on the remote control, dab glow-in-the-dark nail varnish onto buttons so that they're easy to see. You can also use polish to mark keys and keyholes and other hard-to-spot items as well as thermostats and shower settings.

- **Label your sports gear** Put a dot of bright nail varnish on your ball supply to avoid confusion with other people. Mark other belongings in the same way.

- **Label poison containers** Use dark red or other easily visible nail varnish to label anything that may be harmful. Draw an unmistakable X on the label as well as the lid or spout.

- **Seal an envelope** If you don't trust the security of self-sealing envelopes, brush some nail varnish underneath the flap, seal it, and it won't open even if you steam it with a kettle.

N ...around the house

- **Smudgeproof important medicine labels** Preserve the important information on prescription medicines and other important medicine labels with a coat of clear varnish, and they won't smudge if they come into contact with water.

- **Mark levels inside a bucket** When you are mixing in a big bucket, you can't usually lift the bucket to check the quantity. And it may not have the measurements clearly marked at all. Make sure you know you are using the right amounts by marking levels with lines of nail varnish. Use a colour that stands out against the surface of the bucket.

- **Waterproof address labels** When you are sending a parcel on a rainy day, a little clear varnish brushed over the address label will ensure your package goes to the right place.

- **Prevent rust rings from metal containers** Brush nail varnish around the bottom of shaving cream cans and other metal containers to avoid any unsightly stains developing. You can also paint screws with nail varnish to prevent them from rusting.

- **Prevent tarnish on costume jewellery** Inexpensive costume jewellery can add sparkle and colour to an everyday outfit, but not if it gets tarnished and the tarnish rubs off the jewellery and onto your skin. To keep fake jewels and your skin sparkling clean, brush clear nail varnish onto the back of each piece and allow it to dry before wearing.

did you **KNOW?**

Unless you work in a lab, you probably won't know that clear nail varnish is used for mounting microscopic slides. It is the preferred substance used around a cover glass to seal it onto a slide, protecting the specimen from air and moisture.

- **Seal out scuffs on shoes** The back and toes of leather shoes take the brunt of surface wear and tear. Next time you buy a new pair of shoes, give these areas extra protection. Paint a little clear nail varnish on the outside of the back seam and over the toes. Rub polish in to feather out the shine of the varnish. After it dries, you will be a step ahead of 'driver's heel' and 'footballer's toe'.

- **Keep laces from unravelling** Neaten the appearance of frayed shoelaces and extend their life. Dip the ends in clear nail varnish and twist the ravelled ends together. Repair the laces in the evening so that the polish will dry overnight.

- **Get rid of a wart** Warts are unsightly and infectious. To get rid of them and prevent spreading the virus, cover them with nail varnish. The wart should be gone or greatly diminished in a week.

- **Protect a belt buckle's shine** Cover new or just-polished belt buckles with a coat of clear varnish. You will prevent oxidation of the metal and guarantee a gleaming first impression.

- **Make a gleaming paperweight** To create paperweights that look like gemstones, or interesting rocks for the base of potted cacti, find some palm-size, smooth clean rocks. Put about 1.25cm water into a pie tin, and put 1 drop clear nail varnish onto the water. The polish will spread out over the water surface. Holding a rock with your fingertips, slowly roll it in the water to coat it with the polish. Set the rock on newspaper to dry.

TIP using nail varnish

- To keep nail varnishes fresh and easy to use, store them in the fridge. Keep them together in a little square plastic container.
- Shaking a nail varnish bottle to mix the colour can cause bubbles. Roll the bottle between your palms instead.
- Wipe the inside threads of your nail-varnish bottle and cap with a cotton-wool ball dipped in nail-varnish remover before closing them. It will open more easily.

...making repairs

- **Mend a fingernail** If you have split a nail, open an unused teabag, remove the tea, cut a piece of the bag into the shape of your nail and cover it with clear nail varnish. Press it onto the nail; apply coloured nail varnish. It will last until the break grows out.

- **Stop a windscreen crack from spreading** If a small crack has developed in the windscreen, working in the shade, brush the crack on both sides of the glass with nail varnish to fill it well. Move the car into the sun so the windscreen can dry. You will need to replace it, but this repair will give you time to shop around for the best estimate.

- **Fill small nicks on floors and glass** If children have been playing hockey or skating on wooden floors, you can fill the resultant chips and nicks by dabbing them with some clear nail varnish. It will be shiny when it dries, so sand the spot gently with some fine sandpaper. A thick coat of clear nail varnish also helps to soften the sharp edge on a nicked mirror or glass pane.

- **Repair lacquer** To fix a chip on a lacquered item, try mixing several colours of varnish to match the piece and paint over the chip to make it less noticeable.
  WARNING: you may lower the value of an antique by doing this, so only make this repair with inexpensive items.

- **Reset loose stones in jewellery** A stone can be reset using a little drop of clear nail varnish as the 'glue'. It will dry quickly and the repair will be invisible.

- **Temporarily repair a pair of glasses** If you've cracked a lens in your glasses, seal the crack on both sides with a thin coat of clear nail varnish. It will hold together until you get a replacement.

- **Plug a hole in a cooler bag** A small hole inside a cooler bag doesn't mean you have to throw it away just yet. Seal the hole with two coats of nail varnish – leave the first one to dry before applying the second – to hold in ice and other melted substances.

- **Keep chipped car paint from rusting** If a car has several small dents and chips, you can keep them from rusting or getting larger by dabbing clear nail varnish onto the damaged areas.

- **Smooth wooden hangers** Brush nail varnish over the rough edges to smooth the surface again and keep coat linings and delicate garments safe.

- **Fix torn window blinds** If you notice a small tear in a roller blind, you can usually seal it with a dab of clear nail varnish.

- **Tighten loose screws** Keep knobs on drawers and cabinets in place by brushing a little clear polish on the screw threads. Then insert the screws, and let them dry before using again. This is also a great solution if you have been keeping a Phillips screwdriver in the kitchen for loose saucepan handles. You can also use clear nail varnish to keep nuts on machine screws or bolts from coming loose and if you need to take the nuts off, a twist with a wrench will break the seal. Clear nail varnish will also keep the tiny screws on a pair of spectacles in place.

did you **KNOW?**

Nail varnish is certainly not a recent concept. As early as 3000 BC, ancient Chinese nobles are believed to have coloured their long nails with polishes, made from gum arabic, beeswax, gelatin and pigments. The nobility wore shades of gold, silver, red or black, while lower classes were restricted to pastel shades. Coloured nails were also popular with ancient Egyptians, who often dyed their nails with henna or stained them with berries. Polish wasn't just for women. In both Egypt and Rome, military commanders painted their nails red before going into battle.

...in the sewing room

- **Prevent loss of buttons** Keep a brand-new shirt in good shape by putting a drop of clear nail varnish on the thread in the buttons. It prevents the thread from fraying. Put a dab on just-repaired buttons as well.

- **Make needle threading easier** Do you fumble with your needle and thread, licking and re-licking the frayed thread end until it is too floppy to go through the eye? Try dragging the cut thread end through the nail-varnish application brush once or twice and then roll the thread end between your thumb and forefinger. It will dry in a second and the thread end will stay stiff enough to thread in a flash.

- **Keep ribbons from fraying** Brush the cut ends of gift and hair ribbon with a little clear nail varnish to stop them from unravelling. If you store them, you can always cut the ends off when you use them if you don't want the nail varnish to show.

- **Prevent frayed fabric from unravelling** If frayed wisps are peeking out from the bottom of your skirt or the lining of your jacket is fraying at the cuffs, you can stop the fraying getting worse by brushing the frayed strands into place with some clear nail varnish.

- **Stop a run in your tights** It can be a helpless feeling, realising that a small run in your tights is about to turn into a big embarrassment. Luckily you can stop runs permanently and prolong the life of fragile stockings with a dab of clear nail varnish. Simply apply polish to each end of a run (no need to remove the tights) and let it dry. This invisible fix stops runs and lasts through many hand washes.

- **Protect pearl buttons** Delicate pearl buttons – both real and fake – will keep their brand-new sparkle with a protective coat of clear nail varnish.

Oatmeal

- **Treat chickenpox or an itchy rash** Grind 200g oatmeal in a blender to make a fine powder, then pour it into a piece of cheesecloth or the foot of a clean nylon stocking or tights. Knot and tie the bag around a tap so it hangs under the running water. Run a lukewarm bath and soak in it for 30 minutes. Apply the oatmeal pouch directly to the rash or pox for additional relief. For a non-medicinal soothing bath, add a scented oil to the oatmeal. You can also use the bag to exfoliate your skin.

- **Make a face mask** An oatmeal facial is an excellent quick pick-me-up. Combine 100ml hot – not boiling – water and 75g oatmeal. Leave it to settle for 2 or 3 minutes, then mix in 2 tablespoons plain yoghurt, 2 tablespoons honey, 1 small egg white. Apply a thin layer of the mixture to your face and let it sit for 10-15 minutes. Rinse with warm water.

- **Make a dry shampoo** Put 200g oatmeal in a blender and grind it into a fine powder. Add 200g bicarbonate of soda and mix well. Rub some of the mixture into your hair. Give it a minute or two to soak up the oils, then brush or shake it out. This mixture is ideal if you are in a hurry or bedridden.

did you **KNOW?**

Oatmeal can take up to 30 minutes to cook depending on how the oats were made into oatmeal. After the inedible hull is removed, the oat is called a 'groat'. If the groats are cut in four pieces, the oatmeal takes about 30 minutes to cook. If the groats are steamed and rolled but not cut, it takes about 5 minutes. They take a minute or so if they are steamed, rolled and cut, but this breaks down the fibre. To maximise the fibre, use 30-minute oatmeal and cook it until it is chewy, not mushy.

Olive oil

- **Remove paint from hair** If you've got almost as much paint in your hair as on the walls when decorating, you can easily remove it by moistening a cotton-wool ball with some olive oil and gently rubbing it into your hair. The same approach is also effective for removing mascara; just be sure to wipe your eyes with a tissue when you have finished.

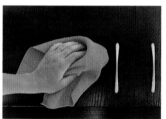

- **Make your own furniture polish** Restore lost lustre to wooden furniture by whipping up some homemade furniture polish that's just as good as anything you can buy commercially. Combine 2 parts olive oil and 1 part lemon juice or white vinegar in a clean recycled spray bottle, shake it up and squirt on. Leave on the mixture for a minute or two, then wipe off with a clean cloth or paper towel. If you're in a hurry, get fast results by applying olive oil straight from the bottle onto a paper towel. Wipe off any oil that remains with another paper towel or an absorbent cloth.

- **Use as a hair conditioner** Put the moisture back into dry and brittle hair by heating 100ml olive oil (don't boil it) and then liberally applying it to the hair. Cover hair with a plastic bag, then wrap it in a towel. Let it set for 45 minutes, then shampoo and rinse thoroughly.

TIP less virgin more vamp

Expensive extra virgin olive oil is made from olives crushed soon after harvest and processed without excessive heat. It's ideal for culinary uses where the taste of the oil is important. But for everyday cooking and nonfood applications, lower grades of olive oil work just as well and will save you money.

- **Clear up acne** Although the notion of applying oil to your face to treat acne does sound a bit eccentric, it's a remedy that many people swear by. Make a paste by mixing 4 tablespoons salt with 3 tablespoons olive oil. Pour the mixture onto your hands and fingers and work it around your face. Leave it on for a minute or two, then rinse it off with warm, soapy water. Apply this treatment daily for one week, then cut back to two or three times weekly. You should see a noticeable improvement in the condition of your skin. (The principle is that the salt cleanses the pores by exfoliation, while the olive oil restores the skin's natural moisture.)

- **Clean greasy hands** To remove motor oil or paint from your hands, pour 1 teaspoon olive oil and 1 teaspoon salt or sugar into your palms. Vigorously rub the mixture into your hands and between your fingers for several minutes; then wash it off with soap and warm water. Not only will your hands be cleaner, you will find they are softer as well.

- **Substitute for shaving cream** If you run out of shaving cream, don't waste time trying to make do with soap which can be rough on the skin. Olive oil, on the other hand, is a great substitute for shaving cream. It not only makes it easier for the blade to glide over your face or legs, but it will moisturise the skin as well. In fact, after trying this, you may not bother to use shaving cream again.

Onions

- **Eliminate the smell of new paint** If your bedroom is freshly painted and looks great, but the smell is keeping you up all night, place several freshly cut slices of onion in a dish with a drop of water; it will absorb the smell within a few hours.

- **Stop pet destruction** If Rover or Kitty is not respecting your property, whether it be by chewing, tearing or soiling, you may be able to get the message across by leaving several onion slices where the damage has been done. Neither cats nor dogs are particularly fond of the smell of onion and they should avoid returning to the scene of their crimes.

- **Remove rust from knives** Forget about using steel wool or harsh chemicals – this is an easy way to get the rust off a kitchen or utility knife. Plunge the rusty knife into a large onion three or four times (if it's very rusty, it may require a few extra stabs). The only tears you shed will be ones of joy over the rust-free blade.

- **Soothe a bee sting** If you have a nasty encounter with a bee at a barbecue, take one of the onion slices intended for your burger and place it over the sting. It will ease the soreness. (If you are severely allergic to bee or other insect stings, seek medical attention at once.)

- **Use as smelling salts** If you are with someone at a party or in a restaurant who feels faint – and you don't normally carry smelling salts – use a freshly cut onion instead. The strong odour is likely to bring them round.

- **Use as a natural pesticide** Create your own highly effective insect and animal repellent for the flowers and vegetables in your garden. In a blender, purée 4 onions, 2 cloves garlic, 2 tablespoons cayenne pepper and 1 litre water. Set the mixture aside. Now dilute 2 tablespoons soap flakes in 8 litres water. Pour in the contents of the blender, shake or stir well, and you have a potent, environmentally friendly solution to spray on your plants.

- **Make mosquito repellent** Some people find that increasing their intake of onions or garlic in the summer, or rubbing a slice of onion over their exposed skin, is a good way to keep away mosquitoes and other biting insects.

did you **KNOW?**

How can you keep your eyes from watering painfully when cutting onions? Suggestions range from wearing protective goggles while chopping, to placing a fan behind you to blow away the onion's tear-producing vapours, to rubbing your hands with vinegar before you start slicing. Another trick from the experts is to chill onions in the freezer for 30 minutes prior to slicing them. Or cut off the top portion and peel off the outer layers. The idea is to leave the root end intact, because it has the highest concentrations of the sulphur compounds that cause your eyes to water.

Oranges

- **Use for kindling** Dried orange and lemon peels are far superior kindling than newspaper. Not only do they smell better and produce less creosote, but the flammable oils in the peels enable them to burn much longer than paper.

- **Cook up a potpourri** Fill your home with a refreshing citrus scent by simmering several orange and/or lemon peels in 200-400ml water in a saucepan for a few hours. Add water as needed during the simmering. This process freshens up the pan as well as the air in your home.

- **Keep cats off the lawn** Make a mixture of orange peel and coffee grounds and distribute it around the cats' favourite haunts. If they don't take the hint, lay down a second batch and try moistening it with a bit of water to keep the smell strong and fresh – they should stop making a mess on your lawn.

- **Apply as a mosquito repellent** If you don't fancy the idea of rubbing onions over yourself to repel mosquitoes (see page 209), you may be happy to know that you can often get similar results by rubbing fresh orange or lemon peel over your exposed skin.

- **Show ants the door** Get rid of the ants in the garden, on the patio and along the foundations of your home. In a blender, make a smooth purée with a few pieces of orange peel in 200ml warm water. Slowly pour the solution over and into the places where the ants tend to congregate.

- **Make a pomander** Pomanders have been used for centuries to fill small spaces with a delightful fragrance as well as to combat moths. They are also incredibly easy to make. Stick cloves into an orange, packing them tightly until you have covered the whole surface. Suspend the pomander using a piece of ribbon, string or monofilament fishing line inside a wardrobe or cupboard and it will keep the space smelling fresh for years.

Oven cleaner

- **Put the style back in a curling iron or straightener**
Is your curling iron or hair straightener buried under a layer of caked-on styling gel or conditioner? Before you use it next time, spray on a light coating of oven cleaner. Let it sit for an hour, then wipe it off with a damp rag, and dry with a clean cloth.
  WARNING: do not use the curling iron or straightener until it is completely dry.

- **Clean grimy tile-grout lines** Make a full-scale attack on grubby grout. First, make sure you have plenty of ventilation – use an extractor fan to suck air out of a small bathroom. Put on rubber gloves and spray oven cleaner into the grout lines. Wipe the cleaner off with a sponge within five seconds. Rinse thoroughly with water to reveal sparkling white grout lines.

- **Clean a cast-iron pot** If you need to clean and re-season an encrusted cast-iron grill pan, start by spraying it with oven cleaner and placing it in a sealed plastic bag overnight. (This keeps the cleaner working by preventing it from drying.) The next day, remove the pan and scrub it with a stiff wire brush. Then wash it thoroughly with soap and water, rinse well and immediately dry it with a couple of clean, dry cloths. Note: this technique will eliminate built-up dirt and grease, but not rust. For that, you'll need to use vinegar. Don't leave it on too long. Prolonged exposure to vinegar can damage your cast-iron utensil.

TAKE CARE

Most oven cleaners contain highly caustic lye, which can burn the skin and damage the eyes. Always wear long rubber gloves and protective eyewear when using oven cleaner; even the mist from oven-cleaner spray can irritate nasal membranes. Ingestion can cause corrosive burns to the mouth, throat and stomach that require immediate medical attention. Store oven cleaner well out of the reach of children.

Oven cleaner

- **Remove stains from concrete** Get rid of unsightly grease, oil and transmission-fluid stains from a concrete driveway or garage floor by spraying them with oven cleaner. Let it settle for 5-10 minutes, then scrub the stains with a stiff brush and rinse the oven cleaner off with a garden hose at high pressure. Severe stains may need a second application.

- **Strip paint or varnish** For an easy way to remove paint or varnish from wooden or metal furniture, try using a can of oven cleaner; it costs less than commercial paint strippers and is easier to apply (that is, if you spray rather than brush it on). After applying, scrub off the old paint with a wire brush. Neutralise the stripped surface by coating it with vinegar, and then wash it off with clean water. Allow the wood or metal to thoroughly dry before repainting.

  WARNING: never use oven cleaner to strip antiques or expensive furnishings; it may seriously darken the wood or discolour the metal.

- **Clean ovenproof glass cookware** When you have tried everything to scrub baked-on stains off Pyrex cookware but they are still there, try this. Put on rubber gloves and cover the cookware with oven cleaner. Then place the cookware in a heavy-duty bin liner, close it tightly with twist ties and leave overnight. Open the bag outdoors, keeping your face away from the dangerous fumes. Use rubber gloves to remove and then thoroughly wash the cookware.

Paintbrushes

- **Use for delicate dusting** A small natural-bristle paintbrush can be indispensable when you need to dust the tiny cracks and crevices of chandeliers, wicker furniture or baskets, and knick-knacks. The soft bristles are ideal for cleaning areas that are hard to reach and also for dusting delicate items such as porcelain.

- **Brush off beach chairs** If your family are regular visitors to the seaside, keep a clean, dry paintbrush in the car for return trips. Use it to remove sand from beach chairs, towels, toys, the children and the dog before you open the car door or boot. You'll end up with a lot less sand to vacuum up the next time you clean the car.

- **Brush on the sauce** You can use a small synthetic-bristle paintbrush to brush on glazes, marinades and sauces while baking or roasting. You can also use it to paint on barbecue sauce when grilling burgers and steaks on a barbecue. A paintbrush is also easier to clean than most conventional pastry brushes.

- **Apply stain remover to clothes** Use a small paintbrush to apply liquid stain remover to stains and dirty shirt collars and cuffs. It's less wasteful than just pouring from the bottle.

- **Cover up seeds when sowing** When planting seeds in rows, use a large paintbrush to gently brush them over with soil. This lets you distribute the exact amount of soil needed and prevents overpacking the soil.

TIP brushes

Natural-bristle brushes work best with oil-based paints such as gloss. But use a synthetic-bristle brush with emulsion paint because the water in the paint can ruin natural bristles. Before cleaning a brush, wipe the excess paint onto newpaper. Clean a brush used with gloss paint in turpentine or white spirit until you get out all the paint. To clean emulsion paint, wash the brush thoroughly with soapy water, rinse clean and shake out.

Paper bags...

...around the house

- **Dust off a mop** Place a large paper bag over the mop head;
  use a piece of string or a rubber band to keep it from slipping off.
  Now give it several good shakes and gentle bumps. Lay the mop
  on its side for a few minutes to let the dust in the bag settle. Then
  carefully remove the bag for easy disposal of the dust.

- **Clean artificial flowers** Silk flowers are actually quite rare
  these days, but regardless of whether they're made of silk or
  another fabric, you can easily freshen them up by placing them
  in a paper bag with 50g salt. Give the bag a few gentle shakes and
  your flowers will emerge as clean as the day you bought them.

- **Make your own wrapping paper** When you need to wrap
  a present in a hurry, don't rush out to buy wrapping paper. Just
  cut a large glossy or colourful paper bag along the seams and
  make a flat rectangle. Position it so that any printing is facing up
  towards you so it will be inside when you wrap your gift. Put your
  gift on top and wrap it up. If you wish, personalise your wrapping
  paper by decorating it with markers, paint, ribbons or stickers.

- **Cover school textbooks** A sturdy paper bag makes a strong book cover. First, cut along the seams to open the bag out into a rectangle. Place the book in the centre. Fold in the top and bottom edges so the bag is slightly wider than the book's height. Cut off the excess, leaving 4-5cm on either side to slide over the front and back covers. Tape on the top and bottom of each paper sleeve to keep it on tight. Name and decorate as appropriate.

- **Store bed-linen sets** Have you ever emptied the contents of your linen cupboard looking for pillowcases to match the duvet cover you have just pulled out? Use medium-sized paper bags to store complete sets of bed linen. Not only will your shelves be better organised, but you can also keep the bed linen smelling fresh by placing a used fabric-softener sheet in each bag.

- **Bag your recycled newspapers** Double up on your recycling efforts by using large paper bags to hold newspapers for collection. It not only spares you the time and effort needed to tie up your bundles with string, but it also makes it easier to sort out magazines and newsprint.

- **Use as a pressing cloth** If your ironing-board cover is on its last legs, make a temporary pressing cloth by splitting open one or two paper bags. Dampen the bags and lay them over the ironing board to get the last few shirts or skirts pressed for work.

- **Reuse as gift bags** The small gift bags with handles that you get from most boutiques are ideal for holding items such as bath supplies, jewellery, perfume and even books. Simply add crêpe paper and a card. Stick a rectangle of coloured paper leaving a border around the edge to cover up any names or logos.

- **Make tidying easier** Cut open one or two paper bags and spread them out over the worktop when peeling potatoes or carrots, husking corn, shelling peas and beans or any other messy task. When you have finished, simply fold up the paper and throw it in the dustbin.

...in the kitchen

- **Keep bread fresh** If your kitchen tends to be hot and steamy, your bread will stay fresher when stored inside a paper bag rather than a plastic one. The paper's ability to 'breathe' will keep the crust crisp while allowing the centre of the loaf to stay soft and moist, ready for you to enjoy.

- **Store potatoes** Stop potatoes from going green and sprouting by keeping them in a strong paper bag. Potatoes always keep better when stored in a dark place and the breathability of the paper will stop them from getting damp and rotting.

- **Use to ripen fruit** Many fruits, including avocados, bananas, pears, peaches and tomatoes, will ripen more quickly when they are placed in a paper bag. To hasten the ripening process of any fruit, place an already ripe apple or a banana skin in the same bag and store at room temperature. To ripen green bananas, wrap them in a damp tea towel before placing them in the bag. Once the fruit has started to ripen, you can halt the process by putting them in the fridge.

did you **KNOW?**

Are paper shopping bags better for the environment than their plastic counterparts? Apparently not: paper bags generate 70 per cent more air pollutants and 50 times more water pollutants than plastic bags. What's more, it takes four times as much energy to make a paper bag as it does to manufacture a plastic bag, and 91 per cent more energy to recycle paper than plastic. On the other hand, paper bags come from a renewable resource (trees), while most plastic bags are made from non-renewable resources (polyethylene, a combination of crude oil and natural gas). And paper bags will degrade naturally, rather than clogging up landfill sites for years. The most eco-friendly solution is to use your own fabric or string bags.

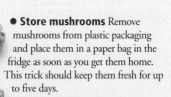

- **Store mushrooms** Remove mushrooms from plastic packaging and place them in a paper bag in the fridge as soon as you get them home. This trick should keep them fresh for up to five days.

- **Make dried herbs** To dry fresh herbs, wash each plant under cold water and dry thoroughly with paper towels to reduce the risk of mould. Take five or six plants, remove the lower leaves and place them upside down inside a large paper bag. Close the bag around the stems and tie it up. Punch a few holes in the bag for ventilation, then store it in a warm, dry area for at least two weeks. Once the plants have dried, inspect them carefully for any signs of mould. If you find any, throw away the entire bunch. Once you have removed the stems, you can grind them up with a rolling pin or a full soft-drink bottle. Alternatively, keep them whole to retain the flavour longer. Store dried herbs in airtight containers and keep them away from sunlight.

(KIDS' STUFF)
Make a body poster

Make a life-size body poster of your child using sturdy paper bags. Start by cutting up 4-6 paper bags so they lie completely flat (any print should be facing down). Arrange them into one big square on the floor and tape the undersides together. Then get the child to lie down in the middle and use a crayon to trace the outline of his or her entire body. Give him or her crayons or watercolour paints to fill in the face, clothing and other details. When it is finished, hang it up in your child's room as a wall decoration.

...for the DIY-er

- **Build a bag kite** Make a simple bag kite for your children to play with by folding over the top of a paper bag to keep it open. Glue on several pieces of party streamers under the fold. Reinforce the kite by gluing in some strips of balsa wood or a few thin twigs along the length of the bag. Poke a couple of holes above the opened end and attach two pieces of string or wool (put a piece of masking or transparent tape over the holes to prevent them from tearing) and tie the ends onto a roll of kite string. Take the kite out onto a beach, a heath or a windy hill and watch it fly.

- **Move ice and snow off your windscreen** If you are tired of having to constantly scrape ice and snow off your car's windscreen during the winter months, keep some paper bags in the car. When snow or ice is forecast, go out to the car and turn on the wipers. Then, shut off the engine with the wipers positioned near the middle of your windscreen. Split open a couple of paper bags and use the car's wipers to hold them in place. After the last snowflake falls, pull off the paper to instantly clear your windscreen. Note: to prevent damaging your car's wipers, do not attempt to turn on the ignition until you have removed the snow and paper from the windscreen.

- **Make a fire starter** For an easy way to get a fire going, fill a paper bag with some crumpled-up newspaper and perhaps some bits of candle wax. Place the bag under the logs, light it, then sit back and enjoy a roaring fire.

- **Spray-paint small items** There is no need to make a mess when you need to spray-paint a small item. Place the object to be painted inside a large paper bag and spray away; the bag will contain the excess spray. Once the item has dried, remove it and throw away the bag.

...in the garden

- **Store geraniums in winter** Although they are considered to be annuals, geraniums are easy to keep going over the winter. First, remove the plants from their pots or carefully dig them up, shake off as much soil as possible and place each plant in its own paper bag. Cover each bag with a second paper bag, turned upside down, and store them in a cool, dry place. In the spring, cut off all but 2.5cm of the stem and repot. Place them in a sunny spot, water regularly and watch the geraniums spring back to life.

- **Feed your plants** Bone meal is an excellent source of nutrients for all the plants in your garden. You can easily make your own by first drying leftover chicken bones in a microwave oven (depending on the quantity, cook them for 1-4 minutes on High). Then place the dried bones in a sturdy paper bag and grind them up using a mallet, hammer or rolling pin. Scatter the powder around the plants to help them to thrive.

- **Add to compost** Brown paper bags are a great addition to any garden compost heap. Not only do they contain less ink and pigment than newsprint, but they will also attract more earthworms to your pile (in fact, the only thing the worms like better than paper bags is cardboard). It is best to shred and wet the bags beforehand. Also, be sure to mix them in well to prevent them from blowing away after they have dried.

Paper clips

- **Open shrink-wrapped CDs** Save your fingernails and teeth from destruction; twist out the end of a paper clip and use it to slice the wrapping off the CD. To prevent scratches, slip the clip under the folded section of wrap and lift up.

- **Make a bookmark** Paper clips make excellent bookmarks because they don't fall out. A piece of ribbon or colourful string attached to the clip will make it even easier to use and find.

- **Stone cherries** If you need seedless cherries or don't like to stone cherries as you are eating them, use a paper clip. Over a bowl or sink, unfold a clean paper clip at the centre and, depending on the size of the cherry, insert either the clip's large or small end through the top. Loosen the stone and pull. To stone cherries but leave the stems intact, insert the clip at the bottom. Cherry juice stains badly, so watch your clothing.

- **Extend a ceiling-fan chain** To extend the chain, just fasten a chain of paper clips to the end.

- **Hold the end of clear tape** Stick a paper clip under the end of the tape and the next time you use the roll, you'll have no trouble finding and pulling back the end.

(SCIENCE FAIR)
The astounding floating paper clip

Challenge your friends to make a paper clip float on water. When they fail, show them how to do it. Place a piece of paper towel – larger than the clip – on top of the water in a cup. Put the paper clip on top of the paper towel and wait a few seconds. The towel will sink, leaving the clip floating. It may look like magic, but it is actually the surface tension of the water that allows the clip to float. As the paper towel sinks, it lowers the paper clip onto the water without breaking the surface tension.

Paper towels

- **Microwave bacon with no mess** Here is a fail-safe way to cook bacon in a microwave oven. Lay two paper towels on the bottom of the microwave. Lay the slices of bacon side by side, on top. Cover with two more paper towels. Run the microwave on High at 1-minute intervals, checking for crispness. It should take 3-4 minutes to cook. There is no grill pan to clean and the towels will absorb the grease – and can be thrown away.

- **Clean silk from fresh corn** If you find it hard to clean the silk off a freshly husked ear of corn, a paper towel can help. Dampen one and run it across the ear. The towel will pick up the silk and the corn will be ready for boiling or grilling.

- **Strain grease from broth** Use a paper towel to absorb the fat from a homemade broth or stock. Place another pot in the sink. Put a colander (or a sieve) in the new pot and put a paper towel in the colander. Pour the hot broth through the towel into the waiting pot. You'll find that the fat stays in the towel, while the broth streams through. Wear oven gloves or use potholders to avoid burning your hands with the boiling-hot liquid.

- **Keep produce fresh longer** If you are always opening the crisper drawer in your fridge to find last week's mouldy carrots mixed with yellowing lettuce or broccoli, line the crisper drawers with paper towels. They absorb the moisture that causes fruit and vegetables to spoil and rot. The contents will last a lot longer and it will be easier to clean the drawer as well.

- **Keep frozen bread from getting soggy** If you like to buy bread in bulk, this tip will help you to freeze and thaw each loaf more easily. Place a paper towel in each bag of bread to be frozen. When you are ready to eat the frozen loaf, the paper towel will absorb the moisture as the bread thaws.

Paper towels

- **Keep cast-iron pots rust-free** Stop rust from invading a prized collection of cast-iron pots. After they're clean, place a paper towel in each to absorb any moisture. Store lids separately from the pots, separated by a lining of paper towels. There should be no rusty surprises the next time you use them.

- **Clean a can opener** Have you ever noticed the unpleasant debris that collects on the cutting wheel of a can opener? It is not something that you want to get into your food. Clean the can opener by 'opening' a paper towel. Close the wheel on the edge of a paper towel, close the handles and turn the crank. The paper towel will clean off the gunk as the wheel cuts through it.

(SCIENCE FAIR)
Explore how colours work

Learn how all other colours are actually mixes of the primary colours of red, blue and yellow. Cut a paper towel into strips. With a coloured marker, draw a rectangle or large circle on one end of each strip. Try interesting shades of orange, green, purple or brown. Black works well too. Place the other end of the strip into a glass jar filled with water, leaving the coloured end dry and draped over the side of the jar. As the water from the jar slowly (about 20 minutes) moves down the towel and into the colour blot, you will see the colours separate. This also demonstrates capillary attraction, the force that allows the porous paper to soak up the water and carry it over the side of the jar.

- **Test the viability of old seeds** To find out whether the two-year-old, expired seeds that you have just found are worth planting, dampen two paper towels and lay down a few seeds. Cover with two more dampened paper towels. Over the next two weeks, keep the towels damp and keep checking on the seeds. If most of the seeds sprout, plant the rest of the batch in the garden.

- **Clean a sewing machine** If your sewing machine is good as new after a recent service, but you are worried about getting grease from the machine on your fabric, thread the machine and stitch several lines up a paper towel first. It should take care of any residual grease so you will be able to resume your sewing projects.

- **Make a place mat for children** If you are hosting your children's boisterous friends or your grandchildren are coming for an extended visit, paper towels can help you to weather the storm that they create at mealtimes. Use a paper towel as a place mat. It will catch spills and crumbs during the meal and makes cleaning up the table and the children very easy.

- **Make a butterfly** Use coloured markers to draw a bold design on a paper towel. Then lightly spray water on the towel. It should be damp enough so that the colours start to run, but do not soak in. When the towel is dry, fold it in half, open it up and then gather it together using the fold line as your guide. Loop a pipe cleaner around the centre to make the body of the 'butterfly' and twist it closed. To make antennae, fold another pipe cleaner into a V shape and slip it under the first pipe cleaner at the top of the butterfly.

Peanut butter

- **Get chewing gum out of hair** Apply some peanut butter to the matted gum and hair and rub the gum until it comes out. Your child's hair may smell like peanut butter until you wash it, but it is a better solution than having to cut the gum out.

- **Remove price-tag adhesives** Even though you have removed the price tag from a new glass or ceramic item, you may still be left with a residue of gummy glue. Remove it easily by rubbing peanut butter on it.

- **Bait a mousetrap** If you have a mouse problem, try laying traps at night baited with peanut butter. Mice love it and it is nearly impossible for them to get at the tasty bait without tripping the trap. Remember to get to the trap before any children do in the morning.

- **Eliminate fishy smells** If you are trying to eat more fish for health reasons, but hate the smell that stays in the house after you have cooked it, try this trick. Put a good-sized dollop of peanut butter in the pan when frying fish. The peanut butter will absorb the odour instead of your carpet, curtains and furniture.

- **Plug an ice-cream cone** Ice-cream cones are fun to eat but can be a bit messy. For a delectable solution, plug up the bottom of an ice-cream cone with a bit of peanut butter. Now, when munching through a scoop of double chocolate fudge, you will be protected from leaks. And there will be a delicious surprise at the end of the treat.

Pencils

- **Ease a new key into a lock** If you can't fit a new key into a lock, rub a pencil over the teeth of the key. The graphite powder should help the key to open the door.

- **Use as hair accessory** If you don't have a wide-toothed comb, a pencil can help to give a lift to curly hair without making it frizz out. Two pencils crossed in an X-shape can also stabilise a bun.

- **Decorate a picture frame** Make a frame for your children's class photograph with pencils. Glue two new brightly coloured sharpened pencils lengthways to the frame. Sharpen down two other pencils to fit the width of the frame.

- **Repel moths with pencil shavings** Empty the shavings from an electric pencil sharpener into little cloth sacks and use as sachets in drawers and wardrobes. The cedar shavings are an effective moth repellent.

- **Lubricate a sticky zip** When a zip is refusing to budge, no matter how hard you tug and pull, run a pencil lead along the teeth of the zip. In no time at all you should be able to pull up the zip with ease.

(**SCIENCE** FAIR)
Make your own animation

Are your eyes deceiving you? Cut a small piece of paper, about 5cm square. Turn the square so it becomes a diamond. On one side, draw or stick on a picture of an animal or a person. On the other side, draw or stick a setting for the animal or a hat and hair for the person. Examples are a cheetah and grasslands or a boy with a hat. Next tape the bottom point of the diamond onto the point of a pencil. Then, holding the pencil so that the picture is upright, twirl the pencil rapidly between your hands. You should see both images from the two sides of the paper at the same time.

Pencil erasers

- **Shine up coins** If you have just inherited a rather grimy coin collection, but you'd like to see it with more lustre, try using an eraser to shine up the coins.

  WARNING: don't do this to rare and valuable coins; you may erase their value along with their surface patina.

- **Store pins or drill bits** A box is not the most handy place to keep sewing pins. Here is an alternative: stick pins in an eraser. They won't fall out and it is easy to grab the ones you need. This is also a good tip if you are storing several fine drill bits.

- **Clean off crayon marks** Your toddler has gone wild with the crayons, but he has scribbled all over the walls instead of on paper. To repair the damage, gently rub an eraser over the crayon marks to get the wall back to its original state.

- **Remove scuff marks on vinyl floors** If new shoes with dark soles have left black streak marks all over the kitchen floor, rub them with an eraser to get them off quickly and cleanly.

- **Cushion picture frames** Glue erasers to the bottom corners of the frame. The pictures will now hang straighter and not leave their mark.

- **Clean piano keys** Whether it is a baby grand, a more conventional upright or just a fold-away electronic keyboard, cleaning the keys can be a nightmare project of dust and finger marks. Find an eraser that fits between the ivories and the black keys and simply rub away the ingrained dirt. This works as well whether you have a piano with real ivory keys or the more common plastic ones.

- **Remove residue from stick-on labels** When the gummy substance on a new picture frame will not come off with plain soap and water, rub the residue with an eraser and watch it just peel away.

Pepper

- **Stop a car-radiator leak** If your car is overheating because of a pinhole leak, pour a handful of pepper into the radiator before you take your car to a mechanic for a more thorough repair. It will plug the leak until you can get some professional help.

  WARNING: if you have just been driving the car, wait until the radiator has cooled down before touching it.

- **Use as a decongestant** Cayenne pepper will sort out a bunged-up nose or blocked ears. Sprinkle some on your food and grab some tissues.

- **Keep colours bright** To stop cheerful colours fading and running, add a teaspoon of pepper to the wash load.

- **Keep ants out of the kitchen** Deter ants looking for sugar by sprinkling cayenne pepper in the places where they go, such as in your cupboards or along the backs of your kitchen worktops.

- **Deter deer from your garden** If your freshly budding country garden is attracting the neighbourhood deer, they'll soon go elsewhere if you spray bushes with a cayenne-water mixture.

- **Get insects off plants** There is nothing more frustrating than a swarm of insects nibbling at a fledgling garden. Mix black pepper with flour. Sprinkle around your plants and the ants, aphids and earwigs should find another source of food.

did you **KNOW?**

Black pepper has been used to add flavour to food since ancient times and it is still the world's most commonly used spice. The black pepper in the grinder actually starts out as a red berry on a bush. When the pea-size berry is placed in boiling water for 10 minutes, it shrinks and turns black, becoming the familiar peppercorns that fill our pepper grinders.

Petroleum jelly...

...for personal grooming

- **Moisturise your lips and much more** Petroleum jelly can safely soothe lips or take off foundation, eyeshadow, mascara and more. It can even be used as a moisturiser on your face.

- **Make emergency make-up** Add a bit of food colouring to petroleum jelly and apply as usual. This is a quick way to make stopgap blusher, lipstick or eyeshadow.

- **Remove a stuck ring** Apply some petroleum jelly and your ring will glide right off.

- **Soften chapped hands** If you are constantly applying hand lotion to tired, chapped hands, but then removing it so you can get on with your work, try this tip. Apply a liberal amount of petroleum jelly to your hands just before you go to bed. Wear a pair of cotton gloves if you don't want to get grease on the sheets. By morning, they will be soft and smooth.

- **Stop hair dye runs** To avoid dying your hairline and forehead, run a bit of petroleum jelly across your hairline. If dye starts to seep off your hair, the petroleum jelly will catch it.

- **No more messy manicures** Petroleum jelly can help a home manicure to look more professional. Dab some along the base of your nails and the sides. If polish seeps off the nail during application, all you have to do is wipe off the petroleum jelly and the sloppy nail polish will completely vanish.

- **Heal windburned skin** if you have windburn after an autumn country hike, liberally apply petroleum jelly to your face and hands. The jelly will help to relieve the soreness.

- **Help prevent nappy rash** Painful nappy rash is one of the downsides of being a baby, but help is just a few moments away. A layer of petroleum jelly will set up a protective coat on the skin so acid is not absorbed.

- **Lengthen the life of perfume** If you are going out and don't want to take your perfume with you, dab a bit of petroleum jelly on your pulse points. Then spray on the perfume.

- **No more shampoo tears** Don't buy special no-tears shampoo for your child. Petroleum jelly is a far cheaper solution. Rub a fair amount into your baby's eyebrows. It acts as a protective shield and will stop shampoo and suds running down into his eyes.

...around the house

- **Get rid of lipstick stains** Before you wash lipstick-stained napkins, blot petroleum jelly on the stain. Launder and, hopefully, the stains will be gone.

- **Eject wax from candlesticks** To make it easier to remove wax from candleholders, apply petroleum jelly to the insides before you put the candles in. The wax will pop out easily.

- **Remove chewing gum from wood** Squeeze some petroleum jelly onto the offending lump, rub it in until the gum starts to disintegrate, then remove.

...around the house

- **Soothe sore pet paws** If your cat or dog's paw pads get cracked and dry, squirt a little petroleum jelly on the pads.

- **Keep ants away from pet-food bowls** Make a ring around poor Tiddles' bowl with petroleum jelly to keep ants at bay.

- **Make vacuum cleaner parts fit together** Apply a small amount of petroleum jelly to the rims of the tubes and the parts will easily slide together and apart.

- **Shine patent-leather shoes** Polish patent leather with petroleum jelly to keep it lustrous for longer.

- **Keep a bottle lid from sticking** If you are having a hard time unscrewing a bottle of glue or nail varnish, remember this tip for when you finally do get it open. Rub a little petroleum jelly along the rim of the bottle. Next time, the top won't stick.

- **Remove watermarks on wood** Apply petroleum jelly to water rings on wooden furniture and let it sit overnight. In the morning, wipe the watermark away with the jelly.

- **Restore leather jackets** You don't need fancy leather cream to take care of a favourite leather jacket. Petroleum jelly does the job just as well. Apply, rub it in, wipe off the excess and the jacket will stay smooth and supple.

- **Keep squirrels away from bird feeder** Keep squirrels off the pole of a bird feeder by greasing it with petroleum jelly. They will slide straight off, leaving the birds to eat in peace.

...for the DIY-er

- **Seal a plumber's plunger** Before unblocking the bathroom toilet, apply some petroleum jelly along the rim of the plunger and the blockage will disappear far more quickly.

- **Mask doorknobs when painting** If you don't want to remove door or window furniture when you are painting, rub them over with petroleum jelly to prevent paint from sticking. When you have finished painting, just wipe off the jelly and the unwanted paint will be gone.

- **Stop a battery terminal corroding** Car batteries often die on the coldest winter day because low temperatures increase electrical resistance and thicken engine oil, making the battery work harder. Corrosion on the battery terminals also increases resistance. Before winter starts, disconnect the terminals, clean with a wire brush, reconnect and smear with petroleum jelly. The jelly will prevent corrosion and help to keep the battery working.

- **Protect stored chrome** If you are getting ready to store children's bikes for the winter, or pack away a pushchair until the next baby comes along, take some petroleum jelly and apply it to the chrome parts of the equipment. When it is time to take the items out of storage, they will be free of rust. The same method works for other chrome-trimmed machinery stored in the garage.

- **Keep an outdoor light bulb from sticking** Have you ever unscrewed a light bulb and found yourself holding the glass while the metal base remains in the socket? It won't happen again if you remember to apply petroleum jelly to the base of the bulb before screwing it into the fixture. This is an especially good idea for light bulbs that are used outdoors.

- **Lubricate cabinets and windows** If you can't stand the sound of a medicine-cabinet door creaking along its runners or having to force a window every time you want a breeze through the house, then using a small paintbrush, apply petroleum jelly to window-sash channels and cabinet-door runners.

- **Stop squeaking door hinges** Squeaking doors at ill-timed moments are very annoying. Put petroleum jelly on the hinge pins of the door for no more squeaks.

Pillowcases

- **Wash lettuce in washing machine** If you are expecting lots of people for an outdoor lunch and have lots of lettuce to wash, place one pillowcase inside another. Pull apart the lettuce heads and fill the inside case with lettuce leaves. Close both pillowcases with string or a rubber band and throw the whole package in the washing machine with another large item, such as a towel, to balance it. Now run the rinse and spin cycle. Your leaves will come out rinsed and dried more effectively than in a salad spinner.

- **Dust ceiling-fan blades** Have you ever seen bundles of dust flying off a ceiling fan when you turn it on for the first time in weeks? Take an old pillowcase and place it over one of the ceiling-fan blades. Slowly pull off the pillowcase. The blades will get dusted and the dust will stay in the pillowcase, instead of parachuting to the floor and spreading all around the house.

- **Clear out cobwebs** Before you take a broom to a cobweb high up in the corner of a room, cover the bristles with an old pillowcase. Now you can wipe away the cobweb without scratching the paint. It is also easier to remove the cobweb from the pillowcase than to pull it out of the broom bristles.

- **Cover a baby's changing table** Use a cheap white pillowcase to cover the pad on a changing table. When it gets soiled, you can just slip it off and replace it with a clean one.

- **Use for wrapping difficult shapes** If you are trying to wrap a football, a vase, a large cuddly toy or an awkwardly shaped piece of artwork and wrapping paper isn't up to the task, place the gift in a cheap, brightly coloured pillowcase and tie it closed with a ribbon.

- **Make a set of linen napkins** Who needs formal linen napkins that need to be pressed every time you use them? Pillowcases are available in a wide array of colours and designs. Pick a colour or design you like, cut it into eight matching squares and make a 1.25cm hem on each edge. You can make a new set of colourful napkins for a fraction of the cost of regular cloth napkins and they iron easily too.

- **Store your sweaters** Stored in plastic, winter sweaters may get musty. But stored just in a wardrobe or drawer, they're prey to moths. The solution can be found in the linen cupboard. Put the sweaters in a pillowcase for seasonal storage. They will stay free from dust but the cotton fabric will allow them to breathe.

- **Store leather accessories** Stop leather handbags or suede shoes from getting dusty by storing items that you use only occasionally in a pillowcase. They'll be clean and ready to use when the occasion arises.

- **Keep matching sheets together** Your recently arrived overnight guests want to go to bed, but it is not made. You go to the linen cupboard, but you can't find a matching set of sheets. To prevent this from happening next time, file away your bed linens. Place newly laundered and folded sheets in a matching pillowcase before putting them in the cupboard.

- **Protect clothing hanging in a wardrobe** You've just washed a favourite dress shirt or skirt but you know you won't be wearing it again for a while. To protect the garment, cut a hole in the top of an old pillowcase and slip it over the hanger and item of clothing.

Pillowcases

- **Machine-wash your delicates** Sweaters and tights can get pulled out of shape when they twist around in the washing machine. To protect these garments during washing, put them into a pillowcase and close it with string or a rubber band. Set the machine on the delicate setting and you won't have to worry about tangles.

- **Machine-wash stuffed animals** Your child's soft-toy collection is sweet but very dusty. When it is time for a bath, place washable toys (check the labels) in a pillowcase and put them in the washing machine. The pillowcase will ensure they get a gentle but thorough wash. If any parts fall off the stuffed animals, they'll be caught in the pillowcase so you can reattach them once they're clean again.

- **Use as a travelling laundry bag** When you are travelling, it is natural to want to keep your dirty laundry separate from your clean clothes. Pack a pillowcase in your suitcase and use it to store the dirty laundry as it accumulates. When you get home, just empty the pillowcase into the washing machine.

(KIDS' STUFF)
Create a wall hanging

Children love to personalise their bedrooms. You can help kids as young as 4 or 5 do just that by making a pillowcase into a wall hanging. Let the child choose a pillowcase colour and then slit a hole about 2cm long in each side seam. Use fabric paints to create a design or scene or let your child rubber-stamp a picture on the pillowcase. Slot a dowel rod through the seam openings. Cut a length of wool about 75cm long. Tie one end of the wool to each end of the dowel. Hang on the wall and let the little one collect the compliments.

Pipe cleaners

- **Decorate a ponytail** Pull hair into a ponytail, then twist a coloured pipe cleaner around the hair band for an alternative hair decoration. Twist a couple of different coloured ones together for an even brighter effect.

- **Use as an emergency shoelace** When you break a shoelace just as you are about to go out onto the squash or tennis court, or out for a run, a pipe cleaner can be a good stopgap lace. Just thread it through your shoe as you would with a shoelace and twist it closed at the top.

- **Safety pin holder** Safety pins come in so many sizes, it is hard to keep them together and organised. Thread safety pins – arranged according to size – onto a slim pipe cleaner, through the bottom loop of each pin, for easy access.

- **Clean gas burners** Have you noticed that your hob burners are not firing on all jets? Can you see an interrupted circle of blue when you turn a burner on? Poke a pipe cleaner into the little vents. This will clean the burner and allow it to work more efficiently. This also works for pressure-cooker safety valves on pressure cookers.

- **Use as a twist tie** When you want to close a bag of kitchen rubbish but are out of twist ties, a pipe cleaner will work just as well instead.

did you **KNOW?**

According to reliable sources, pipe cleaners were invented in the late 19th century in Rochester, New York, by J. Harry Stedman. Although pipe smoking has declined dramatically since then, pipe cleaners have flourished, having been co-opted by the arts-and-crafts community. Technically, craft pipe cleaners are called chenille stems. They come in various colours and widths and are much furrier than the simple pipe cleaners smokers use.

Pipe cleaners

- **Make napkin rings** Colourful pipe cleaners are an easy and fast way to make napkin rings. Just twist around the napkin and place on the table. If you want to get adventurous, use two, one for the napkin ring, then attach the other pipe cleaner to it, shaped into a heart, shamrock, flower, curlicue or other inventive creation.

- **Use as a travel toy** If you are worried about having a bored, fidgeting child on your hands during your next long car or plane ride, take a bunch of pipe cleaners along. Whip them out when the 'Are we there yet?' questions start coming. Colourful pipe cleaners can be bent and shaped into fun figures, animals and flowers. They even make cool temporary bracelets and necklaces.

- **Use as a mini-scrubber** Pipe cleaners are great for cleaning in tight spaces. Use one to remove dirt from the wheel of a can opener or to clean the bobbin area of a sewing machine.

- **Decorate a gift** To give a special touch to a birthday or holiday present, shape a coloured pipe cleaner into a bow or a heart. Poke one end through a hole in the card and secure it to the package with a spot of glue.

super item **32 uses!**
Plastic bags...

...around the house

- **Line a cracked flower vase** If your vase leaks, line it with a strong plastic bag before you fill it with water and add the bouquet to give fresh life to a treasured heirloom.

- **Make party decorations** Cut coloured plastic bags into strips starting from the open end and stopping short of the bottom. Attach each bag to the ceiling, bottom side up.

- **Drain bath toys** Don't let your child's bath toys go mouldy. After the bath, gather them up in a plastic bag pierced with a few holes. Hang the bag on a tap to let the water drain out. The toys will be clean, dry and all in one place, ready for next time.

- **Keep kids' mattresses dry** There is no need to buy an expensive mattress guard if bed-wetting is a problem. Instead, line the mattress with plastic rubbish bags. Big bags are also useful to protect car seats or upholstery from toilet-training toddlers or damp children coming home from a swimming lesson.

- **Treat chapped hands** If your hands are cracked and scaly, rub a thick layer of petroleum jelly on your hands. Place them in a plastic bag. The jelly and your body's warmth will help to make your hands supple in about 15 minutes.

P ...for storing things

- **Collect clothes for the charity shop** If you are always setting aside clothes for charity, but then find them back in your wardrobe, try this. Hang a large plastic rubbish bag in your wardrobe. Each time you find something you want to give away, put it in the bag. Once it is full, take it to the local charity shop.

- **Cover clothes for storage** If you want to protect a suit or jacket, take a large, unused rubbish bag. Slit a hole in the top and push the hanger through to make an instant garment cover.

- **Store your skirts** If you find you have an over-flowing wardrobe but plenty of room to spare in a chest of drawers, do a clothes transfer. Roll up your skirts and place them each in a plastic bag. That will help them to stay crease-free until you are ready to wear one.

- **Keep handbags in shape** Do you ever notice that if you change handbags and leave an empty one in the cupboard, it deflates and loses its shape? Fill your handbag with plastic bags to retain its original shape.

TIP storing plastic bags

If a plethora of plastic shopping bags are spilling out of a drawer in the kitchen, here are some better ways to store them:
- Stuff them inside an empty tissue box for easy retrieval.
- Push a bunch into a cardboard tube, such as a paper towel or posting tube or even a section of a carpet tube.
- Fill a clean, 4 litre plastic milk carton. Cut a 10cm hole in the bottom. Stuff it with bags and hang by its handle on a hook. You can pull the bags out of the spout.
- Make a bag 'sock'. Fold a kitchen towel lengthways with the wrong side facing out. Stitch the long edges together. Sew 1.25cm casings around the top and bottom openings and thread elastic through them, securing the ends. Turn the sock right side out, sew a loop of ribbon or string onto the back to hang it up, then stuff plastic bags into the top opening. Retrieve them by pulling them out from the bottom.

...for keeping things clean

- **Protect your hand when cleaning the toilet** When you are cleaning the toilet, first wrap your hand in a plastic bag. You will be able to do all the necessary scrubbing without your hand getting splashed in the process.

- **Prevent steel wool from rusting** To prolong the life of a new steel-wool pad, put it into a plastic bag after you have finished. It won't rust and you'll be able to use it again and again.

- **Create a high-chair floor cloth** A shop-bought floor cloth to place under a child's high chair is expensive. Split the seams of a large bin bag and place it under the high chair to catch all the drips and dribbles. When it gets filthy, take it outside and shake or just throw it away.

- **Line the litter tray** Nobody enjoys changing the cat's litter tray. Make the job quick and easy by lining the box with an open plastic bag before pouring in the litter. Use two bags if you think one is too flimsy. When it is time to change the litter, just remove the bags, tie them up and throw into the bin.

- **Needle-free Christmas-tree removal** When it is time to take down the tree, place a large bin bag over the top and pull down. If it doesn't fit in one bag, use another from the bottom and pull up. You can quickly remove the tree without needles trailing behind you. Then make sure you take it to be recycled.

- **Keep polish off your hand** To polish a pair of sandals without getting more polish on your hands than on your shoes, wrap your hand in a plastic bag before inserting it into the sandal. Then when polish runs off the sandal straps, your hand will be protected. Leave the bag in the sandal until the polish is completely dry.

...in the kitchen

- **Bag the phone** You are doing something messy in the kitchen and the phone rings. Quickly wrap your hands in a plastic bag and answer it.

- **Replace a mixing bowl** If you are short of mixing bowls, try using a plastic bag instead. Place all the dry ingredients to be mixed in the bag, gather it up and gently shake. If the ingredients are wet, use your hands to mix.

- **Spin dry salad greens** Wash lettuce and other greens and shake out as much water as you can in the sink. Line a plastic bag with paper towel and place the greens inside. Grab the handles and spin the bag in large circles in the air. After several vigorous whirls, the lettuce will be dry.

- **Ripen fruit** To ripen rock-hard peaches and similar soft fruits, place the unripe fruits with a few already ripe pieces or some ripe bananas in a plastic bag. The ripe fruit will help to soften the others through the release of natural gas. But don't leave them for more than a day or two or they will turn purple and mouldy.

- **Cover a cookbook** You're trying a new recipe from a borrowed cookbook that you don't want to get splattered. Cover the book with a clear plastic bag and you will be able to read the instructions, while the book stays clean.

...in the garden

- **Protect plants from frost** When frost is forecast, use plastic bags to protect small garden plants. Cut a hole in the bottom of each bag. Slip one over each plant and anchor it inside using small rocks. Then pull the bags over the plants, roll them closed and secure them with clothespegs or paper clips. You can open the bags up again if the weather gets warmer.

- **Protect your shoes from mud** If it has rained hard in the night, but you still need to do the weeding, cover your shoes in plastic bags. The mud gets on the bag, not on the shoes, and your feet stay dry so you can stay out in the garden longer.

- **Clean a grill easily** After a brilliant barbecue, your grill is probably a sorry mess. To clean it, take the racks off and place them in a bin bag. Spray oven cleaner on the grill and close up the bag. The next day, open the bag, making sure to keep your face well away from the fumes. All the burned-on food should wipe straight off.

- **Protect fruit on the tree** To protect apples or plums that need a little more time to ripen, slip the fruit into clear plastic bags while it is still on the trees. You'll keep out insects and deter birds while the fruit continues to ripen.

did you **KNOW?**

Worried about the growing number of plastic bags filling landfills, countries across the globe have started putting restrictions on the seemingly indispensable item. Bangladesh has banned plastic bags, blaming them for clogging drainage pipes and causing flooding. Some Australian towns also have banned plastic bags, and the country is pushing shops to halve their use of bags (estimated at 7 billion annually) in a few years. If you want to use a plastic bag in Ireland, you will be charged about 11p a bag. In Taiwan, it's 20p a bag.

P

...in the garden

- **Cover car-boot sale signs** If you have gone to the trouble of advertising an upcoming car-boot sale with signposts but worry that rain may hurt your publicity campaign before even the early birds show up, protect the signs by covering them with pieces cut from clear plastic bags. Passers-by can still see the lettering, which will be protected from the rain.

- **Store outdoor equipment manuals** Your lawnmower has lost a cutting blade and you need to replace it. If you store all your outdoor equipment's warranties and owner's manuals in a plastic bag and hang it in the garage, you will know exactly where to look for advice on how to fix it.

- **Protect your car mirrors** Be a step ahead of snow or ice by covering your car's wing mirrors with plastic bags before a storm starts. When you are cleaning off the car the next morning, just remove the bag.

(SCIENCE FAIR)
Test the strength of a shopping bag

It is said that a plastic bag can carry about 9kg of groceries before you need to double-bag. Find out how much a bag can hold without its handles breaking. For this, you will need bathroom scales, a plastic bag and some stones. Place the bag on the scales. Fill it with stones until the scale reads 4kg. Lift the bag. Does it hold? Add more stones in 1kg increments, testing the bag's strength after each addition. When the handles start to tear, you will know the bag's actual strength.

...on the move

- **Store a wet umbrella** When you are out in the rain and running to your next appointment, who wants to deal with a soggy umbrella dripping all over your clothes and car? One of the plastic bags that magazines are delivered in is the perfect size to cover your umbrella the next time it rains. Just fold the umbrella up and quickly slip it into the bag

- **Pack your shoes** If a smart holiday means you have to take shoes for all occasions, but you are worried that packing them in the suitcase will get everything else dirty, wrap each pair in its own plastic bag. It will keep the dirt off all your clothes and you can rest assured that you have packed complete pairs of shoes.

- **Make an instant poncho** Keep a large bin bag in the car. The next time it rains unexpectedly, cut some slits for arms and one for your head. Slip on your impromptu poncho and stay dry.

...for the DIY-er

- **Store paintbrushes** If you are halfway through painting the living room and it is time to break for lunch, there is no need to clean the paintbrush. Just put it in a plastic bag and it will remain wet and ready to use when you return. If you are planning to finish next weekend, put the bag-covered brush in the freezer. Defrost it next weekend and you will be ready to start again.

- **Contain paint overspray** If you have a few small items to spray-paint, use a plastic bag to control any overspray. Just place one item at a time in the bag, spray-paint, then remove it to a spread-out newspaper to dry. When you have finished, throw away the bag to make cleaning up fast and easy.

Plastic bottles...

...around the house

● **Make a foot warmer** Fill a 1 or 2 litre drink bottle with hot – but not boiling – water, then sit down and roll it back and forth under your feet.

● **Use as a boot tree** Stop long boots from getting crumpled. Insert a clean 1 litre drink bottle into each boot. For extra tautness, put a couple of old socks or towels around the bottles.

● **Storing sugar** Decant a 2kg bag of sugar into a clean, dry 4 litre plastic bottle with a handle. The sugar is far less likely to harden and stick together and the handle will make pouring much easier.

● **Cut down on water when you flush** If you have an older toilet that uses a lot of water for each flush, save money on water bills by filling an empty 1 litre soft-drink bottle with water and placing it in the toilet cistern to reduce the amount of water used in each flush.

● **Fashion a funnel** Cut a clean milk bottle with a handle in half across its midsection. Use the top portion (with the spout and handle) as a funnel for easy pouring of paints, rice, coins and other materials.

...away from home

- **Make a scoop or boat bailer** Cut a clean plastic 2 litre bottle with a handle diagonally from the bottom so that you have the top three-quarters of the bottle intact. You now have a handy scoop that can be used for everything from removing leaves and other debris from your gutters, to cleaning out a cat-litter tray and cleaning up after your dog.

- **Keep a cooler cold** Fill a few clean plastic bottles with water or juice and keep them in the freezer to use when transporting food in a cooler. As well as keeping food cold, you can drink the water or juice as it melts.

- **Use for emergency road kit in winter** Keep a couple of clean 4 litre bottles with handles filled with sand or cat litter in the boot of your car. You will be prepared to sprinkle the material on the road surface to add traction under your wheels if you need to get moving on a slippery road. The handle makes pouring easier.

...in the garden

- **Use as a portable rubbish bin or harvesting basket** Cut a large hole opposite the handle of a large container and loop the handle through a belt or rope on your waist. Use it to collect debris you encounter as you mow the lawn or stroll through the garden. You can also make a basket for harvesting berries, cherries and other small fruits or vegetables.

TIP safe rotary cutter

Cutting plastic containers can be a tricky, dangerous business – especially when you use a sharp kitchen knife. But you can greatly minimise the risk by using a rolling cutter knife from a craft shop. Be careful as these knives use razor-sharp blades, but they make life much easier when it is time to cut into a hard plastic container.

P

...in the garden

- **Feed the birds** Take a clean 2 litre bottle and carve out an opening in one side, about half to two-thirds of the way down the bottle. Then make two small holes on either side of the opening to insert a sturdy twig or dowel for a perch and push it through. Poke a hole in the middle of the cap and suspend the bottle from a tree with a piece of string or monofilament fishing line. Fill it up to the opening with birdseed.

- **Create a drip irrigator for plants** During dry spells, a good way to get water to the roots of plants is to place several drip irrigators around the garden. You can make them from clean 4 litre bottles. Cut a large hole in the bottom, then drill two to five tiny (1.5mm) holes in or around the cap. Bury the closed bottles upside down about three-quarters submerged beneath the soil near the plants you need to water and fill with water through the hole on top. Refill as often as needed.

- **Space seeds** Use an empty soft-drink bottle as a guide. Find the distance that the seed company recommends between seeds and then cut off the tapered top of the bottle so that its diameter equals that distance. Firmly press the bottle, cut edge down, into the soil and place a seed in the centre of the circle it makes. Line up the bottle so that its edge touches the curve of the first impression and press down again. Plant a seed in the centre and repeat until you've filled up all the rows.

- **Isolate weeds when spraying herbicides** To isolate the weed you want to spray, cut a 2 litre plastic bottle in half and place the top half over the weed. Then direct the herbicide pump's spraying wand through the opening in the top of the bottle and spray. After the spray settles down, pick up the bottle and move on to your next target.

  WARNING: you should always wear goggles and gloves when spraying any chemicals in the garden.

- **Set up a garden sprayer** Cut three 2.5cm vertical slits in one side of a clean 2 litre soft-drink bottle. Or make the slits at different angles so the water will squirt in different directions. Attach the nozzle of a hose to the bottle top with gaffer tape (make sure it is fastened on tight). Turn on the tap and let the fun begin.

- **Keep flies and wasps away with a trap** Use an empty 2 litre bottle to make an environmentally friendly trap. First, dissolve 100g sugar in 100ml water in the bottle. Add 200ml cider vinegar and a banana skin (squash it to fit it through). Give the mixture a good shake before filling the bottle halfway with cold water. Cut a 2cm hole near the top of the bottle for the insects to enter. Hang it close to where they seem especially active. When the trap is full, throw it away and replace it.

...for the DIY-er

- **Store your paints** Keep paints clean and fresh in plastic containers. Use a funnel to pour the paint into a clean, dry milk or water container and add a few marbles (they help mix the paint when you shake the container before your next paint job). Label each one with a piece of masking tape, noting the paint manufacturer, colour name and the date.

- **Use as a level substitute** Make sure the shelf you are about to fix is straight even if you don't have a spirit level to hand. Fill a 1 litre soft-drink bottle about three-quarters full with water. Replace the cap, then lay the bottle on its side. When the water is level, the shelf will be too.

- **Make a weight for anchoring or lifting** Fill a clean, dry 4 litre bottle with a handle with sand and put on the cap. You now have an anchor that is suitable for holding down a painting cloth, securing a shaky patio umbrella or steadying a table for repair. Or use a pair of sand-filled bottles as exercise weights, varying the amount of sand to meet your lifting capacity.

Plastic lids

- **Stop a sink or bath** If the plug has disappeared, but you need to stop the water in a sink or bath, here is a stopgap solution. Place a plastic lid over the drain. The vacuum created keeps the water from draining away.

- **Keep the fridge clean** Drippy bottles and leaky containers can create a horrible mess on the shelves of a fridge. Make coasters from plastic lids to keep things clean. Place the lids under food containers to stop any potential leaks. If they get dirty, you can wash them off easily, while the fridge shelves stay free from any sticky mess.

- **Use as kids' coasters** When you are entertaining a crowd of children and want to make sure your tabletops survive, give them plastic lids to use as coasters. Write their names on the coasters so they won't get their drinks mixed up.

- **Use as coasters for plants** Plastic lids are the perfect water catchers for small houseplants. One under each plant will help to keep watermarks off the furniture.

- **Scrape nonstick pans** Unfortunately, food often tends to stick to so-called nonstick pans. Though using steel wool to get it off is not advisable, try scraping off the mess with a plastic lid which shouldn't scratch the surface.

- **Separate frozen hamburgers** Prepare homemade hamburgers for a barbecue in advance. Season the meat as desired and shape it into patties. Place each patty on a plastic lid. Then stack them up, place in a plastic bag and freeze. When the grill is fired up, you will have no trouble separating the pre-formed hamburgers.

- **Prevent paintbrush drips** If you are concerned about getting messy paint drips all over yourself while you are touching up a repair job on the ceiling, try this trick. Cut a slot in the middle of a plastic lid. The kind of plastic lid that comes on catering size tins is the perfect size for most paintbrushes. Insert the handle of the paintbrush through the lid so that the lid is on the narrow part of the handle just above your hand. The lid will catch any paint drips. Even with this shield, always be careful not to put too much paint on your brush when you are painting overhead.

- **Close a bag** When you have run out of twist ties but need to take a bin bag out of the house, take a plastic lid, cut a slit in it, gather the top of the bag and thread it through. The bag will be completely sealed and ready for disposal.

Plastic tablecloths

- **Make a shower curtain** A colourful tablecloth can make an attractive shower curtain to match your bathroom. Punch holes about 15cm apart and 1.25cm from one edge of a hemmed tablecloth. Insert shower curtain rings or loop strings through the holes and loosely tie to the curtain rod.

- **Make a high-chair drop cloth** It is par for the course for a baby or young toddler to get more food on the floor than in his or her mouth when learning to feed themselves. Catch the debris and protect your floor by spreading a plastic tablecloth under the high chair.

- **Save bending at leaf-raking time** Don't pick the leaves up to put them in a wheelbarrow to transport them to the leaf pile. Just rake the leaves onto an old plastic tablecloth, gather up the four corners, drag the tablecloth to the leaf pile and deposit.

Plungers

- **Remove dents in a car** Before spending money to have a mechanic remove a dent from your car, try this. Wet a plumber's plunger, push it over the dent and then pull it out sharply.

- **Catch chips when drilling ceiling** Before you use a drill to make an overhead hole, remove the handle from a plunger and place the cup over the shank of the drill. The cup will catch falling chunks of plaster, cement or brick.

- **Use as an outdoor candleholder** If you are looking for a place to put an insect-repelling citronella candle, plant a plunger handle in the ground and put the candle in the rubber cup.

Polystyrene foam

- **Make a buoyant tray for a swimming pool** Polystyrene foam is nearly unsinkable. Use the scraps from a building project to make a drinks holder or tray that will float in the pool:

  - To make a drink-can holder, cut two pieces to the size you want the finished holder to be, then cut holes the same size as a drink can in one piece. Glue the piece with holes on top of the other piece, using a glue gun.

  - To make a tray with a rim, just glue small strips of foam that are at least 2.5cm high around the edge of a larger tray-size section of the material.

- **Make your own protective pellets** If you'd like to use foam chips to post some fragile items, but all you have got is sheets or blocks of foam, not pellets, just break up what you have into pieces small enough to fit in a blender and pulse it on and off to shred the foam into perfect packing material.

- **Hold treats for freezing and serving** To prepare a quantity of ice-cream cones in advance, cut a foam block to a size that will fit flat in your freezer. Cut holes just large enough and close enough to hold cones so they won't touch, fall over or poke through the bottom. Fill the cones and slip them into the waiting holes. Then pop the whole thing into the freezer ready for serving at a moment's notice.

- **Make a swimming float** A sharp kitchen knife is all you need to cut a scrap of polystyrene insulation into a float to use when practising swimming strokes.

- **Keep nail varnish smooth** When applying nail varnish, a polystyrene pellet or a small chunk cut from a block of foam packaging placed between each finger or toe will help to spread them apart and keep the varnish unblemished until it can dry.

- **Help shrubs withstand winter** Sometimes shrubs need a little help to survive winter. Leftover sheets of polystyrene foam insulation are perfect for the job. They're rigid, waterproof and block wind and road salt. Here are two ways to use the material:

  - To give moderate protection, cut two polystyrene foam sheets and lash them together to form a 'tent' over the plant. To hold the pieces in place, drive bamboo garden stakes through the bottom of each piece and into the ground.

  - For more substantial protection, fit pieces of foam together so that you can box in the plants on four sides. Put a stake inside each corner and join the pieces with gaffer or packing tape. Plants in containers that overwinter outdoors are more likely to survive with polystyrene protection too.

TIP recycling foam pellets

Even with lots of creative reuse, sometimes polystyrene packing pellets just come in faster than they go out again. If you have got more than you can handle, remember that packing and shipping businesses may accept clean pellets for reuse. Call to confirm before you bring them in.

Potatoes

- **Extract salt for soup** Cut a few potatoes into large chunks. Add them to the soup while it is still cooking. When they start to soften, in about 10 minutes, remove them and the excess salt they have absorbed. Save them for another use, such as potato salad.

- **Remove stains on your hands** Hard-to-remove stains on hands from peeling carrots or handling pumpkins will come straight off if you rub your hands with a potato.

- **Remove a broken light bulb** If you are changing a light bulb and it breaks off, leaving the stem still inside, unplug the lamp, then cut a potato widthwise and place it over the broken bulb. Twist and the rest of the light bulb should come out easily.

- **Remove tarnish on silverware** Boil some potatoes. Remove them and place the silverware in the remaining potato water. Let it sit for an hour. Remove and wash. The tarnish should be gone.

- **Keep ski goggles clear** You can't keep a good lookout for trees and other skiers through snow goggles that fog up during a downhill descent. Rub raw potato over the goggles before you get on the ski lift and the ride down should be crystal clear.

- **End puffy morning eyes** Apply slices of raw, cold potatoes to your eyes and they will quickly get rid of the puffiness.

- **Make a decorative stamp** Forget expensive rubber stamps – a potato can provide the right medium for making your own stamp for decorating festive cards and envelopes. Cut a potato in half widthways. Carve a design on one half. Then start stamping as you would with a wooden version.

- **Feed new geraniums** A raw potato can give a fledgling geranium all the nutrients it could ever desire. Carve a small hole in a potato. Slip a geranium stem into the hole. Then plant the whole thing, potato and all.

- **Lure worms in houseplants** When worms are crawling in and out of the roots of your houseplants and the roots are suffering, slice raw potato around the base of the plant to act as a lure for the worms. They'll crawl up to eat and you can grab them and throw them into the garden.

- **Hold a floral arrangement in place** If you have a small arrangement of flowers that you'd like to stabilise but have no floral foam to stick the flower stems into, use a large baking potato. Cut it in half lengthways and place it cut side down. Poke holes where you want the flowers and insert the stems.

- **Restore old, beat-up shoes** If old shoes are too scuffed to take a shine anymore, but are otherwise in good repair, cut a potato in half and rub them. After that, polish them and they should come out nice and shiny.

- **Make a hot or cold compress** Potatoes retain heat and cold well. The next time you need a hot compress, boil a potato, wrap it in a towel and apply to the area. Refrigerate the boiled potato if you need a cold compress.

(**SCIENCE** FAIR)
Demonstrate the power of air pressure

Grasp a plastic straw in the middle and try to plunge it into a potato. It will crumple and bend, unable to penetrate the potato. Now grasp another straw in the middle, but this time, put your finger over the top. The straw will plunge right into the tuber. When the air is trapped inside the straw, it presses against the straw's sides, stiffening the straw enough to plunge into the potato. In fact, the deeper the straw plunges, the less space there is for the air and the stiffer the straw becomes.

Rubber bands

- **Anchor a chopping board** Does your chopping board move around when you are cutting up vegetables? Give the board some traction by putting a rubber band around each end.

- **Reshape your broom** If the bristles are splayed with use, wrap a rubber band around them a few centimetres from the bottom. Leave for a day or so and the bristles should get back in line.

- **Childproof kitchen and bathroom cabinets** Temporarily childproof bathroom and kitchen cabinets that you don't want visiting children to get into. Just wrap the bands tightly around pairs of handles.

- **Stop a sliding spoon** To stop a wooden spoon slipping into the mixing bowl, wrap a rubber band around the top of the handle. It will catch the spoon before it falls.

- **Thumb through papers with ease** Don't lick your finger. Wrap a rubber band around your index finger a few times the next time you need to shuffle papers. Don't make it too tight or you'll cut off circulation to your fingertip.

- **Extend a button** If a top shirt button is a little too tight, put a small rubber band through the buttonhole, then loop the ends over the button to give yourself a little breathing space.

- **Cushion a remote control** To protect furniture from scratches and nicks, wrap a wide rubber band around both ends of the television remote control. You'll be protecting the remote too; it will be less likely to slide off a table and get damaged.

- **Secure bed slats** Wrap rubber bands around the slat ends to make them stay in place.

- **Tighten furniture casters** The casters on furniture legs can become loose with wear. To tighten up a caster, wrap a rubber band around the stem and re-insert.

- **Gauge your liquids** Slip a rubber band around the liquid containers in your workshop to indicate how much is left and you will always know at a glance.

- **Wipe your paintbrush** To avoid paint accumulating and getting messy every time you wipe the excess against the side of the tin, wrap a rubber band around the can from top to bottom, going across the middle of the can opening. Now, when you fill your brush, you can just tap it against the rubber band and the excess paint will fall back into the can.

- **Get a grip on drinking glasses** Does arthritis make it difficult for you to grasp a drinking glass securely? Wrap a couple of rubber bands around the glass to make it easier to grip. This works well for young children, too.

- **Get a grip on twist-off tops** Some twist-off tops can dig into your hand when you undo them. Wrap the top in a rubber band to save the pain. This also works well for smooth, tough-to-grip bottle tops.

- **Make a holder for your car visor** Snap a couple of rubber bands around the sun visors on your car to make a handy place to slip parking receipts, directions or even a CD.

did you **KNOW?**

The first rubber band was patented in 1845 by Stephen Perry, who owned a rubber manufacturing company in London. A key ingredient is sulphur. When it is added to the rubber and heated – a process known as vulcanisation – it makes the rubber strong and stretchy and prevents it from rotting. The process of making rubber bands is surprisingly similar to making bread. First the dry ingredients are mixed with natural rubber. The resulting friction and chemical reaction heats and partially vulcanises the rubber. The rubber is cooled, then rolled out like bread dough. It is extruded into a long tube, and the tube is heated to finish the vulcanisation. Then it is rinsed, cooled and sliced into bands.

Rubber flip flops

- **Remove pet hair** Slip a rubber flip flop onto your hand and rub carpets and rugs in the direction of the pile. The pet hair will form into balls that can be vacuumed up. This works well on upholstery, too, including car seats.

- **Stop that banging door** Cut a piece of rubber from an old flip flop and use it to keep a door wedged open on a breezy day.

- **Prevent rattling windows** If your older sash or casement windows rattle in their frames whenever it is windy, cut slivers of rubber from an old flip flop and wedge them between the window and the frame.

- **Keep furniture steady** Stop the wobbles in a wonky table by cutting a piece of old flip flop to shape and gluing it beneath the offending leg.

did you **KNOW?**

Flip flops were inspired by the traditional woven or wooden soled 'zori' used by the Japanese. They were first used as beach wear in New Zealand in the 1930s, where they were known as 'jandals' or 'Japanese sandals'. They were made from rubber and plastic in the 1950s and Maurice Yock patented the design in New Zealand in 1957.

Rubber jar rings

- **Keep rug from slipping** If you have a rug that tends to skate across a polished wooden floor, keep it in place by sewing a rubber jar ring or two in each corner on the wrong side of the rug.

- **Play indoor quoits** Turn a stool or small table upside down and let children try to toss rubber jar rings over the legs.

- **Protect table tops** Protect table tops from scratches and watermarks by placing a rubber jar ring under vases and lamps.

Salt see page 258

Salt shakers

- **Cut back on sugar** Oddly enough, you can cut back on your sugar intake but still keep your sweet tooth happy if you fill up a salt shaker with sugar. The idea is that the shaker dispenses less sugar and, for sugar-restricted diets, is a useful alternative to dipping fruit into the sugar-bowl. Sprinkle just a small amount lightly over your food or, using icing sugar, over the top of a sponge cake.

- **Use for flour-dusting** Baking can be a messy job, but you can make at least one part of it tidier by putting flour into a large salt shaker. It is perfect for dusting cake tins. Keep it neat and close to hand in the cupboard with all your other ingredients for baking.

- **Use to apply dry fertiliser** If you use dry fertiliser, try putting it in a salt shaker to use when you are fertilising seedlings. It gives you plenty of control over how you can apply it and will help you to prevent fertiliser from burning tender young plants.

TIP coloured salt

To bring a little unexpected fun to the dinner table, try coloured salt. Put a few tablespoons of salt into a plastic sandwich bag and add a few drops of food colouring. Work it gently with your fingers to mix and let dry in the open bag for about a day. Cut a hole in the corner of the bag to pour the festive salt into the shaker. As a bonus, the coloured salt makes wonderful homemade glitter, but make sure that young children do not eat it as too much salt is not good for their digestive systems.

Salt...

...around the house

● **Make your own brass and copper polish** When exposure to the elements dulls brass or copper items, there is no need to buy specialist cleaning products. To shine candlesticks or remove green tarnish from copper pans, make a paste by mixing equal parts salt, flour and vinegar. Use a soft cloth to rub the paste over the item, then rinse with warm, soapy water and buff back to its original shine.

● **Remove residue from a vase** Once a bouquet has wilted, you will probably find deposits of minerals on the vase interior. To get rid of them, rub the offending ring of deposits with salt, then wash with soapy water. If your hand won't fit inside, fill the vase with a strong solution of salt and water, shake it or brush gently with a bottle brush, then wash.

● **Clean artificial flowers** You can quickly freshen up artificial flowers, of silk or synthetic fabric, by placing them in a paper bag with 50g salt. Give the bag a few gentle shakes and the flowers will emerge crisp and bright.

● **Hold artificial flowers in place** Salt is an excellent medium for keeping artificial flowers fixed in an arrangement. Fill a vase or container with salt, add a little cold water and arrange the artificial flowers. The salt will solidify and the flowers will stay in place.

● **Keep wicker looking new** Untreated wicker furniture often yellows with age and exposure to the weather. To keep the natural tone, scrub the item with a stiff brush dipped in warm salt water. Let it dry in the sun. Repeat this process every year or two.

- **Remove wine from a carpet** Red wine spilled on a light-coloured carpet can be fixed. While the red wine is still wet, pour a little white wine or mineral water onto it to dilute the colour. Then clean the spot with a sponge and cold water. Sprinkle the area with salt and wait for about 10 minutes. Then vacuum up the residue and wait for the carpet to dry.

- **Clean grease stains from rugs or carpets** Greasy marks on a rug or carpet can be hard to see, but they're not impossible to remove if you treat them correctly. Mix up 1 part salt to 4 parts methylated spirits and rub it over the grease stain, being careful to rub in the direction of the rug's natural nap.

- **Remove watermarks from wood** Watermarks from damp glasses or bottles left on a wooden surface are very unattractive. Make them disappear by mixing 1 teaspoon salt with a few drops of water to form a paste. Gently rub the paste onto the ring with a soft cloth or sponge and work it over the spot until it is gone. Then restore the lustre of the wood with furniture polish.

- **Clean a fireplace with ease** When you go to bed, dowse the glowing embers with salt. The fire will burn out more quickly, so there will be less soot than if it smouldered. Cleaning is easier, too, because the salt helps the ashes and residue to gather into piles so that they can be swept up easily.

did you **KNOW?**

Salt may be the key to life on Mars. Thanks to Mars missions, scientists have confirmed two things about the Red Planet. There's lots of ice and lots of salt. Of course, life as we know it requires water. And while temperatures on Mars are either too high or too low for fresh water, the presence of salt makes it possible that there is life-sustaining salt water below the planet's surface.

...around the house

- **Make brooms last for longer** A new straw broom will last longer if you soak the bristles in a bucket of hot, salty water. After about 20 minutes, remove the broom and let it dry.

- **Restore a sponge** Hand sponges and mop sponges usually become horribly filthy long before they are really worn out. To restore sponges to a pristine condition, soak them overnight in a solution of about 50g salt per litre of water.

- **Keep windows and windscreens frost-free** Salt greatly decreases the temperature at which ice freezes. Keep the windows in your home frost-free by wiping the outsides with a sponge dipped in salt water, then letting them dry. In the winter, keep a small cloth bag of salt in the car. When the windscreen and other windows are wet, rub them with the bag. The next time you go out to your car, the windows won't be covered with ice or snow.

- **Deodorise your trainers** Trainers and canvas shoes can get pretty smelly, especially if you wear them without socks in the summer. Cut down the odour and soak up the moisture by occasionally sprinkling a little salt into the shoes.

- **Relieve stings, bites and nettle rash** Salt can help to reduce the pain of bee stings, mosquito bites and nettle rash:

  - If you've been stung by a bee, immediately wet the sting and cover with salt. It will lessen the pain and reduce the swelling. If you are allergic to bee stings, you should get immediate medical attention.

  - For relief from an itchy mosquito bite, soak the area in salt water, then apply a coating of vegetable oil.

  - If you've blundered into a patch of stinging nettles, relieve the itching by soaking in hot salt water.

- **Make a scented air freshener** Perfumed air fresheners can be expensive and the smell is often synthetic. Here is a wonderful way to make your room smell delightful at any time of year. Layer rose petals and salt in a pretty jar with a tight-fitting lid. Remove the lid to release the perfume and freshen the room.

- **End the ant parade** If ants are beating a path to your larder, intercept them by sprinkling salt across the door frame or directly on their paths. They will be discouraged from crossing this barrier.

- **Give goldfish a parasite-killing bath** Mix 1 teaspoon plain (non-iodised) salt into a litre of fresh water. As with tank water, let tap water sit overnight to let the chlorine evaporate before submerging fish in it. Submerge the fish for no more than 15 minutes. The salt water kills parasites on the fish's scales and absorbs electrolytes. Don't add salt to the fish's tank, though. Goldfish are freshwater fish and should not spend a lot of time in salt water.

- **Clean a fish tank** To remove mineral deposits from hard water in a fish tank, rub the inside of the tank with salt, then rinse the tank well before re-installing the fish. Note: be sure to use only plain, not iodised, salt, which is safe for aquariums.

- **Repel fleas in pet habitats** Keep fleas at bay by washing down the interior walls and floor of the kennel with a solution of salt water every few weeks.

did you **KNOW?**

The world's leading salt producer is the USA. In 2002, the US produced 43.9 million metric tons of salt. China was second, with 35 million metric tons. Other nations producing significant amounts of salt were Germany, with 15.7 million metric tons; India, with 14.8 million metric tons, and Canada, with 13 million metric tons.

...in the kitchen

- **Freshen your waste disposal** Is your waste-disposal unit emitting an unpleasant smell? Freshen it up with salt. Pour in 100g salt, run the cold water and start the disposal. The salt will dislodge stuck waste and neutralise any odours.

- **Clean greasy iron pans** Grease can be hard to remove from iron pans, because it is not water-soluble. Sprinkle salt in the pan before you wash it and it will absorb most of the grease. Then wipe off the grease and salt and wash as usual.

- **Remove baked-on food** You can remove food that has been baked onto pans or serving plates by lifting it with a pre-treatment of salt. Before washing, sprinkle the stuck-on food with salt. Dampen the area, let it sit until the salt lifts the baked-on food, then wash it away with soapy water.

- **Soak stains off enamel pans** You can run out of elbow grease trying to scrub burned-on stains off enamel pans. Instead, soak the pan overnight in salt water. Then boil salt water in the pan the next day. The stains should lift straight off.

- **Brighten up chopping boards** After washing breadboards and chopping boards with soap and water, rub them with a damp cloth dipped in salt. The boards will come out lighter and brighter in colour.

did you **KNOW?**

Salt was surely the first food seasoning. Prehistoric peoples got all the salt they needed from the meat that made up a large portion of their diet. When humans began turning to agriculture as a more reliable food source, they discovered that salt, probably taken from the sea, gave vegetables a salty taste they craved. As the millennia passed, salt gradually made life more comfortable and certain as people learned to use it to preserve food, cure hides and heal wounds.

- **Keep oven spills from hardening** The next time food bubbles over in the oven, don't give it a chance to bake on and cool. Throw some salt on the drips while it is still liquid. When the oven cools, you will be able to wipe up the spill with a cloth. The same technique works for spills on the hob. The salt will remove unpleasant smells as well, and if you would like to add a sweet scent, you can mix a little cinnamon in with the salt.

- **Clean away messy dough** Here is a way to make short work of cleaning up after you've rolled out dough or kneaded bread. Sprinkle the floured worktop with salt and you can neatly wipe away everything with a sponge.

- **Scrub off burned milk** Burned milk is one of the toughest stains to remove, but salt makes it a lot easier. Wet the burned pan and sprinkle it with salt. Wait about 10 minutes, then scrub the pan. The salt will absorb the burned-milk smell too.

- **Erase tea and coffee stains** You can easily scrub away brown rings by sprinkling salt onto a sponge and rubbing in little circles across the ring. If the stain persists, mix white vinegar with salt in equal proportions and rub with the sponge.

- **Clean a cast-iron wok** No matter how thoroughly you dry them, cast-iron woks tend to rust when washed in water. Instead, when you have finished cooking, but while the wok is still hot, pour in about 50g salt and scrub it with a stiff wire brush. Wipe it clean, then apply a light coating of sesame or vegetable oil before putting it away. Don't clean a wok with a nonstick coating in this way, as it will scratch the finish.

- **Clean discoloured glass** Have the dishwasher and a good scrub failed to remove stubborn stains from glassware? Mix a handful of salt in a litre of vinegar and soak the glassware overnight. The stains should wipe off in the morning.

...in the kitchen

- **Remove lipstick marks from glassware** Lipstick smudges on glassware can be hard to remove, even in the dishwasher. That is because the emollients designed to help lipstick stay on your lips do a good job of sticking to glassware as well. Before washing wine glasses or tumblers, rub the edges with salt to erase lipstick stains.

- **Revive overcooked coffee** Before you throw out stewed coffee, try adding a pinch of salt to a cup to restore the flavour.

- **Clean the fridge** After removing the food and the wire shelves from the fridge, mix up a handful of salt in 4 litres of warm water and use it with a sponge to clean the inside of the fridge. The mixture isn't abrasive, so it won't scratch surfaces. And you won't be introducing chemical fumes to a place where you keep food.

- **Shine a teapot spout** Teapots with seriously stained spouts can be cleaned with salt. Pack the spout with salt and let it sit overnight or for at least a few hours. Then run boiling water through the pot, washing away the salt to reveal the old sparkle. If the stain persists, treat the rim with a cotton bud dipped in salt.

- **Prevent grease from splashing** Add a few dashes of salt to the pan before starting to fry fatty foods that can splash. You won't have to clean grease off the hob.

- **Shell hard-boiled eggs with ease** Is there a secret to peeling hard-boiled eggs without breaking the shell into dozens of tiny pieces? There is: just add a teaspoon of salt to the water before placing the eggs in it to boil.

- **Test an egg's freshness** If you are in doubt about the freshness of your eggs, add 2 teaspoons salt to 200ml water and gently place the egg in the cup. A fresh egg will sink. An old one floats.

- **Make perfect poached eggs** You know it is possible to keep the whites intact when you poach eggs – you've had them in a restaurant. But no matter how careful you are, the whites always diffuse into the water when you poach eggs at home. Here is the secret that restaurant chefs use. Sprinkle about ½ teaspoon salt into the water just before you put in the eggs. This helps to 'set' the whites in a neat package. A dash of vinegar also helps and improves the taste of the eggs, too.

- **Wash spinach more easily** Fresh spinach leaves are an ideal health food, but their curving, bumpy surface makes it difficult to wash away all the dirt that collects in the crevices. Wash spinach leaves in salted water: the dirt is driven out along with the salt in the rinse water and you should get away with a single rinse.

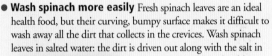

- **Keep salad crisp** When you need to prepare leafy salad in advance for a dinner party, lightly salt the salad immediately after you prepare it and you can rest assured that it will remain crisp for several hours.

- **Prevent mould on cheese** Cheese is much too expensive to throw away because it has a touch of mould. Prevent it from getting mouldy in the first place by wrapping the cheese in a napkin soaked in salt water before storing it in the fridge.

did you **KNOW?**

One of a number of words that salt has added to our language is salary. It comes from the Latin word salarium, which means 'salt money' and refers to that part of a Roman soldier's pay that was made in salt or used to buy salt, a life-preserving commodity. This is also the origin of the phrase 'worth one's salt'.

...in the kitchen

- **Revive shrivelled apples** If you discover that the apples in the fruit bowl are past their best, soak them in mildly salted water to make the skin smooth again.

- **Stop cut fruit from going brown** To ensure that fresh-cut fruit for a dessert looks appetising when you serve the dish and that cut apples and pears don't go brown, soak them briefly in a bowl of lightly salted water.

- **Keep your milk fresh** Add a pinch of salt to a carton of milk to help it stay fresh for longer. This tip will work for cream as well.

- **Speed up cooking time** When you are in a hurry, add a pinch or two of salt to the water you are boiling food in. This makes the water boil at a higher temperature so the food you are cooking will require less time to finish.

(KIDS' STUFF)
Make your own craft dough

Make a craft dough that can be made into detailed ornaments, miniature food and dolls. In a bowl, slowly stir 200g salt into 200ml boiling water. After the salt dissolves, stir in 400g white flour. Turn the dough out onto a work surface and knead until smooth. If the dough is still sticky, add flour by the tablespoon until it is pliant. It should be easy to shape into balls, tubes, wreaths and other shapes. When they are finished, you can air-dry your creations or bake them in the oven at 110°C/gas mark ¼ for up to 2 hours; the time depends on thickness. Or microwave on High for 1-2 minutes. Apply paint, then protect and shine with clear nail varnish.

- **Use to whip cream and beat eggs**
The next time you whip cream or beat eggs, make sure that you add a pinch of salt first. The cream will whip up more lightly and the eggs will beat more quickly, take in more air and firm up better when you cook them.

- **Pick up spilled eggs** If you have ever dropped an uncooked egg, you will know how messy it is to clean up. To clean it up much more easily, cover the spill with salt. It will draw the egg together and you can wipe it up with a sponge or paper towel.

- **Extinguish grease fires** Keep a box of salt next to the cooker. If a grease fire erupts in a grill pan or frying pan, throw plenty of salt on it to extinguish the flames. Salt is also the solution when barbecue flames from meat drippings become too high. Sprinkling salt on the coals will quell the flames without causing a lot of smoke and cooling the coals as water does.

    WARNING: never pour water on a grease fire; it will cause the grease to splatter and will spread the fire.

did you **KNOW?**

The concentration of salt in the human body is nearly a third of the concentration found in seawater. This is why blood, sweat and tears are so salty. Many scientists believe that humans, as well as all animals, need salt because all life evolved from the oceans. When the first land dwellers crawled out of the sea, they carried the need for salt – and a bit of the supply – with them and passed it on to their descendants.

...in the laundry

- **Make a quick pre-treatment** If you drop a spot of grease onto your clothes, quickly rub salt over the spot to absorb the grease. Wash the garment as usual.

- **Remove stubborn perspiration stains** Dissolve 4 tablespoons salt in a litre of hot water. Then just sponge the garment with the solution until the stain disappears.

- **Set the colour in new towels** The first two or three times you wash new coloured towels, add 200g salt to the wash. The salt will set the colours so the towels will remain bright for longer.

- **Clean your iron's metal soleplate** Turn the iron onto High. Sprinkle table salt onto a piece of newspaper on the ironing board. Run the hot iron over the salt and you should iron away the bumps.

...in the garden

- **Stop weeds in their tracks** The weeds that pop up in the cracks of a garden path or patio can be difficult to eradicate. But salt can do the job. Bring a solution of about 200g salt in 400ml water to the boil. Then pour directly onto the weeds to kill them. Another equally effective method is to spread salt directly onto the weeds or unwanted grass that appear between patio bricks or blocks. Sprinkle with water or wait until rain does the job for you.

- **Rid the garden of snails and slugs** Take a container of salt out into the garden and put a ring of salt around your plants. Salt is lethal to soft-bodied animals and they shouldn't attempt to breach the salt 'defences'.

...in the bath

- **A pre-shampoo dandruff treatment** The abrasiveness of ordinary table salt works well for scrubbing out dandruff before you wash your hair. Shake some salt onto your dry scalp. Then work it through your hair, giving your scalp a massage. You should find you have worked out the dry, flaky skin before you start to shampoo your hair.

- **Give yourself a salt rubdown.** To remove dead skin particles and boost your circulation, give yourself a massage with dry salt either in or just after a bath, when your skin is still damp. Ordinary salt works well; the larger sea-salt crystals also do the job.

- **Condition your skin** Instead of using bath salts which contain colourings and a host of additional ingredients, dissolve 200g table salt in the bath and soak as usual. Your skin will be noticeably softer. For a real treat use sea salt.

- **Open drains blocked with hair** It is difficult to keep hair and shampoo residues from collecting in the drain of the bath and blocking it. Dissolve the mess with 200g salt, 200g bicarbonate of soda and 100ml white vinegar. Pour the mixture down the drain. After 10 minutes, follow up with 2 litres of boiling water. Run the hot-water tap until the drain flows freely.

- **Remove spots on bath enamel** Yellow spots on an enamel bath or sink can be reduced by mixing up a solution of salt and turpentine in equal parts. Using rubber gloves, rub away the discoloration and then rinse thoroughly. Don't forget to ventilate the bathroom.

- **Freshen your breath the old-fashioned way** Mix 1 teaspoon salt and 1 teaspoon bicarbonate of soda into 100ml water. Rinse and gargle.

Sand

- **Clean a narrow-necked vase** Once a colourful bouquet is dead, it is time to thoroughly clean the vase. If the opening is too narrow for your hand, put a little sand and warm, soapy water in the vase and swish gently. The sand will do the work of cleaning the residue inside for you.

- **Hold items while gluing** Repairing small items, such as broken china, with glue would be easy if you had three hands, one for each piece along with one to apply the glue. Since you only have two hands, try this. Stick the biggest part of the item in a small container of sand to hold it steady. Position the large piece so that when you set the broken piece in place, the piece will balance. Apply glue to both edges and stick on the broken piece. Leave the mended piece and the sand will hold it steady until the glue dries.

- **Protect and store garden tools** Garden tools are meant to last longer than perennials, so keep them clean and protected from the elements. Fill a large (10-15 litre) bucket with builder's sand (available at builders' merchants) and pour in about a litre of clean motor oil. Plunge spades, hoes, rakes and other tools into the sand a few times to clean and lubricate them. To prevent rust, you can also leave the tool blades in the bucket of sand for storage. A large coffee can filled with sand and a little motor oil will give the same protection to secateurs and trowels.

- **Carry in the car for traction** A bag of sand in the boot of the car is good insurance against getting stuck or spinning out from a parking spot in icy weather. Take a clean margarine tub vas well, to use as a scoop. For those with rear-wheel-drive vehicles, a bag or two of sand will also give you some extra traction.

270

Sandpaper

- **Remove pilling on sweaters** If you are fighting a losing battle with the fuzz balls on your sweaters, a little sandpaper will handle them. Use any grade and rub lightly in one direction.

- **Remove scorches on wool** Take some medium-grade sandpaper to any small scorch spots on woollen clothing. The mark left by a careless spark will be less noticeable with some light sanding around the edges.

- **Hold pleats while ironing** If you like to keep pleats perfect, keep some fine or medium-grade sandpaper alongside the iron. Put the sandpaper under the pleat to hold it in place while you iron in a sharp fold.

- **Roughen slippery leather soles** New shoes with slippery soles can send you flying, so take a little sandpaper and a little time to sand across the width of the soles and roughen up the slick surface. It is easier than taking new shoes to a repair shop to have new rubber soles put on.

- **Sharpen scissors** Do your scissors cut less than crisply? Try cutting through a sheet of fine sandpaper to finish off the edge and keep every cut clean and sharp.

- **Sharpen sewing needles** Think twice before throwing out a used piece of fine sandpaper; the unused edges or corners are perfect for tucking into a sewing box. Running your sewing needles through sandpaper a few times or twisting them inside a folded piece of sandpaper, will keep them sharp.

- **Make an emery board** If you don't have an emery board handy the next time you need to smooth your nails, use a piece of ultra-fine sandpaper instead.

- **Use to deter slugs** Stop slugs from getting into potted plants by placing used sanding discs under the bases of pots, making sure the sandpaper is wider than the pot base.

Sandpaper

- **Remove ink stains and scuff marks from suede** A little fine-grade sandpaper and a gentle touch will help to minimise an ink stain or small scuff mark on suede clothing or shoes. Afterwards, bring up the nap with a toothbrush or nailbrush. It may avoid an expensive trip to the dry-cleaner.

- **Remove stubborn grout stains** Sometimes a bathroom abrasive cleaner is just not abrasive enough. Get tough on grout stains with fine-grade sandpaper. Fold the sandpaper and use the folded edge to sand in the grout seam. But be careful not to sand the tiles and scratch the finish.

- **Open a stuck jar** If you are having a hard time opening a jar, take a piece of sandpaper and place it, grit side down, on the lid. The sandpaper should improve your grip enough to twist off the lid more easily.

(KIDS' STUFF)
Make a designer T-shirt

You or a junior artist can make a beautiful one-of-a-kind T-shirt. Get the child to use crayons to draw a simple, bold design on the rough side of a sheet of sandpaper. Lay the T-shirt on the ironing board and slip a sheet of aluminium foil inside, between the front and back of the shirt. Place the sandpaper onto the T-shirt, design side down. Using an iron on the warm setting, press the back of the sandpaper in one spot for about 10 seconds and then move on to the next spot until the entire design has been pressed. Let the shirt cool to set the design, wash on a cool setting, then hang up to dry.

super item **25 uses!**
Sandwich and freezer bags...

...around the house

- **Freeze a facecloth for a cold pack** It is hard to predict when you will need a cold compress for a burn, teething pain or bruise. Be ready; freeze a wet facecloth in a sandwich or freezer bag. Get it out the next time someone needs a cold pack.

- **Make baby wipes for pennies** Make your own wipes by placing soft paper towels in a sealable bag with a mixture of 1 tablespoon gentle anti-bacterial soap, 1 teaspoon baby oil and 75ml water. Use enough of the mixture to make the wipes damp but not completely drenched.

- **Mould soap scraps into a new bar** Collect leftover slivers of soap in a sealable plastic bag. When you have several (ideally of the same colour and fragrance), place the bag in a pan of warm, but not boiling, water. Let the soap pieces melt and pour the mixture into a small mould. Turn it out when it is cool.

- **Protect a padlock** When the weather is cold enough to freeze padlocks on an outdoor shed or garage, placing a sandwich bag over the lock will stop it from getting frozen.

...in the kitchen

- **Make a piping bag** Place the food that you want to pipe into a sealable bag. Push out the air and close the top. Snip off a corner to the size you want – start conservatively – and start squeezing.

- **Dispose of cooking oil** Instead of clogging the drain with oil, wait for it to cool, place it in a plastic bag and throw it in the bin.

- **Colour dough without staining your hands** Place the dough in a bag, add the food colouring and squish it around until you get an even colour. Use the dough at once or freeze it.

- **Stop ice crystals on ice cream** It is annoying to open up a container of ice cream from the freezer to find crystals forming on the frozen dessert. Place the half-full ice-cream container in a sealable bag and no crystals will form.

- **Store grated cheese** Pasta or pizza always tastes better with freshly grated Parmesan cheese. Save time and grate it all at once. Double-bag it in two self-closing bags to keep it completely fresh.

- **Soften hard marshmallows** Marshmallow puffs can become as hard as rocks if stored too long. Warm some water in a pan. Place the marshmallows in a sealable plastic bag, seal and place in the pan. The warmth will quickly soften them up.

(KIDS' STUFF)
Make coloured pasta

Dyed dry pasta in different shapes and sizes is great for getting children's creative juices flowing. They can use it to make string jewellery or to decorate a picture frame or pencil holder. To dye the pasta, put a handful of pasta in a sealable plastic bag. Add several drops of food colouring. Next squirt in a few drops of methylated spirits. Seal the bag. Shake it up so the colouring dyes the pasta. Spread the pasta out on foil to dry.

- **Grease a cake tin** If you don't like using your fingers when greasing a cake tin or biscuit tray, place a sandwich bag over your hand, scoop up a small amount of butter or margarine and start greasing the tin.

- **Use as children's gloves** Helping hands are always welcome in the kitchen. But if they are little hands that will leave dirty fingerprints all over the place, place small sandwich bags over their hands before they start 'helping' you make chocolate chip cookies or cupcakes.

- **Make a funnel** Fill a bag with the contents you need funnelled. Snip off the end and transfer into the required container.

- **Keep a fizzy drink from going flat** If you can't finish a fizzy drink, zip the opened bottle or can into a large self-closing bag. It should help to keep it fizzy until you are thirsty again.

...for storing things

- **Save your sweaters** Give clean sweaters extra protection when storing and seal them in a sealable plastic bag. They will be clean and moth-free when you need them again.

- **Protect your fragile breakables** If an item needs some extra padding when it is being put into storage, place it in a self-closing bag. Close the bag most of the way, blow into it and seal it. The air forms a protective cushion around the memento.

- **Create a sachet** If your drawers sometimes smell musty, fill a small sealable bag with potpourri. Punch a number of small holes in the bag. Then place in the drawer. Your drawers should soon smell fresh again.

- **Mothproof a wardrobe with cedar** Fill a sealable bag with cedar chips (often sold at pet shops as bedding for small animals). Zip it closed and punch several small holes in it. Hang the bag in your wardrobe and the cedar smell will deter moths.

...for storing things

- **Make a pencil bag** Help your children keep track of pencils, pens and rulers. Puncture two holes along the bottom edge of a sealable freezer bag so it will fit in a two-ring binder and they can zip their supplies in and out of the bag.

...out and about

- **Create a beach hand cleaner** Need to clean sandy hands before lunch? Baby powder in a sealable plastic bag is the key. Cover your hands, rub and the sand will be gone.

- **Carry wet facecloth for cooling off** When out hiking, use a sealable bag to carry a few wet facecloths that have been soaked in water and lemon juice.

- **Apply insect repellent to your face** Put some cotton-wool balls into a plastic bag, squirt in the repellent, seal and shake. You can now use the cotton wool to apply the repellent easily.

- **Use as a portable water dish** If you take the dog with you on a long walk, bring some water for him in a sealable plastic bag. Just hold the bag open while your dog has a refreshing drink.

- **Keep your valuables dry and afloat** Avoid disaster by putting valuables in a sealable bag before you set off in a dinghy or a kayak. Blow air into it before you seal the bag so it will float. A sealable bag is perfect for keeping valuables dry by the seaside as well.

...in the bathroom

- **Make a bath cushion** Blow up a large sealable plastic bag to make a comfortable cushion to rest your head on during your soak. Use two bits of looped gaffer tape to stick it to the bath.

Shampoo

- **Lubricate a zip** If a zip gets stuck, don't tug at it until it breaks. Put a drop of shampoo on a cotton bud and dab it onto the zip. The shampoo will help the zip to slide free and any residue will come out in the next wash.

- **Resize a shrunken sweater** You can often bring a 'downsized' sweater back to full size again with baby shampoo and warm water. Fill a basin with warm water, squirt in some baby shampoo, and swish once with your hand. Lay the sweater on top of the water and let it sink on its own and soak for 15 minutes. Gently take your sweater out without wringing it and put it in a container, then fill the sink again with clean water. Lay the sweater on top and let it sink again to rinse. Take the sweater out, place it on a towel, and roll the towel to take out most of the moisture. Lay the sweater on a dry towel on a flat surface and gently start to reshape it. Come back to the sweater while it is drying to reshape a little more each time. Your patience should be rewarded with a full-size sweater.

- **Wash houseplant leaves** Houseplants get dusty, but unlike furniture they need to breathe. Make a soapy solution with a few drops of shampoo in a pot of water, immerse a cloth and wring it out and wipe the dusty leaves clean.

did you **KNOW?**

The word 'shampoo' was first used in the 18th century and derives from the Hindi word, champna, meaning 'to massage'. The earliest shampoos in the UK were made by boiling soap in water with fragrant herbs to make a cleansing solution for the hair. Kasey Hebert, a Londoner, is thought to have been the first actual manufacturer of shampoo; he sold bottles of 'shaempoo' in the streets near his home.

In Indonesia, rice husks and rice straw were burned to create ash, which was then mixed with water to create a lather for cleaning the hair. The solution was very drying so coconut oil was then applied to the hair to add back moisture.

Shampoo

- **Lubricate stubborn nuts and bolts** Do you have a nut and bolt that won't come apart? If a spot lubricant isn't to hand or you have run out, try a drop of shampoo. Let it seep into the threads and the bolt will be much more cooperative.

- **Revitalise leather shoes and handbags** Bring life back to leather shoes and handbags with a little shampoo and a clean rag. Rub shampoo into worn areas in circles to clean and bring back the colour of your accessories. It will protect your shoes from salt stains as well.

- **Revitalise your feet** Give your feet a pick-me-up while you sleep. Rub a little shampoo all over your feet and put on a light pair of cotton socks. When you wake up, your feet will feel smooth and silky.

- **Remove sticking plasters painlessly** You don't have to brace yourself for pain when removing a plaster. Rub just a drop of shampoo on and around the plaster to let it seep through the airholes and it will come off easily.

- **Remove eye make-up** You can't beat no-tears baby shampoo for a good-value eye make-up remover. Put a drop on a damp cotton-wool pad to gently remove the make-up, then rinse clear.

- **Clean your car** The grease-cutting power of shampoo works for washing a car as well. Use about 50ml shampoo to a bucket of water and sponge the car as usual. Use a dab of shampoo directly on a rag or sponge for hard-to-remove spots.

- **Have bubble bath** Shampoo makes a nice and sudsy bubble bath. It is especially relaxing if you love the scent of your favourite shampoo and the bath will be easier to rinse out.

- **Clean grimy hands** In place of soap, a little undiluted shampoo works wonders for cleaning stubborn or sticky grime from your hands. It even works well to remove water-based paint.

- **Clean the bath and taps** When you need to clean the bath quickly before guests arrive, use the handiest item – your shampoo. It does a great job on soap scum because it rinses clean. You can also use it to buff chrome taps to a shine.

- **Substitute for shaving cream** If you are travelling and forget to bring shaving cream, don't use soap to lather up. With its softening agents, shampoo is a much better alternative.

- **Remove hair spray from walls** If you have been using hairspray to kill flies or you have just noticed hairspray deposits on the bathroom walls, use some shampoo. Put some on a wet sponge to clean. Then wipe off the suds with a clean, wet sponge. Shampoo is tailor-made to handle any build-up from hair products.

did you **KNOW?**

Martha Matilda Harper was one of the pioneers of the idea of personal grooming and pampering as an experience that could be marketed and sold to a willing audience, rather than as simply a part of the personal grooming that took place in the home. She emigrated from Canada to the USA as a young girl, bringing with her a recipe for a hair 'tonic' (shampoo). Eventually, she went from making her tonic in a shed to opening her own shop, where she offered the Harper Method. She encouraged wealthy women to leave their homes for a luxurious salon experience where their hair would be washed and dressed and they would be pampered by professionals.

Shampoo

- **Use to wash delicates** Shampoo makes a great cleanser for delicate clothing that needs hand-washing. It foams up well with just a drop and you get two cleaning products for the price of one.

- **Clean brushes and combs** Oils from skin and hair can build up on combs and brushes faster than you realise. And if you keep them in a handbag or pocket, they're accumulating dust and dirt as well. Clean them thoroughly with a bath of shampoo. First comb any loose hair out of the brush, then rub a little shampoo around the bristles or along the teeth of the comb. Put a small squirt of shampoo into a tall glass of water, let the comb and brush sit for a few minutes, swish and rinse clean.

- **Remove sticky substances from pet fur** Has Rex or Fluffy stepped on something sticky or rolled in chewing gum? Rub a tiny amount of shampoo on the spot and gently draw out the sticky mess towards the end of the fur. Rinse with a wet cloth.

did you **KNOW?**

Johnson & Johnson introduced the world's first shampoo made specifically for infants in 1955 – containing its now-famous No More Tears formula. The company has promoted its baby shampoo to be 'as gentle to the eyes as pure water'. But, in fact, like most baby shampoos, Johnson's contains many of the same ingredients found in adult formulations, including citric acid, PEG-80 sorbitan laurate and sodium trideceth sulphate. The lack of baby tears has less to do with the shampoo's purity than it does with its relatively neutral pH.

Shaving cream

- **Use to clean hands** Save your water for cooking and drinking when you are camping. Rub dirty hands with shaving cream as you would with liquid soap and wipe them dry with a towel.

- **Prevent bathroom mirrors from fogging** Before taking a shower, wipe shaving cream on the mirror to stop it fogging up.

- **Remove stains from carpet** Blot the damp stain, pat it with a wet sponge, squirt shaving cream on it, and wipe clean with a damp cloth. Use the same technique for small stains on your clothes – especially if you notice them just before you go to work.

- **Silence a squeaky door hinge** A squeaky door hinge can ruin a child's peaceful nap. If you dab a little shaving cream on the hinge, you will be able to check on a baby undetected.

Sheets

- **Make a beanbag bull's-eye** To diffuse youthful energy on a rainy day, draw a large bull's-eye on an old sheet. Tape the sheet to a wall and let children throw beanbags at it.

- **Repel deer from your garden** Circle the garden with a cord set about 1 metre above the ground, then tie small strips of old white sheeting to it every 60cm; a tail-height flash of white is a danger sign to a deer.

- **Scoop up autumn leaves** Don't strain your back by constantly lifting piles of leaves into a wheelbarrow or bag. Rake the leaves onto an old sheet laid on the ground. Then gather the four corners and drag the leaves to the leaf pile.

- **Wrap up an old Christmas tree** After removing the decorations, wrap an old sheet around your Christmas tree so that you can carry or pull it out of the house without leaving a trail of pine needles behind you.

Shoe bags

- **Bring order to a cleaning cupboard** A pocketed hanging shoe bag is a brilliant organiser in a cleaning cupboard. Use the pockets to store sponges, scrubbing brushes and other cleaning utensils, and even some bottles of cleaning products. It is also good for separating dusters and cleaning cloths so you will always have the right one for the job.

- **Tidy up an office area** Free up some valuable drawer space in the office with an over-the-door shoe holder. Its pockets can store lots of supplies that you need to keep handy, like scissors, staples and markers. You can use the pockets to organise bills and other 'to do' items as well.

- **Banish clutter from the bathroom** A shoe bag can keep lots of everyday bathroom items handy and tidy. Brushes, shampoo, hand towels, hair spray – almost everything can be stored at your fingertips instead of cluttering the shower or edge of the bath.

- **Keep a bedroom tidily sorted** Instead of lifting a hanger to get at a belt, or rummaging through a drawer for a scarf, try organising clothing accessories with an over-the-door shoe bag. The pockets can be used in the bedroom for keeping socks, gloves, scarves, ties and other accessories tidy and accessible.

- **Organise a child's room** A shoe bag hung over the bedroom door is a great way to help your children to organise their small toys. Whether your child likes dolls, dinosaurs or different-coloured building bricks, a shoe bag puts the toys on display and the children can keep them sorted themselves.

- **Keep car toys and games to hand** Cut a shoe bag to fit the back of a car seat, fill it with toys, books and games and let children make their own choices for back-seat entertainment.

Shoe boxes

- **Get everything organised** There are lots of ways shoe boxes can help you to get organised besides collecting old photos and receipts. Label the boxes and use them to store treasures, bank statements, pay slips, bills to be paid and other items you want to keep track of. For a neater appearance, cover the boxes with wrapping paper or any other decorative paper.

- **Pack yummy gifts** Shoe boxes are the perfect size to carry loaves of homemade bread, biscuits and homemade cakes.

- **Use as a whelping box** If your dog or cat is expecting puppies or kittens, reduce the risk of the mother rolling onto a newborn creature and smothering it by placing the puppies or kittens in a towel-lined shoe box while the others are being born.

- **Make a gift ribbon dispenser** Use a shoe box to make a ribbon dispenser so you always have a good selection to hand when you are wrapping presents.

1 Take a used broom handle or piece of a bamboo garden cane – anything you can use as a small dowel – and cut it a little longer than the length of the shoe box.

2 Cut two holes for the dowel, one in each short end of the box, at a height where a spool of ribbon slipped onto the dowel would spin freely.

3 Slip the ribbon spools onto the dowel as you poke it from one end of the shoe box through to the other. Once the dowel is in place, you can gaffer tape it at either short end to keep it from slipping out.

4 You could also cut holes along one long side of the shoe box for each spool of ribbon, and pull a little bit of each ribbon through the hole.

Shower curtains

- **Line cabinet shelves** Don't discard old vinyl shower curtains or tablecloths. Turn them into easy-to-clean shelf liners.

- **Durable painting dust sheet** Use an old shower curtain as a protective cloth the next time you paint a room. It's heavier and more durable than the plastic dust sheets you can buy.

- **Cover picnic tables and benches** When you are having a picnic, use an old shower curtain as a makeshift tablecloth. An extra shower curtain can be folded over a sticky or dirty picnic bench before you sit down to eat.

- **Protect a table when cutting fabric** Next time you cut out a sewing pattern on the dining-room table, put a shower curtain or plastic tablecloth under it before you cut. The scissors will glide more easily across the surface and you will protect the table top from an accidental nick.

- **Block weeds in mulched beds** Old shower curtains will also come in handy if you do any landscaping using a mulch such as gravel or bark chips. Place the curtain under the mulching material to prevent weeds from poking through.

did you **KNOW?**

In the early 1920s, Waldo Semon, a rubber scientist, was none too thrilled when he first discovered polyvinyl chloride, commonly known as vinyl. He was trying to develop a new adhesive and it didn't stick at all. But Waldo was quick to recognise the material's potential and began experimenting with it, even making golf balls and shoe heels out of it. Soon vinyl products like raincoats and shower curtains reached the consumer. Today, vinyl is the second-largest-selling plastic in the world, used for everything from wallpapers, to roofing and cladding materials, plastic sheeting and countless other products.

Soap

- **Loosen a stuck zip** Rub a jammed zip loose with a bar of soap along the teeth. The lubricants in the soap will get it moving.

- **Unstick furniture drawers** If you have a sticky drawer, rub the bottom of the drawer and the supports it rests on with a bar of soap and you will find that it slides more easily.

- **Prevent cast-iron marks** Rub the bottom of a cast-iron pot with a bar of soap before heating it over a sooty open flame and you won't get any dirty marks on the base during cooking.

- **Remove a broken light bulb** If a bulb breaks while it is still screwed in, don't chance nicks and cuts trying to remove it. First, turn off the power. Insert the corner of a large, dry bar of soap into the socket. Give it a few turns and the base will unscrew.

- **Lubricate screws and saw blades** Lubricating with soap makes metal move through wood much more easily. Rub some soap on a handsaw blade for easier cutting and twist a screw into a bar of soap before screwing it in.

- **Say farewell to fleas** If you have a flea infestation in the carpet, put a few drops of liquid soap and some water on a plate. Place the plate on the floor next to a lamp. Fleas love light – they will jump onto the plate and drown in the soap.

TIP homemade soap

Handcrafted soap makes a great gift and is easy to make. You need a solid bar of soap base (either glycerine or a vegetable base); soap moulds; a clean, dry can; a double boiler; food colouring; and essential oil. Place the soap base in the can and put the can in a double boiler, which has water in the top as well as the bottom, and heat gently until it melts. To add colour, mix in food colouring. Spray a mould with nonstick cooking-oil spray and fill it halfway with melted soap base. Add a few drops of essential oil and fill the rest with glycerine. Let it harden.

Soap

- **Deodorise a car** If you want the car to smell nice, but are tired of tree-shaped pine deodorisers, place a little piece of your favourite-smelling soap in a mesh bag and hang it from the rearview mirror.

- **Mark a hem** Don't buy marking chalk. A thin sliver of soap, like the ones left when a bar is just about finished, works just as well when you are marking a hem and the markings will wash straight out with no fuss.

- **Make a pin holder** Here is an easy-to-make alternative to a pincushion. Wrap a bar of soap in fabric and tie the fabric in place with a ribbon. Stick in the pins. As a bonus, the soap lubricates the pins, making them easier to insert.

- **Save those soap slivers** When soap slivers get too small to handle, don't throw them away. Make a small slit in a sponge and put the slivers inside. The soap will last for several more washings. Or make a facecloth that is easy for children to hold by putting the soap slivers in a towelling sock.

- **Keep stored clothes fresh** Pack a bar of your favourite scented soap when you store clothes or luggage. It will keep clothes smelling fresh until next season and prevent musty odours developing in your luggage.

did you **KNOW?**

Hanging a perfumed bar of soap has been touted as one way to keep deer off your property. But how long or how well soap works as a repellent depends on a number of factors, including the type of plant you are protecting and the location of the soap. However, some studies have shown that soap, especially tallow-based soap, will stop deer from making lunch out of your shrubbery.

Socks

- **Protect stored breakables** Slip fragile china into an old sock to help to protect it from breaking or chipping.

- **Apply or buff polish** A big soft old sock makes a perfect hand mitt for buffing the wax on your car after you have cleaned it or for applying or buffing off furniture polish to wooden furniture or floors. Also handy as a general cleaning mitt.

- **Keep hands clean when changing a tyre** Keep a pair of socks in the car and put them on your hands while handling the tyre and your hands will remain clean.

- **Protect floor surfaces** Put socks over the legs of a piece of heavy furniture and you should be able to slide it easily.

- **Store a pair of protective goggles** Goggles won't fit in a glasses case, so put them in a sock to stop them getting scratched.

- **Make a wash bag** To protect your best underwear in the washing machine, slip it into a sock and tie the ends.

- **Clean shutter and blind slats** Just slip a sock over your hand and gently rub the dust off the slats.

- **Clean rough plaster walls** Use nylon socks instead of a sponge or cloth to clean rough plaster walls. They won't leave specks of lint as a cotton cloth would.

- **Wash small stuffed animals** When your child's favourite stuffed toy needs a bath, slip it, and any other small stuffed animals into a sock and tie the end to prevent buttons, eyes and hair from coming off.

- **Protect a wall from ladder marks** Place socks over the top ends of a ladder when you are leaning it against a wall to avoid making marks.
    WARNING: always make sure that someone is holding the ladder.

Soft drinks

- **Clean car-battery terminals** The acidic properties of fizzy drinks will help to eliminate corrosion from a car battery. Nearly all carbonated soft drinks contain carbonic acid, which helps to remove stains and dissolve rust deposits. Pour a soft drink over the battery terminals and let it sit for a while. Remove the sticky residue with a wet sponge.

- **Loosen rusted-on nuts and bolts** Don't struggle with rusted-on nuts and bolts. A fizzy drink can help to loosen them. Soak a rag in the fizzy drink and wrap it around the bolt for several minutes. Then try to loosen it again with a spanner. It should move more easily.

- **Make cut flowers last longer** Don't throw away the last drops of a bottle of soft drink. Pour about 50ml into the water in a vase full of cut flowers. The sugar in the drink will make the blossoms last for longer. Note: if you have a clear vase and want the water to remain clear, use a transparent drink such as clear lemonade.

- **Clean the toilet** Eliminate dirt and smells with a can of soft drink. Pour it into the toilet, let it sit for an hour or so, then scrub and flush.

did you **KNOW?**

Ginger has long been a traditional remedy for nausea, and recent scientific research has shown that ginger ale does work better than a placebo. Ginger ale was first made in Ireland in 1851, but it was not until 1907 that it was commercially marketed by a Toronto pharmacist named John McLaughlin. McLaughlin kept trying new formulas until he patented what is now known throughout the world as Canada Dry Ginger Ale. McLaughlin was one of the pioneers of the technology of mass bottling, which allowed customers to take fizzy drinks home in bottles, rather than drinking them at a soda fountain.

- **Keep drains from blocking** If you have a slow drain and no drain cleaner in the house, pour a 2 litre bottle of cola down the drain to help to remove the blockage.

- **Get gum out of hair** When a child gets gum in his or her hair, put the gummy hair in a bowl with some cola. Let it soak for a few minutes and then rinse.

- **Make a roast ham moist** To make a ham juicier, pour a can of cola over the traditional ham recipe and follow your baking instructions as usual.

- **Remove oil stains from concrete** Here is an effective way to remove oil stains from concrete driveways and garage floors. Take a small bag of cat litter, a few cans of cola, a stiff bristle broom, bucket, liquid laundry detergent, bleach, eye protection and rubber gloves. Cover the stain with a thin layer of cat litter and brush it in. Sweep up the litter and pour cola to cover the area. Work the cola in with a bristle broom, and leave the cola for about 20 minutes. Mix 50ml laundry detergent with 50ml bleach in 4 litres warm water and use it to mop up the mess.

- **Clean coins** If coin collecting is your hobby, you can use cola to clean your hoard. Place the coins in a small dish and soak in cola for a brilliant shine.
    WARNING: don't attempt to do this with any very rare and valuable coins.

Sparkling mineral water

- **Make pancakes fluffier** If you like pancakes to be fluffy, substitute sparkling mineral water for the liquid called for in the recipes. You'll be amazed at how light and fluffy they turn out.

- **Give plants a mineral bath** Don't throw out leftover mineral water. Use it to water indoor and outdoor plants. The minerals in the water help green plants to grow. For maximum benefit, try to water your plants with sparkling mineral water about once a week.

- **Clean precious gems** Soak diamonds, rubies, sapphires and emeralds in sparkling mineral water to give them a bright sheen. Simply place them in a glass full of sparkling mineral water and let them soak overnight.

- **Remove fabric stains** Clean grease stains from synthetic knitted fabrics by pouring sparkling mineral water on the stain and scrubbing gently. Scrub more vigorously to remove stains on carpets or less delicate articles of clothing.

- **Clean a car windscreen** Keep a spray bottle filled with sparkling mineral water in the boot of your car. Use it to help to remove bird droppings and greasy stains from the windscreen. The fizzy water speeds the cleaning process.

- **Restore hair colour** If your blonde hair turns greenish when you swim in a pool with too much chlorine, don't panic. Rinse your hair with sparkling mineral water and it will change back to its original colour.

- **Help shell oysters** If you love oysters but find removing them from their shells nearly impossible, try soaking them in sparkling mineral water before you try to open them. The oysters won't exactly jump out of their shells, but they will be much easier to prise apart.

- **Tame your tummy** Cold sparkling mineral water with a dash of bitters will work wonders on an upset stomach that is caused by indigestion or a hangover.

- **Clean worktops and fixtures** Pour sparkling mineral water directly onto stainless-steel worktops, ranges and sinks. Wipe with a soft cloth, rinse with warm water and wipe dry. To clean porcelain fixtures, simply pour sparkling mineral water over them and wipe with a soft cloth. There is no need for soap or rinsing and the mineral water will not mar the finish. Give the inside of the fridge a good clean with a weak solution of sparkling mineral water and a little bit of salt.

- **Remove rust** To loosen rusty nuts and bolts, pour some sparkling mineral water over them. The carbonation bubbles the rust away.

- **Eliminate urine stains** When a child or pet has had an accident, blot up as much urine as possible, then pour sparkling mineral water over the stained area and immediately blot again. It will get rid of the stain and help to reduce the unpleasant smell.

- **Make cleaning cast iron simple** Food tastes delicious when it is cooked in cast iron, but cleaning heavy pots and pans with a sticky mess inside is a pain. You can make cleaning easier by pouring some sparkling mineral water in the pan while it is still warm. The bubbly water will keep the mess from sticking.

did you **KNOW?**

Bubbling water has been associated with good health since the time of the ancient Romans, who enjoyed drinking mineral water almost as much as they liked bathing in it. Many Europeans now drink more than 100 litres of bottled water each year. It takes 1.3 million metric tons of carbon dioxide to provide all the fizz for the mineral waters and other drinks consumed annually in Europe.

Spices

- **Make a hair tonic** Enhance your natural hair colour and give it shine. For dark hair, use 1 tablespoon crumbled sage or 1 sprig chopped fresh rosemary or a mixture of 1 teaspoon allspice, 1 teaspoon ground cinnamon and ½ teaspoon ground cloves. For blonde hair, use 1 tablespoon chamomile. Pour 200ml boiling water over the herb or spice mix and let it steep for 30 minutes. Strain it through a coffee filter and let it cool. Pour it repeatedly over your hair as a final rinse after shampooing.

- **Keep feet smelling sweet** Sage is great for preventing foot odour because it kills the odour-causing bacteria that grow on your feet in the warm, moist environment inside your shoes. Crumble a leaf or two into your shoes before you put them on. At the end of the day, just shake the remains into the bin.

- **Scent your home** Instead of using commercial air fresheners, throw a handful of whole cloves or a cinnamon stick into a pan of water and simmer on the stove for half an hour. Or place a teaspoon or two of the ground spices on a baking sheet and place it in a 110°C/gas mark ¼ oven with the door ajar for 30 minutes. Either way, your house will have a delicious natural fragrance.

- **Keep woollens whole** Woollen clothing can last a lifetime – if you keep the moths away. Preserve them using sachets of cloves. Fill some small drawstring muslin bags (you can buy them at a health-food store or make your own) with a handful of whole cloves. To protect the clothing from oil or colour transfer, put the sachet in a small plastic bag, but don't seal it. Attach it to a hanger in your wardrobe or tuck one in your chest of drawers to protect your woollens from the attentions of hungry moths.

- **Keep your Thermos fresh** If you have a musty Thermos, place a whole clove inside the flask before putting the cap on to stop it from happening next time. A teaspoon of salt works, too. Empty and rinse the Thermos before using it.

- **Stamp out silverfish** These insects frequent places with lots of moisture, such as kitchens, bathrooms and laundry rooms. Hang an aromatic sachet containing sage or bay leaves on a hook and behind the washing machine or keep a few in decorative baskets along windowsills.

- **Control insects in the garden** Don't use harsh pesticides to control small-insect infestations outdoors. If you have an ant problem, add 1 tablespoon ground black pepper (or another strong-smelling ground spice, such as ground cloves or dry mustard) to 200g sifted white flour and sprinkle the mixture on and around the ants. They will vanish within the hour. Sweep the dry mix into the garden instead of trying to hose it off; water will just make it gooey.

- **Deodorise bottles for reuse** To reuse jars that retain a lingering smell, add 1 teaspoon dry mustard to 1 litre of water, fill the jar and let it soak overnight. It will smell fresh by morning. This solution banishes strong odours, including pickle, garlic and tomatoes.

did you **KNOW?**

What is the difference between a spice and a herb? The basic guideline is this: if it is made from a plant's leaf, it is a herb; if it is made from the bark, fruit, seed, stem or root, it is a spice. Parsley and basil are typical herbs because we eat their leaves. Cinnamon (the bark of a tree) and pepper (the fruit of a vine) are considered spices. Salt, perhaps the most essential food enhancer of all but not a plant product at all, is a seasoning – the word that describes anything used to flavour foods, regardless of its origin.

Spices

- **Shield your vegetable garden** For centuries, gardeners have used companion planting to repel insect pests. Aromatic plants such as basil, marigolds and sage are all reputed to send a signal to insects to go elsewhere. Mint, thyme, dill and sage are historic favourites to be planted near cabbage-family plants (cabbage, broccoli, cauliflower and brussels sprouts) to fend off cabbage-munching moths.

- **Keep ants at bay** Flour, sugar and paprika can all fall prey to ants. Keep them safe by taping a bay leaf to the inside of the storage lid. This also works inside cabinets, where sachets of sage, bay, stick cinnamon or whole cloves will smell pleasant while discouraging ants.

- **Deter plant-eating animals** Hot peppers affect everyone – in fact, they are the basis for many commercial rodent repellents. Chop up the hottest pepper you can find and combine it with 1 tablespoon ground cayenne pepper and 2 litres water. Boil the mixture for 15-20 minutes, then let it cool. Strain it through cheesecloth, add 1 tablespoon washing-up liquid and pour it into a spray bottle. Spray vulnerable plants liberally every five days or so. The spray works best for rabbits, but may also deter deer, especially if used in combination with commercial products.

TIP toothache and oil of cloves

If you have a toothache, get to a dentist as soon as possible. Meanwhile, oil of cloves may provide temporary relief (although it tastes unpleasant). Place a drop directly into the aching tooth or apply it with a cotton bud. But don't put it directly on the gums. Eugenol, an active ingredient in the spice oil, is a natural pain reliever.

Sponges

- **Keep your veggies fresh** Moisture that collects at the bottom of the crisper drawer in the fridge will make vegetables go off. Extend the life of fresh vegetables by lining the drawers with dry sponges. When you notice that the sponges are wet, wring them out and let them dry before putting them back in the fridge. Every now and then, between uses, let them soak in some warm water with a splash of bleach to discourage the growth of mould.

- **Make flowerpots hold water longer** If you find that houseplants dry out too quickly after watering, try this simple trick for keeping the soil moist longer when you repot them. Tuck a damp sponge in the bottom of the pot before filling it with soil. It will act as a water reservoir. And it will also help to prevent a gusher if you accidentally overwater.

- **Make an 'unwelcome' mat for garden visitors** Anyone who has ever cleaned a floor with ammonia knows that the smell of this strong, everyday household cleaner is overpowering. Throw browsing animals off the scent of ripening vegetables in a vegetable garden by soaking some old sponges in your floor-cleaning solution and distributing them wherever you expect the next garden raid.

- **Mop up drips from soggy umbrellas** When it has been raining, the family has been tramping in and out with umbrellas all day and your umbrella stand has only a shallow receptacle to catch drips, protect the hall floor from major flooding by placing a large sponge in the base of the stand. Even if you forget to squeeze it out, the sponge should dry on its own as soon as the weather clears.

Sponges

- **Stop soap getting slimy** A shower is so refreshing in the morning, until you reach for the soap and are treated to the slimy sensation of a bar that has been left to marinate in its own suds. Your soap will last longer if you place a sponge on the soap dish. It will absorb moisture so the soap can dry out.

- **Lift lint from fabric** To remove lint and pet fur from clothes and upholstery, give the fabric a quick wipe with a dampened and wrung-out sponge. Just run your fingers over the sponge and the unwanted fluff will come off in a ball for easy disposal.

- **Protect fragile items** If you are posting or storing small, fragile valuables that won't be harmed by a little contact with water, sponges are a clever way to cushion them. Dampen a sponge, wrap it around the delicate item and use a rubber band to secure it. As it dries, the sponge will conform to the contours of your crystal ashtray or porcelain figurine. To unpack it, just dip the item in water again. You can use the sponge again.

(KIDS' STUFF)
Make a children's garden

Making seeds grow seems magical to young children. For an easy and renewable play garden with a minimum of mess, all you need is an old soap dish, a sponge, and seeds of a plant such as lobelia. Cut the sponge to fit the dish, add water until it is moist but not sopping, and sprinkle the seed liberally over the top. Prop an inverted glass bowl over it until the seeds begin to grow. A bright window and a daily watering will keep it going for weeks.

Spray and squirt bottles

- **Mist your houseplants** Keep houseplants healthy and happy by using an empty trigger-type spray bottle as a plant mister. Clean the bottle by filling it with equal parts water and vinegar; don't use liquid soap, as you may not be able to get it all out, let the solution sit for an hour, and rinse it out thoroughly with cold water. Repeat if necessary. Then, fill the bottle with lukewarm water, and use it frequently to give your plants a soothing, misty shower.

- **Help with the laundry** Use clean, recycled bottles to spray water on clothes as you are ironing. Or fill a spray bottle with stain-remover solution so that you can apply it to your garments without having to blot up drips.

- **Spray away garden pests** Keep a few recycled spray bottles on hand to use around the garden. Here are two immediate uses:

  - Fill one with undiluted white vinegar to get rid of weeds and grass poking out of cracks in concrete, as well as ants and other insects, but be careful not to spray it on the plants; the high acidity could kill them.

  - For an effective homemade insecticide recipe that works on most slugs and snails, but won't harm plants, mix several cloves of crushed garlic, 50ml sunflower oil, 3 tablespoons hot pepper sauce and ½ teaspoon mild liquid soap in 4 litres of water. Pour some into your spray bottle and shake well before using.

- **Keep car windows clean** Include a spray bottle filled with windscreen cleaner in the boot of your car as part of a roadside emergency kit. Use it to clean the car's headlamps, mirrors and windows whenever necessary. During the winter months, mix in ½ teaspoon antifreeze and you can spray it on to melt the ice on your windscreen or mirrors.

Spray and squirt bottles

- **Stop cooking-oil drips** Fill a squirt bottle with olive oil or another favourite cooking oil. It is a lot easier to handle than a jar or bottle and you can spray precisely the right amount of oil over your salads or into a frying pan without having to worry about drips or spills.

- **Substitute for a baster** Simply squeeze some air out of a cleaned squirt bottle, and use it to suck up the fat from roasts and soups. You can even use it to distribute marinades and drippings over meat.

- **Dispense condiments** Recycled squirt bottles are good for storing condiments and other foods typically sold in jars, such as mayonnaise, salad dressing, jam and honey. In addition to having fewer sticky jars in the fridge or cupboard, you will also reduce the washing-up load by eliminating the need for knives or spoons. Do make sure you give the bottles a thorough cleaning before using them.

- **Clean out crevices** A clean, empty squeeze bottle may be just the cleaning tool you need to get the dust out of the corners of picture frames and other tight spaces. Use it to give a good blast of air to blow out the dirt you can't otherwise reach.

- **Let children have a squirt party** Fill up a few clean squeeze bottles with water, then give them to your children to squirt each other with in the garden on a hot summer day. It will help them to stay cool while they burn off some energy.

- **Cool off in summer** Whether you are jogging around the park, taking a breather between tennis matches, or just sitting out in the sun, a recycled spray bottle filled with water can make a refreshing summer companion. Use it to cool off during and after a workout or while sunbathing on the beach or in the garden.

Steel wool

- **Scrub filthy trainers** Moisten a steel-wool soap pad and gently scrub away at stains and stuck-on grime. Wipe them clean with a damp sponge and you may be able to enjoy many more months of wear. (It is never a good idea to put trainers that you use for serious sport in the machine as it may cause them to fall apart.)

- **Shoo heel marks away** The black marks that rubber soles leave behind don't come off with a mop, no matter how hard you try. To rid a vinyl floor of smudges, gently rub the surface with a moistened steel-wool soap pad. When the heel mark is gone, wipe the floor clean with a damp sponge.

- **Rebuff rodents** Mice and rats are experts at finding every conceivable entrance into a house. When you discover one of their entry points, stuff it full of steel wool. Steel wool is much more effective than foam or newspaper because even dedicated gnawers are unlikely to try to chew through such a sharp blockade.

- **Keep garden tools in good shape** Nothing will extend the life of gardening tools like a good clean at the end of each growing season. Use a piece of fine steel wool, saturate it with household oil such as WD-40 that you would use on a squeaky door hinge, and rub the rust off garden shears, secateurs, spades, forks, hoes and anything else with metal parts. Wipe them clean with a dry rag, sharpen the blades and reapply a little oil before storing them for the winter.

TIP not for stainless steel

Steel wool may make stainless steel look better, but it scratches the surface and will ultimately hasten rusting. Most cutlery manufacturers caution against using any abrasive on stainless steel. The safest way to care for stainless steel is to wash with a sponge and mild soap and water.

Straws

- **Fix loose veneer** When the veneer on a favourite piece of furniture is coming away at the edges, although a dab of glue is a simple remedy, veneer can be very brittle and you may break off a piece by lifting it up. As a solution, cut a length of plastic drinking straw and press it to flatten it slightly. Fold it in half and fill one half with glue, slowly dripping the glue in from the top. Push the filled half carefully under the veneer and gently blow in the glue. Wipe off any excess, cover the area with greaseproof paper and a wood block, and clamp it overnight to dry.

- **Keep jewellery chains** To stop necklaces and pendants from getting tangled and kinked, run each chain through a straw cut to just under half the length of the chain, and close the clasp before putting it away.

- **Give flowers needed height** To perfect a flower arrangement where just a few of the flowers aren't tall enough, stick each of the too-short stems into plastic straws, trimming the straw to get the desired height and inserting them into the vase.

- **Get slow ketchup flowing** If the ketchup is recalcitrant, insert a straw all the way into the bottle and stir it around a little to get the flow started.

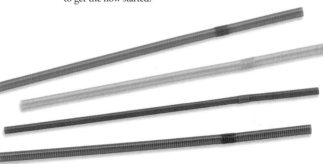

- **Have seasonings, will travel** Perhaps you are on a low-salt diet and need a low-salt alternative to use when dining out or you want salt and pepper to season your packed sandwich or salad just before you eat it. Straws provide an easy way to take along small amounts of dry seasonings. Fold one end over and tape it shut, fill it, and fold and tape the other end. If moisture may be a problem, use a plastic straw.

- **Improvise some foamy fun** To make a cheap and easy game that will work even with a large group of children, cut the ends of some plastic straws at a sharp angle and set out a shallow dish of washing-up liquid diluted with a little bit of water. Dip a straw in the liquid and blow through the other end. All children love the piles of bubbles that result.

- **Make a pull-toy protector** Pull-along toys are perennial favourites of young children, but you can spend all day untying the knots that a toddler will inevitably put in the pull string. By running the string through a plastic straw (or a series of them), it should stay untangled.

did you KNOW?

It was the quest for a perfectly cold mint julep that led to the invention of the drinking straw. Mint juleps are served chilled and their flavour diminishes as they warm up. Holding a glass heats the contents, so the custom was to drink mint juleps through natural straws made from a section of hollow grass stem, usually rye. But the rye imparted an undesirable 'grassy' flavour. In 1888, Marvin Stone, a manufacturer of paper cigarette holders, fashioned a paper tube through which to sip his favourite drink. When other mint julep aficionados began clamouring for paper straws, he realised that he had a hot new product on his hands.

String

- **Polish silverware more easily** Polishing silver can be curiously satisfying – but it can be difficult to get a good result with intricate implements. Run a length of string through some silver polish and use it to get at the hard-to-reach spots between the tines of a fork.

- **Stop the sound of a dripping tap** If a leaky tap is keeping you awake at night, you can silence it until a plumber arrives. Tie a piece of string to the fixture with one end at the point where the water is dripping out and the other end hanging down to the bottom of the sink. The water droplet will travel silently down the string instead of driving you to distraction.

- **Measure irregular objects** A cloth tape measure is the ideal tool for measuring odd-shaped objects, but you may not have one if you don't sew. String is a useful substitute. Wrap a piece around the item instead, cut or mark with a pen, then hold it up to a ruler to get the measurement you need.

- **Stop slamming doors** When a slamming door is getting on your nerves, you can use string in two ways to control the way a door closes:

    - A piece of light string tied to both sides of a door knob and running around the door edge will provide just enough friction to slow the door down and prevent a loud slam when it shuts.

    - Use thicker rope in the same way to temporarily prop open a door that automatically locks when it closes or to make sure pets or small children don't get trapped in one room of the house.

- **Use as a straight-line guide** Trimming a long hedge straight is a near-impossible feat unless you use a visual guide. Drive two stakes into the ground, one at each end of the hedge. Measure the height you want the trimmed hedge to be, then run the string between the two stakes, tying it to each one at that exact height. As you clip away, cut down to the string line but no further; the top of your hedge will be completely straight and true.

- **Plant perfectly straight rows** It is harder than it looks to make straight garden rows freehand. String can be used in two ways to keep plants in line:

    - For planting heavy seeds such as beans, put sticks in the ground at each end of a row and run a piece of string between to guide you as you plant.

    - To plant dozens of lightweight seeds quickly, cut string to the length of a row, wet it thoroughly, then sprinkle the seed directly on it. The moisture will allow the seeds to stick long enough to lay the string in a prepared furrow. Just cover the string with soil to finish.

- **Outline garden features** When you are planning a design for a new garden, lay white string on the ground to outline paths and beds.

String

From an upstairs window or other high vantage point, you will be able to tell at a glance if the borders are straight and whether the layout is working.

● **Make wicks for watering plants** To keep potted plants watered while you are away for the weekend, fill a large container with water and place it next to the plants. Cut several pieces of string so they are long enough to hang down to the bottom of the container at one end and be buried a few centimetres in the soil of the pots at the other. Soak the strings until they are completely wet and put them in position. As the soil begins to dry, capillary action will draw water from the reservoir to the pots through the strings.

● **Make a quick package opener** Next time you are preparing a box for posting, take a second to make it easier for the recipient to open. Place a piece of string along the centre and side seams before you tape, allowing a tiny bit to hang free at one end. That way, the recipient will just need to pull the strings to sever the tape without having to resort to a sharp blade that might damage delicate contents. Do the same for packing boxes when you are moving house.

Sugar

- **Keep cut flowers fresh for longer** Dissolve 3 tablespoons sugar and 2 tablespoons white vinegar per litre of warm water. When you fill the vase, make sure the cut stems are covered by 7-10cm of the prepared water. The sugar nourishes the plants, while the vinegar inhibits bacterial growth. You will be surprised how long the arrangement stays fresh.

- **Get rid of nematode worms** If your outdoor plants look unhealthy, with ugly knots at the roots, chances are they've been victims of an attack by nematodes. The nematode worm, nemesis of many an otherwise healthy garden, is a microscopic parasite that pierces the roots of plants and causes knots. You can prevent nematode attacks by using sugar to create an inhospitable environment for the tiny worms. Apply 2kg sugar for every 25m² of garden. Micro-organisms feeding on the sugar will increase the organic matter in the soil, thereby eliminating the nematodes.

- **Clean greasy, grimy hands** To clean filthy hands easily and thoroughly, pour equal amounts of olive oil and sugar into the cupped palm of one hand, then gently rub your hands together for several minutes. Rinse thoroughly and dry. The grit of the sugar acts as an abrasive to help the oil to remove grease, paint and grime. Your hands will look and feel clean, soft and moisturised.

- **Make a nontoxic fly trap** Keep the kitchen free of flies with a homemade fly trap that uses no toxic chemicals. In a small saucepan, simmer 400ml milk, 110g raw sugar, and 60g ground pepper for about 10 minutes, stirring occasionally. Pour the mixture into shallow dishes or bowls and set them around the kitchen, patio or anywhere that flies are a problem. They will flock to the bowls and drown in the sticky mixture.

Sugar

- **Exterminate cockroaches** If you hate using smelly, noxious pesticides as much as you loathe cockroaches, scatter a mixture of equal parts sugar and bicarbonate of soda over the infested area. The sugar will attract the cockroaches, and the bicarbonate of soda will kill them. Replace it frequently with a fresh mixture to prevent future infestations.

  WARNING: keep the pesticide well away from pets and small children, as it is poisonous if swallowed.

- **Soothe a burned tongue** To relieve a tongue burned by a hot potato, pizza, coffee, tea or soup, sprinkle a pinch or two of sugar over the affected area. Astonishingly, the pain should begin to subside immediately.

- **Keep desserts fresh** You have used sugar to sweeten a cake mixture; now use it to keep the finished cake fresh and moist. Store the cake in an airtight container with a couple of sugar cubes, and it will stay fresh for days longer. You can also store a few lumps of sugar with cheese to prevent it from going mouldy.

(KIDS' STUFF)
Make your own rock sweets

Make old-fashioned rock sweets with children, with no strings, paper clips, sticks or thermometers needed. Stir 500g sugar into 200ml hot water. Pour the syrup into several open dishes and set aside. Add a grain of sugar to act as a seed crystal in each container. Within days or weeks you should be able to collect glittering crystals of rock. Use a spoon to scoop it out, then rinse and dry the sweet before you eat it.

Surgical spirit

- **Clean bathroom fixtures** Pour some surgical spirit onto a soft, absorbent cloth and clean the taps and other fixtures. There is no need to rinse as the alcohol will just evaporate. It does a superb job of making chrome sparkle, plus it kills any germs in its path.

- **Remove hair spray from mirrors** A quick wipe with surgical spirit will remove sticky residue and leave the mirror sparkling clean.

- **Clean venetian blinds** Surgical spirit does a terrific job of cleaning the dirt off venetian blinds. Wrap a flat tool such as a spatula in a cloth and secure it with a rubber band. Dip it in surgical spirit and wipe backwards and forwards along each slat.

- **Keep windows sparkling and frost-free** Wash windows with a solution of 100ml surgical spirit to 1 litre water.

- **Dissolve frost on the windscreen** Fill a spray bottle with surgical spirit and spray the glass. You will be able to wipe the frost straight off.

- **Prevent rings around collars** To prevent natural oil from your neck making a grimy line on a shirt collar, wipe your neck with surgical spirit each morning before you dress.

- **Clean a phone** When a phone is getting a bit grubby, wipe it with surgical spirit. It will remove the grime and disinfect the phone at the same time.

- **Remove ink stains** If you have spilled ink on a favourite garment, try soaking the spot in surgical spirit for a few minutes before putting the garment in the wash.

- **Erase permanent markers** If a child has decorated your worktop with a permanent marker, as long as it is made from a non-permeable material such as plastic laminate, surgical spirit will dissolve the marker to a liquid state so you can just wipe it off.

Surgical spirit

- **Remove dog ticks** Ticks hate the taste of surgical spirit. Before you pull a tick off Fido, dab it with surgical spirit to make it loosen its grip. Then grab the tick as close to the dog's skin as you can and pull it straight out. Dab again with alcohol to disinfect the wound. This technique will work on people, too.

- **Get rid of fruit flies** The next time you see fruit flies hovering in the kitchen, take a fine-misting spray bottle and fill it with surgical spirit. Spraying the little flies knocks them out and makes them fall to the floor, where you can sweep them up. The alcohol is less effective than insecticide, but it is a lot safer than spraying poison around your kitchen.

- **Make a shapeable ice pack** Make a slushy, conformable pack by mixing 1 part surgical spirit with 3 parts water in a self-sealing plastic bag. The next time a sore knee acts up, wrap the bag of slush in a cloth and apply it to the area.

- **Stretch tight-fitting new shoes** This doesn't always work, but it is worth a try. If new leather shoes are pinching your feet, try swabbing the tight spot with a cotton-wool ball soaked in surgical spirit. Walk around in the shoes for a few minutes to see if they stretch enough to be comfortable.

TAKE CARE

Don't confuse denatured alcohol or methylated spirits with surgical spirit. Denatured alcohol is ethanol (drinking alcohol) to which poisonous and foul-tasting chemicals have been added to render it unfit for drinking. Often, the chemicals used in denatured alcohol are not ones you should put on your skin. Surgical spirit is made from chemicals that are safe for skin contact; the most usual solution is 70 per cent isopropyl alcohol and 30 per cent water.

Talcum powder

- **Keep ants away** For an effective organic ant repellent, scatter talcum powder liberally around the foundations of your house and other known points of entry, such as doors and windows. Other effective organic repellents include cream of tartar, borax, powdered sulphur and oil of cloves. You can also try planting mint close to the foundations.

- **Fix a squeaky floor** Don't let squeaky floorboards drive you crazy. Sprinkle talcum powder or powdered graphite between the boards. If that doesn't do the trick, squirt in some liquid wax to help to fill the gaps.

- **Remove bloodstains from fabric** To remove fresh bloodstains from fabric, make a paste of water and talcum powder and apply. When it dries, brush away the stain. Substitute cornflour or cornmeal if you have run out of talcum powder.

- **Get rid of greasy carpet stain** A greasy stain can spoil the look of the most luxurious carpet. You can remove greasy stains from a carpet with a combination of talcum powder and patience. Cover the affected area with talcum powder and wait at least 6 hours for the talcum to absorb the grease. Then vacuum the stain away. Bicarbonate of soda or cornflour may be substituted for the talcum powder.

- **Get grease stains out of synthetics** To delete greasy marks from synthetic fabrics such as polyester, sprinkle some talcum powder directly onto the spot and rub it in with your fingers. Wait 24 hours, then gently brush. Repeat as necessary until the stain is completely gone.

- **Loosen tangles and knots** Don't break a fingernail trying to untie a knot in your shoelace. Sprinkle some talcum powder on the shoelaces (or any knotted cords) and the knots will pull apart more easily. Use talcum powder to help to untangle chain necklaces as well.

Tape see page 311
Tea see page 316

Tape see page 311
Tea see page 316

Tennis balls

- **Fluff up down-filled jackets, duvets and pillows** These can become flat when you wash them. Fluff them up by placing a couple of tennis balls in the tumble dryer with them.

- **Sand curves in furniture** Wrap a tennis ball in sandpaper and use it to sand curves when you are refinishing furniture.

- **Hide valuables at the gym** Make a 5cm slit along one seam of a tennis ball and insert the valuables inside. Keep the ball in your gym bag among other sporting gear.

- **Massage your back and feet** Fill a long sock with tennis balls, tie the end and stretch it around your back, moving it like a towel. For feet, roll a tennis ball under your toes and soles.

- **Get a better grip on bottle caps** If have arthritic hands, an old tennis ball may help you to remove twist-off bottle caps. Cut a ball in half and use one half to enhance your grip.

(SCIENCE FAIR)
Teach children about gravity

Stand on a chair holding a tennis ball in each hand. Extend your arms so they are at the same distance from the floor. Ask the children to watch as you release both balls at once. Did they hit the floor at the same time? Now repeat using a tennis ball and a much lighter table tennis ball. Ask which will land first. They'll land at the same time because gravity exerts the same force on all objects regardless of their weight. If you try this with a ball and a feather, the kids will also learn that less dense objects fall more slowly due to air resistance.

Tape...

...in the kitchen

- **Create a no-fly zone** Make fly and pest strips that are chemical-free. Cover empty paper-towel or toilet-paper rolls with double-sided sticky tape and hang them where you need them.

- **Mark the start of a cling-film roll** Stick a small loop of clear tape to your finger and touch the film as close to its edge as you can. Lift gently.

- **Prevent salt and pepper spills** If your shakers have to be filled through a hole in the bottom, before you refill, tape over the holes on top so it won't spill when you turn it upside down.

- **Safely pick up glass shards** Don't risk cutting yourself when picking up bits of broken glass. Hold a long piece of clear tape tightly at each end and use it to pick up the shards.

- **Keep your hands free at the supermarket** It's very easy – just tape your shopping list to the handle of the shopping trolley. This will free both your hands and you won't keep mislaying or dropping the list.

...around the house

- **Find your favourite photo negative** Before framing a favourite photograph, tape the negative to the back of the picture. If you ever want to make copies of the photo, you won't have to go searching through piles of old negatives to find the right one.

- **Mark a phone number for quick reference** Use transparent tape to highlight numbers in the phone book that you look up often. The tape will make the page easier to find and you will also be able to spot the number without having to search the whole page.

- **Keep spare batteries handy** Tape a set of extra batteries to the back of a wall clock. When the clock stops and you need wto replace the batteries, they will be immediately to hand.

- **Code your keys** Are you always groping around to find the right key when you get home in the dark? Wrap some tape around the top of your house key and you will be able to feel for the right key when it is too dark to see. Or if you have several similar looking keys that you can't tell apart, colour-code them using tape of different colours.

- **Make candles fit snugly** Don't let wobbly candles spoil a romantic mood or cause a fire at a candlelit dinner. If the candles don't fit snugly into the holder, wrap a few layers of tape around the bottom edges until they slot in firmly.

- **Prevent jewellery tangles** To keep fine chains from tangling when you are travelling, lay the chain along a piece of clear tape. Then place another piece on top to encase it. You can also use the tape trick to keep a pair of earrings from getting separated.

- **End loose ends on spools of thread** Put an end to those time-wasting searches for loose ends of thread. Just tape the ends to the top or bottom of the spool when you have finished sewing and they will be ready to use next time you sew.

- **Contain grease stains on paper** You may never be able to get rid of the grease spots on books or important papers, but you can keep them from spreading with a little help from some clear tape. Put a piece of tape over both sides of the spot to keep the grease from seeping through to other pages or papers.

- **Keep papers from blowing in the wind** If you have to make a speech or accept an award at an outdoor event, bring a roll of clear tape with you. When it is your turn to talk, place some tape on the lectern, sticky side up, to prevent your papers from blowing away.

- **Make sewing easier** Use clear tape to simplify your sewing – use it instead of pins. Hold a zip in place when you are making a garment. (You can sew through the tape and remove it when you have finished.) Keep badges, patches or name tags in place when sewing them onto shirts, uniforms or caps. Tape hooks, eyes and poppers to garments when sewing so they won't slip. Just pull the tape off when you have finished. Tape your pattern to the material and when you cut the pattern, you will have a reinforced edge.

- **Remove lipstick from silk** Why pay for dry-cleaning to remove a lipstick spot from a silk scarf or dress when you can do it yourself for free? Just place a piece of clear tape (or masking tape) over the spot and pull it off. If you can still see some of the lipstick colour, sprinkle on some talcum powder or chalk, and dab until the powder and the remaining lipstick disappear.

- **Keep flowers upright in a vase** To keep cut flowers from sagging in their vase, crisscross several pieces of clear tape across the mouth of the vase, leaving spaces where you can insert the them. They should look perky and fresh for a few extra days.

- **Clean a nail file easily and effectively** Simply place a piece of clear tape over it, press and pull off. The tape will pick up all the dirt embedded in the surface of the file.

...around the house

- **Make safety markers for a car emergency** Wrap strips of brightly coloured reflector tape around two large empty cans. Keep them in the boot of the car to use in an emergency.

- **Mark dark stairways** Stop stumbling on poorly lit cellar or outdoor stairs or worrying about guests tripping and falling. Apply reflector tape along the edges of the steps and you will be able to see exactly where you are going.

- **Make pets visible at night** Don't let your beloved family pet get hit by a car if it is out at night. Put reflector tape on its collar so drivers will be able to see it immediately in the dark.

- **Deter a cat from scratching** Sprinkle ground red pepper on a strip of tape and attach it to the areas you don't want them to scratch. They hate the smell and they will soon keep away.

...for the DIY-er

- **Mend a broken plant stem** Use clear tape to add support to a broken plant stem. Just wrap the break in tape and leave it on until the stem mends. The taped plant will keep growing as long as moisture can continue to travel up the stem.

did you **KNOW?**

Sellotape® dates back to 1937 when Colin Kininmonth and George Gray coated cellophane film with a natural rubber resin to create a 'sticky tape' product, based on a French patent. They had seen this process carried out in France by a company called CIMA and obtained a licence to make it in the UK. When war broke out in 1939 the company made cellulose tape for sealing ration and first-aid packs and a cloth tape for sealing ammunition boxes. They also made a product for covering windows to protect householders from breaking glass that was manufactured in sheet form.

- **Make a seed strip** Sprinkle some seeds in a straight line on a piece of greaseproof paper. After removing the excess, place clear tape over the seeds and lift off. Bury the tape in the garden and you will soon have perfect rows of seedlings.

- **Prevent wall damage from picture-hook nails** Before hammering in a nail, put a piece of masking tape on the wall where you want it. This will prevent the paint from peeling off if you have to remove the nail.

- **Keep screws handy** Stick double-sided tape on a workbench and use it to hold loose screws, nuts and bolts.

...for children

- **Makeshift childproofing** When visiting a home that isn't childproofed, bring a roll of clear tape along, too. Use it to cover electrical outlets as a temporary safety measure. Although it will not provide a lot of protection, it could give you the extra time you need to remove a child from a potentially hazardous situation.

- **Make multicoloured designs** Tape a few different-coloured markers or pencils together and let children draw multicoloured designs. Be careful not to use too many, so the children can keep control of their drawings.

(**KIDS'** STUFF)

The balloon that just won't pop

Stick a piece of clear tape to a blown-up balloon. Hold up the balloon in one hand and a pin in the other.

Pierce the balloon with the pin at the taped spot and remove it. The balloon will not pop! Then pop the balloon in another area. It's guaranteed to leave them laughing and scratching their heads.

Tea...

...around the house

- **Clean wooden furniture and floors** Freshly brewed tea is
  great for cleaning wood furniture and floors. Boil a couple of tea
  bags in a litre of water and let it cool. Dip a soft cloth in the tea,
  wring out the excess and wipe away dirt and grime. Buff dry with
  a clean, soft cloth.

- **Create 'antique' fashions** Soak white lace or garments in
  a tea bath to create an antique beige, creamy or ivory look. Use
  three tea bags for every 2 cups of boiling water and steep for
  20 minutes before removing the bags. Make sure it is cool, before
  soaking the material for 10 minutes or more. The longer you soak
  the fabric, the darker it will become.

- **Give mirrors a shine** Brew a pot of strong tea and allow it
  to cool. Dampen a soft cloth in the tea and wipe it all over the
  surface of the mirrors. Then buff well with a soft, dry cloth to get
  a streak-free shine.

- **Control dust from fireplace ash** Keep dust from rising from the ashes when you clean out a fireplace. Before you begin cleaning, sprinkle wet tea leaves over the area. The tea will keep the ashes from floating around as you lift them out.

- **Perfume a sachet** Next time you make a sachet to perfume a drawer or wardrobe, try using something a little more exotic than lavender or rose petals. Just open a few used herbal tea bags and spread the wet tea on some old newspaper to dry. Then use the dry tea as stuffing for the sachet.

- **Tenderise tough meat** Even the toughest cuts of meat will melt in your mouth after you marinate them in strong black tea. Place 4 tablespoons of black tea leaves in a pot of warm (not boiling) water and steep for 5 minutes. Strain to remove the leaves and stir in 100g brown sugar until it dissolves. Set aside. Season up to 1.5kg meat with salt, pepper, onion and garlic powder and place it in a large cast-iron casserole dish. Pour the liquid over the seasoned meat and cook in a preheated 160°C/gas mark 3 oven until the meat is tender (about 90 minutes).

...in the garden

- **Give roses a boost** Sprinkle new or used tea leaves around rose bushes and cover with mulch to give them a midsummer boost. When you water the plants, the nutrients from the tea will be released into the soil, encouraging growth. Roses thrive on the tannic acid that occurs naturally in tea.

TIP dyeing with herbal teas

Tea has been used to dye fabrics for a long time. It was first used to hide stains on linens. But you can also use herbal teas to dye fabric different colours and subtle hues. Try using hibiscus to achieve red tones and darker herbal teas like liquorice for soft brown tints. Always experiment using fabric scraps until you obtain the desired results.

...in the garden

- **Enhance your compost heap** To speed up the decomposition process and enrich the compost, pour a few cups of strongly brewed tea into the heap. The liquid tea will hasten decomposition and draw acid-producing bacteria, creating a desirable acid-rich compost.

- **Feed your ferns and other acid-loving houseplants** Substitute brewed tea when watering the plants or work wet tea leaves into the soil around the plants to encourage lush, luxuriant growth –they like the extra nutrients from the tea. Note: don't use leftover tea with sugar or milk as these are not good for the plant.

- **Prepare a planter for potting** For healthier potted plants, place a few used tea bags on top of the drainage layer at the bottom of the planter before potting. The tea bags will retain water and leach nutrients into the soil.

...health and beauty

- **Drain a boil** Cover a boil with a wet tea bag overnight and it should have drained without pain by the time you wake up the next morning.

did you **KNOW?**

Legend has it that tea originated some 5,000 years ago with the Chinese emperor Shen Nung. A wise ruler and creative scientist, the emperor insisted that all drinking water be boiled as a health precaution. One summer day, during a rest stop in a distant region, servants began to boil water for the royal entourage to drink when some dried leaves from a nearby bush fell into the pot. As the water boiled, it turned brown. The emperor's scientific curiosity was aroused, and he insisted on tasting the liquid. It was just his cup of tea.

- **Reduce razor burn** When you forget to replace a blunt razor blade before you start to shave and end up with razor burn and painful nicks and cuts, apply a cool wet tea bag to soothe the affected area.

- **Cool sunburned skin** If you forget to use sunscreen and pay the price with painful sunburn, a few wet tea bags applied to the affected skin will take out the sting. This works well for other types of minor burns (such as those from a teapot or steam iron), too. If the sunburn is too widespread to treat this way, put some tea bags in your bath water and soak your whole body.

- **Tan your skin with tea** Give pale skin a tanned appearance without exposure to dangerous ultraviolet rays. Brew 2 cups of strong black tea, let it cool and pour into a plastic spray bottle. Make sure your skin is clean and dry. Then spray the tea directly onto your skin and let it air-dry. Repeat as desired for a glowing tan. This will also work to give a man's face a more even tone after shaving off a beard.

- **Condition dry hair** To give a natural shine to dry hair, use a litre of warm, unsweetened tea (freshly brewed or instant) as a final rinse.

- **Soothe nipples sore from nursing** When breastfeeding a baby leaves your nipples sore, treat them to an ice-cold bag of tea. Just brew a cup of tea, remove the bag and place it in a bowl of ice cubes for about a minute. Then place the wet tea bag on the sore nipple and cover it with a nursing pad. Keep it under your bra for several minutes. The tannic acid in the wet tea leaves will soothe and help to heal the sore nipple.

- **Get the grey out** Turn grey hair dark again without an expensive trip to the hairdresser or the use of chemical hair dyes. Make a natural dye using brewed tea and herbs. Steep 3 tea bags in 200ml boiling water. Add 1 tablespoon each of rosemary and sage (fresh or dried) and let it stand overnight before straining. To use, shampoo as usual and then pour

...health and beauty

or spray the mixture on your hair, making sure to saturate it thoroughly. Take care not to stain your clothes. Blot with a towel and do not rinse. It may take several treatments to achieve the desired result.

- **Relieve a baby's pain from an injection** If your baby's arm is still painful from a recent inoculation, try wetting a tea bag and placing it over the puncture. Hold it gently in place until the crying stops. The tannic acid in the tea will soothe the soreness. Try it on yourself the next time an injection leaves your arm sore.

- **Soothe bleeding gums** Your child's lost tooth has led to bleeding gums that are sore and feel horrible. To stop the bleeding and soothe the pain from a lost or recently pulled tooth, wet a tea bag with cool water and press it directly onto the site of the missing tooth.

- **Stop foot odour** Put an end to smelly feet by giving them a daily tea bath. Soak your feet in strongly brewed tea for 20 minutes a day to cure offensive odours.

- **Relieve your tired eyes** Revitalise tired, achy or puffy eyes by soaking two tea bags in warm water and placing them over your closed eyes for 20 minutes. The tannins in the tea act to reduce puffiness and soothe tired eyes.

- **Make a soothing mouthwash** To ease toothache or a mouth ulcer, rinse your mouth with a cup of hot peppermint tea mixed with a pinch or two of salt. Peppermint is an antiseptic and contains menthol, which alleviates pain on contact with skin surfaces. To make peppermint tea, boil 1 tablespoon fresh peppermint leaves in 200ml water and steep for several minutes.

Tights...

...around the house

- **Keep a hairbrush clean** If you dread the prospect of cleaning out your hairbrush, here is a way to make the job much easier. Cut a 5cm strip from the leg section of a pair of tights, and stretch it over and around the bristles of your new (or newly cleaned) hairbrush. If necessary, use a hairgrip or a comb to push the tights down over the bristles. The next time the brush needs cleaning, simply lift up and remove the tights layer, along with all the dead hair, lint and dirt on top and replace it with a fresh strip.

- **Remove nail varnish** If you can't find any cotton-wool balls, moisten strips of recycled tights with nail-varnish remover to take off your old nail varnish. Cut the material into 8cm squares and store several of them in an old plaster container or make-up bag.

- **Make a ponytail scrunchy** Why buy a scrunchy for a ponytail when you can easily make one for nothing? Cut a horizontal strip about 8cm wide across a stocking leg and wrap it a few times around the ponytail.

- **Buff your shoes** Bring out the shine in freshly polished shoes by buffing them with a medium-length strip from a pair of old tights. Just hold the strip over the shoes at each end and pull down on each side alternately, like 'shoeshines' you see in old films. It works so well, you may never want to use another method again.

...around the house

- **Vacuum a fish tank** If you have a wet-dry vacuum cleaner, you can change the water in your fish tank without disturbing the gravel and tank accessories. (You will still have to relocate the fish, of course.) Pull the foot of an old nylon stocking or pair of tights over the end of the vacuum's nozzle, secure it with a rubber band and you can start sucking out the water.

- **Wrap up wrapping paper** Keep used rolls of wrapping paper from tearing and unravelling by storing them in tubes made by cutting the leg sections off old pairs of tights. (Don't forget to leave the foot section intact.) Or, if you have a number of used rolls, you can simply put one in each leg of a pair of tights and hang them over a hanger in the wardrobe.

- **Keep spray bottles unblocked** If you recycle spray bottles to use with homemade cleaners or furniture polishes, you can prevent any potential blockages by covering the open end of the tube – the part that goes inside the bottle – with a small, square-cut piece of nylon tights held in place with a small rubber band. This works especially well for filtering garden sprays that are mixed from concentrates.

- **Find lost small objects** Have you ever spent hours on your hands and knees searching through a carpet for a lost gemstone,

contact lens or another tiny, precious item? If not, count yourself among the lucky few. Should you ever be faced with this situation, cut a leg off an old pair of tights, making sure that the toe section is intact, and pull it up over the nozzle of the vacuum cleaner hose. (If you want additional security, you can even cut off the other leg and slip that over as well.) Secure the stocking in place with a tightly wound rubber band. Turn on the vacuum, carefully move the nozzle over the carpet, and you will soon find your valuable attached to the homemade filter.

- **Take a citrus bath** Make scented bath oil by drying and grinding orange and/or lemon peel and pouring them into the foot of a pair of old tights. Knot about 2.5cm above the peel and leave another 15cm or so of tights above that before cutting off the remainder. Tie the stocking to a bath tap with the peel suspended below the running water. You can also use the stocking to exfoliate your skin.

- **Hold mothballs or potpourri** For an easy way to store mothballs in a wardrobe or to make sachets of potpourri to keep in your drawers, pour either ingredient into the toe section of a pair of recycled tights. Knot off the contents, then cut off the remainder. If you plan to hang up the mothballs, leave several centimetres of material before cutting.

- **Use to hang-dry sweaters** Avoid getting clothes-peg marks on newly washed sweaters by putting an old pair of tights through the neck of the sweater and running the legs out through the arms. Hang the sweater to dry by clipping the pegs onto the tights instead of the wool.

- **Bundle blankets for storage** For an effortless and foolproof way to keep blankets and duvets securely bundled before they go into temporary storage, wrap them up in large 'rubber bands' made from the waistbands of your used tights.

did you **KNOW?**

Nylon, the world's first synthetic fibre, was invented at E.I. DuPont de Nemours, Inc., and unveiled on October 28, 1938. Instead of calling a press conference, company vice-president Charles Stine chose to make the landmark announcement to 3,000 women's club members at the New York World Fair, introducing it with live models wearing nylon stockings. Stine's instincts were spot on. By the end of 1940, DuPont had sold 64 million pairs of stockings. Nylon had actually made its big-screen debut a year earlier, when it was used to create the tornado that lifted Dorothy out of Kansas in *The Wizard of Oz*.

...around the house

- **Tie up boxes, newspapers, magazines** If you run out of string (or need something stronger – perhaps for a large stack of glossy magazines), tie up bundles of boxes, newspapers and other types of recyclable paper goods using an old pair of tights. Cut off the legs and waistband to make the 'string'.

- **Organise a suitcase** As any seasoned traveller knows, you can sqeeze more of your belongings into any piece of luggage by rolling up your clothes. To keep bulkier rolls from unwrapping, cover them in flexible nylon tubes. Cut the legs off a pair of old tights, snip off the foot sections, and stretch the stockings over the rolled-up garments for a neat and tidy suitcase.

...in the kitchen

- **Dust under the fridge** Catch the dust bundles that lurk underneath and alongside the fridge by rolling up a pair of old tights and attaching it with a rubber band to a coat hanger. The dust and dirt will cling to the nylon, and is easily washed off.

- **Make a pot or dish scrubber** Clean stains off nonstick cookware by making a do-it-yourself scrubbing pad. Crumple up a pair of clean old tights, moisten it with a bit of warm water and add a couple of drops of washing-up liquid. You can also make terrific scrubbers for dishes, as well as walls and other nonporous surfaces, by cutting off the foot or toe section, fitting it over a sponge and knotting off the end.

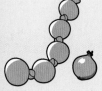

- **Store onions longer** Hang onions in nylon holders that provide good air circulation so they stay fresh. Place an onion in the foot of an old, clean pair of tights; make a knot above it; add another onion and knot. Repeat as necessary. Hang in a cool, dry area of the kitchen. You can easily remove the onions by snipping off each knot, starting from the bottom and working up.

- **Make a flour duster** Here is a simple way to dust baking pans and surfaces with exactly the right amount of flour. Cut the foot section off a clean old tights' leg, fill it with flour, tie a knot in it and keep it in the flour jar. Give your new flour dispenser a few gentle shakes whenever you need to dust flour onto a baking pan or prepare a surface for rolling out dough for breads or pastries.

- **Secure rubbish bags** How many times have you opened the kitchen bin to discover that the liner has slipped and it has been covered over with fresh rubbish? You can prevent this by firmly securing the bin bag or liner to your bin with the elastic waistband from a recycled pair of tights; tie a knot in the band to keep it tight. You can also do this to keep rubbish bags from slipping off the edge of outdoor rubbish bins.

- **Keep a rolling pin from sticking** Getting pie dough to a perfect consistency is an art form in itself. Although you can always add water to dough that is too dry, it often results in a gluey consistency that sticks to your rolling pin. Avoid the hassle of having to scrape the rolling pin by covering it with a piece of nylon stocking. It will hold enough flour to keep even the soggiest pie dough from sticking to the pin.

did you **KNOW?**

Until the late 1950s, women wore nylon stockings attached to a suspender belt. Tights, with the legs fused to pants, were first produced in 1959 by the Gant company in the USA. Their popularity soared in the 1960s when the miniskirt made wearing stockings and suspenders virtually impossible as hemlines were too short to hide them.

Legend also has it that the doll maker Madame Alexander came up with the concept for tights in the early 1950s, when she started sewing tiny pairs of silk stockings onto her dolls' underpants to keep them from slipping down!

...for the DIY-er

- **Apply stain to crevices in wood** Getting wood stain or varnish into the corners and crevices of an unfinished bookcase or table can be a difficult task. Often your brush just doesn't fit into them to give an even coating. Cut a strip from an old pair of tights, fold it over a few times, and use a rubber band to attach it to the tip of a wooden ice-lolly stick. Dip the homemade applicator into the stain or varnish and you should find it easy to get into these inaccessible spots.

- **Test a sanded surface for snags** Wrap a long piece of tights around the palm of your hand and rub it over the wood. If the tights snag on any spots, sand them until you are able to freely move the nylon over the surface without it catching.

- **Clean a swimming pool** To skim the debris off the surface of a swimming pool, cut a leg off a pair of tights and fit it over the pool's skimmer basket. It will catch those tiny dirt particles and hairs that would otherwise get into and possibly clog the pool's filter unit.

- **Make a paint strainer** Cut a leg off some old tights. Clip the foot off and make a cut along the leg's length so you have a flat piece of nylon. Then cut the leg into 30cm sections to make the filters. Stretch the nylon over the container you want to pour the paint into and hold it in place with the waistband from the tights. Slowly pour the paint through the filter into the bucket.

...in the garden

- **Prevent soil erosion in houseplants** When moving a houseplant to a larger container, put a piece of nylon tights at the bottom of the new pot. It will act as a liner to let excess water flow out without draining the soil at the same time.

- **Support melons** Melons are not easy to grow in the UK, but you can help them along. Keep small melons, such as cantaloupes, off the ground by making protective sleeves for them from old tights. Cut the legs off and, as the melons start to develop, slide each one into the foot and tie the leg to a stake so the melon is suspended above the ground. The tights will stretch as the melons mature, while keeping them from touching the damp soil, where they would be susceptible to rot or invasion by hungry insects and other garden pests.

- **Support delicate plants** Use strips of tights to attach young plants and trees to garden stakes. The nylon's flexibility will stretch as your seedlings or saplings fill out and mature – unlike string or twine, which can damage plant stalks if tied too tightly.

...in the garden

- **Store flower bulbs in winter** Legs of tights make great sacks for storing bulbs, since they allow the air to circulate and so prevent mould and rot. Hang them up in a cool, dry place.

- **Cover a kids' bug jar** When making an insect jar, don't punch holes in the jar's metal lid. It is much easier to cut a 15cm square from an old pair of tights and attach it to the jar with a rubber band. The nylon cover lets plenty of air enter the jar, and makes it easier to let insects in and out.

- **Keep deer and foxes out of your garden** Fill the foot sections of some old tights with human hair from a hairbrush or dog hair from a brushing. Tie up the ends and hang them up where the deer tend to snack. They won't be back for more. The hair loses its scent after a while, so replace every few days.

- **Clean up after gardening** Here are two recycling tips in one: save up leftover pieces of soap and put them in the foot of an old stocking. Knot it off and hang it next to an outdoor tap. Use the soap-filled stocking to wash your hands after working outside to avoide getting dirt on handles or bathroom fittings inside.

did you **KNOW?**

You have probably heard that you can temporarily replace a broken fan belt with a nylon stocking in an emergency. Well, don't believe it – it won't work! Pulleys in most vehicles require flat belts, not the rounded shape tights would give. Even on a V-belt pulley, they will fly off as soon as the engine starts. A much better idea is to replace a fan belt before it gets into bad condition.

Tomato juice

- **Deodorise plastic containers** To remove an unpleasant smell from a plastic container, pour a little tomato juice onto a sponge and wipe it around the inside of the container. Then wash the container and lid in warm, soapy water, dry well and store them separately in the freezer for a couple of days. The container will be odour-free and ready to use again.

- **Rid a fridge of odours** If a power failure has caused food to spoil in the fridge, get rid of the resulting smell in your refrigerator and freezer with the help of some tomato juice. After disposing of the spoiled food, thoroughly wipe the insides of the fridge and freezer with a sponge or cloth doused in undiluted tomato juice. Rinse with warm, soapy water and wipe dry. If any traces of the smell remain, either repeat the procedure or substitute vinegar for the tomato juice.

- **Restore the colour to blonde hair** If you are a blonde who has ever gone swimming in a pool treated with chlorine, you know it can sometimes give your hair an unappealing green tint. To restore the blonde colour to your hair, saturate it with undiluted tomato juice, cover with a shower cap and wait 10-15 minutes. Then rinse thoroughly, shampoo, and your hair should be back to its usual shade.

- **Relieve a sore throat** For the temporary relief of sore throat symptoms, gargle with a mixture of 100ml tomato juice and 100ml hot water, plus about 10 drops of a hot pepper sauce.

Toothbrushes

- **Remove tough stains** Try using a soft-bristled nylon toothbrush, dabbing it gently to work in the stain-removing agent (bleach or vinegar, for example) until the stain is gone.

- **Use as all-purpose cleaners** Don't throw out old toothbrushes. Instead, use them to clean a host of diverse items and small or hard-to-reach areas and crevices, including the seams on shoes where the leather meets the sole.

- **Clean silk from ears of corn** Before cooking fresh sweetcorn, take an old toothbrush and gently rub down the ear to brush away the remaining clingy strands of silk. Then you won't have to brush them out from between your teeth after you have eaten the corn.

- **Clean and oil an electric grill** A clean, soft toothbrush is just the right utensil to clean crumbs and grease from the nooks and crannies of an electric grill.

- **Apply hair dye** When dyeing your hair at home, use an old toothbrush as an applicator. It is the perfect size.

- **Clean dirt from appliances** Dip an old toothbrush in soapy water and use it to clean between appliance knobs and buttons, and nameplates with raised lettering.

did you **KNOW?**

The ancient Chinese were apparently the first people to use toothbrushes, which they made with bristles from the necks of long-bristled pigs. William Addis is credited with producing the first mass-produced toothbrush in the UK in 1780. Toothbrushing did not become a two or three-times-a-day habit for many people until after the Second World War when returning soldiers brought home their army-enforced hygiene habits. By then the DuPont company had invented the nylon bristle, which, unlike the natural bristles used earlier, dried completely between brushings and was resistant to the growth of bacteria. Nylon bristles are still used in most toothbrushes made today.

Toothpaste

- **Remove scuffs from shoes** A little toothpaste does an amazing job of removing scuffs from leather shoes. Just squirt a small amount on the scuffed area and rub with a soft cloth. Wipe clean with a damp cloth. The leather will look like new.

- **Clean piano keys** Has too much tickling of the ivories left them a bit dingy? Clean them up with toothpaste and a toothbrush, then wipe them down with a damp cloth. Toothpaste will work just as well on modern pianos that have keys made of plastic rather than real ivory.

- **Remove ink or lipstick stains from fabric** When a pen has leaked in the pocket of a shirt, try this. It may or may not work, depending on the fabric and the ink, but it is certainly worth a try before consigning the shirt to decorating duty. Put white nongel toothpaste on the stain and rub the fabric vigorously together. Rinse with water. If some of the ink has come out, repeat the process a few more times until you get rid of all the ink. The same process should also work for lipstick.

- **Brighten up canvas shoes** Clean and whiten the rubber part of canvas shoes with nongel toothpaste and an old toothbrush. After scrubbing, clean off the toothpaste with a damp cloth.

- **Clean the iron** The mild abrasive in nongel toothpaste is ideal for scrubbing the sticky residue off the soleplate of an iron. Apply the toothpaste to the cool iron, scrub with a rag, then rinse clean.

- **Polish a diamond ring** Put a little toothpaste onto an old toothbrush and use it to make a diamond ring sparkle. Clean off the residue with a damp cloth.

- **Deodorise baby bottles** Over time, baby bottles inevitably pick up a sour-milk smell. Toothpaste will remove the odour effectively. Just put some on a bottle brush and scrub away. Be sure to rinse thoroughly.

Toothpaste

- **Shine bathroom and kitchen chrome** You can buy commercial cleaners with a very fine abrasive designed to shine up chrome, but if you don't have any, the fine abrasive in nongel toothpaste works just as well. Smear on the toothpaste and polish with a soft, dry cloth.

- **Prevent steamed-up goggles** Whether you are woodworking, skiing or scuba diving, nothing is more frustrating (and sometimes dangerous) than goggles that steam up. Prevent the problem by coating the goggles with toothpaste and then wiping them off.

- **Prevent bathroom mirrors from fogging** It is impossible to see clearly in a fogged-up bathroom mirror. Coat the mirror with nongel toothpaste and wipe it off before you get in the shower. When you come out, the mirror won't have misted over.

- **Clean the bathroom basin** Nongel toothpaste works as well as anything else to clean a dirty bathroom basin. Squirt some into the basin, scrub with a sponge or cloth and rinse it out. As a bonus, the toothpaste will also get rid of any smells that are emanating from the drain trap.

did you **KNOW?**

Ancient Egyptians used a mixture of ox-hoof ashes, burned eggshells, myrrh, pumice and water to clean their teeth. For most of history, tooth-cleaning concoctions were used mainly by the wealthy and included such alarming ingredients as salt, pepper, mint leaves, iris flowers, burnt bread, dragon's blood, cinnamon, and burnt alum. In 1850, Dr Washington Sheffield developed a formula we would recognise as toothpaste. He called it Dr Sheffield's Creme Dentifrice. His son, Dr Lucius Tracy Sheffield, observed collapsible metal tubes of paint and decided to use the same idea to make squeezable tubes of toothpaste. Fluoride was first added to toothpaste in 1914 but only became widely accepted in the 1950s.

- **Remove crayon from walls** When children brandishing crayons have been creative on a wall, take a tube of nongel toothpaste and a rag or a scrubbing brush. Squirt the toothpaste on and start scrubbing. The fine abrasive in the toothpaste will rub away the crayon every time. Rinse the wall with water.

- **Remove watermarks from furniture** Even though you leave coasters around, some people just won't use them. To get rid of telltale watermark rings left by sweating drinks, gently rub some nongel toothpaste on the wood with a soft cloth. Then wipe it off with a damp cloth and let it dry completely before applying furniture polish.

- **Remove tar** Getting black tar on your feet at the seaside is annoying, but it is easy enough to remove. Just rub it with some nongel toothpaste and rinse.

- **Clear up pimples** Get rid of an offensive spot by dabbing a bit of nongel, non-whitening toothpaste on the pimple. It should have dried up by morning. The toothpaste dehydrates the spot and absorbs the oil. This remedy works best on spots that have come to a head. But be careful as this remedy may be irritating to sensitive skin.

- **Remove smells from hands** The ingredients in toothpaste that deodorise your mouth will work on your hands as well. If you have been preparing smelly food, wash your hands with toothpaste and the odour will be gone.

TAKE CARE

All toothpastes, including gels, contain abrasives. The amount varies, but too much can damage tooth enamel.

People with sensitive teeth in particular should use a low-abrasive toothpaste. Ask your dentist which is the best toothpaste for you.

Toothpicks

- **Mark cooking times on cuts of meat** When all of your guests want their steaks cooked differently at a dinner or barbecue, you can keep track of exactly who wants what by using a series of different coloured toothpicks to mark the steaks as rare, medium and well-done.

- **Stick through a garlic clove when marinading** If you marinate foods with garlic cloves, stick a toothpick through the clove so you can remove it easily when you are ready to serve.

- **Keep pots from boiling over** To stop a pot from boiling over on the hob, stick a toothpick, laid flat, between the lid and pan. The little space will allow enough steam to escape to prevent the liquid from boiling over. This will also work with a casserole dish that is cooking in the oven.

- **Microwave potatoes faster** The next time you microwave a potato, stick four toothpick 'legs' in one side and stand it up. The suspended potato will cook much faster because the microwaves will reach the bottom as well as the top and sides.

- **Control your use of salad dressing** Instead of removing the foil seal when you open the bottle, take a toothpick and punch several holes in the foil. This will prevent too much dressing running out and make it last longer.

- **Keep sausages from rolling around** When cooking sausages, insert toothpicks between pairs to make turning them over easy and keep them from rolling around in the pan. They'll cook more evenly and will only need to be turned over once.

- **Keep fabrics flat when using a sewing machine** Use a round toothpick to push fabrics, lace or gatherings flat under the pressure foot of the sewing machine as you sew.

- **Apply glue to sequins** If you are working on a project that requires the gluing on of sequins, buttons or beads, squirt a little glue on a piece of paper and dip in a toothpick to apply small dabs of glue. You won't make a mess and you won't waste glue.

- **Use to light candles** When a candle has burned down and the wick is hard to reach, don't burn your fingers trying to use a small match to light it. Light a wooden toothpick instead and use it to light the wick.

- **Repair a bent plant stem** Straighten the plant stem and support it by placing a toothpick against the stem and wrapping the toothpick on with tape. Water the plant and keep your eye on it. Depending on how fast it grows, the stem will regain its strength and you will need to remove the splint so you don't strangle the stem.

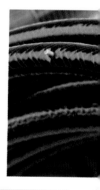

- **Foil cutworms** Cutworms kill seedlings by encircling the stem and severing it. To protect seedlings, stick a toothpick in the soil about 60mm from each stem. This prevents a cutworm from being able to enclose the stem.

- **Repair a leaky garden hose** If a garden hose springs a leak, don't go out and buy another one; just find the hole and insert a toothpick in it. Cut off the excess part of the toothpick. The water will make the wood swell, plugging up the leak every time.

did you **KNOW?**

- Buddhist monks used toothpicks as far back as the 700s and researchers have even found toothpick grooves in the teeth of prehistoric humans.
- Shakespeare mentions a toothpick in *Much Ado About Nothing*.
- In 1872, Silas Noble and J.P. Cooley patented the first toothpick-manufacturing machine.
- One cord of white birch wood (also known as the toothpick tree) can make 7.5 million toothpicks.

Toothpicks

- **Mark the start of a roll of tape** Instead of wasting time trying to find the beginning of some tape, just wrap it around a toothpick whenever you have finished using the tape and the start of the tape will always be easy to find.

- **Repair small holes in wood** When you have driven a nail into the wrong spot, dip the tip of a toothpick into PVA glue. Stick the toothpick in the hole and break it off. Sand the toothpick flush to the surface and you will never notice the repair.

- **Repair a loose hinge screw** To fix a stripped hole on a door hinge, put some glue on the end of a toothpick and stick it in the hole. Break it off. Add one or two more toothpicks with glue until the hole is tightly filled, breaking each one off as you go. Re-drill the hole and screw the hinge back in place.

- **Clean cracks and crevices** To get rid of dirt in hard-to-reach cracks or crevices, dip an ordinary toothpick in some alcohol and run it through the affected area. Also try this to clean around the buttons of your phone.

- **Touch up crevices in furniture** The secret to touching up paint effectively is to use as little paint as possible, because even the right paint may not match exactly. Dip the end of a toothpick into the paint and use it to touch up just the crevice. Unlike a brush, the toothpick won't apply more paint than you need and you won't have to clean it.

TAKE CARE

Overusing toothpicks can damage tooth enamel and gums. If you have crowns or veneers, be extra careful to avoid breakage. Toothpicks also cause wear to tooth roots, particularly in elderly people whose gums have pulled away, exposing the roots.

Twist ties

- **Organise electrical cords** If the top of your computer desk looks like climbing plants have taken over, tame the jungle of electrical wires by rolling each one up neatly and securing the extra length with a twist tie.

- **Make a trellis** You need some twist ties and the plastic rings from four or six-packs of beer or soft drinks. Use the twist ties to join together as many of the rings as you want. Attach the trellis between two stakes, also using twist ties. At the end of the season, roll up the trellis and store it for next year.

- **Tie up plant stems** Twist ties are useful for securing drooping plant stems to a stake or holding climbers onto a trellis. Don't twist the ties too tight, because you might injure the stem and restrict its growth.

- **Temporarily repair a pair of glasses** If your specs are slipping because a tiny screw that holds the earpiece has fallen out, secure it temporarily with a twist tie. Trim the edges off the tie to reveal just the centre wire. After you insert and tie it off, snip off the excess wire with scissors.

- **Use as an emergency shoelace** When you don't have a replacement shoelace handy, use a twist tie across each opposing pair of eyelets.

- **Code your keys** If there are several similar-looking keys on your chain, identify them with twist ties of different colours secured through the holes in the keys.

- **Make an emergency cuff link** If you have packed a smart shirt with double cuffs to wear to a wedding, but forgot to pack cuff links, secure the cuffs with twist ties. Pull the ties through so the twist is discreetly hidden inside the cuff.

- **Bind loose-leaf paper** Hold sheets of loose-leaf paper together by inserting twist ties in the holes.

Tyres

- **Protect vegetables** Plant tomatoes, potatoes, aubergines, peppers or other vegetables inside tyres laid on the ground. The tyres will protect the plants from harsh winds and the dark rubber will absorb heat from the sun and warm the surrounding soil.

- **Make a paddling pool for children** To make an impromptu paddling pool for toddlers, drape a shower curtain or other piece of waterproof material over the centre of a large lorry tyre and fill it with water.

- **Make a classic tyre swing** A swing made from an old tyre is a timeless source of pleasure for children of all ages. To make one for the garden, drill a few drainage holes in the bottom of the tyre. Drill two holes for bolts in the top, bolt two chains or strong pieces of rope to the tyre, and suspend it by the chains from a healthy branch of a large tree. Put some wood chips or other soft material under and around the swing to cushion any falls.

TIP tyre check-ups

Spending 5 minutes a month to check your tyres can protect against avoidable breakdowns and crashes, improve vehicle handling, increase mileage and extend the life of your tyres.

Here are some guidelines:
- Check tyre pressure at least once a month and before going on a long journey.
- Don't forget to take a spare.
- Inspect for uneven wear on tyre treads, cracks, foreign objects or other signs of wear or damage. Remove bits of glass and other objects wedged in the tread.
- Make sure your tyre valves have caps.
- Do not overload your vehicle.

Umbrellas

- **Use as a drying rack** An old umbrella makes a handy clothes drying rack. Strip off the fabric and hang the frame upside down from the shower rail. Attach wet clothing with clothes pegs. Your new drying rack will fold up easily for storage.

- **Clean a chandelier** The next time you climb up to clean a chandelier or ceiling fan, bring an old umbrella with you. Open the umbrella and hook its handle on the fixture so that it hangs upside down to catch any drips or dust.

- **Signal in a crowd** When you and a friend next go to a crowded event, carry a couple of identical brightly coloured umbrellas. If you get separated, you can hold the umbrellas over your head and open them up to find each other in a flash.

- **Block plant overspray** Houseplants always benefit from a misting with water, but walls don't enjoy being soaked as well. Place an open umbrella between the plants and the wall and give your plants a shower.

- **Make plant stakes** If the wind has caught your umbrella, turned it inside out and ripped the fabric, before throwing it away, remove the ribs to make excellent supports for top-heavy garden plants such as peonies.

- **Make an instant trellis** Remove the fabric from an old umbrella and insert the handle into the ground to support climbing vines such as clematis. The umbrella's shape, covered with flowers, will look terrific in the garden.

- **Shield your seedlings** If you thought you had waited long enough before planting your seedlings outside, but a killer frost is now forecast, sacrifice an old umbrella to save the seedlings. Open the umbrella, then cut off the handle. Place the umbrella over the seedlings to keep the frost away from them.

Vanilla extract

- **Freshen up the fridge** If an unpleasant smell is lingering in the fridge even after it has been thoroughly scrubbed, try wiping down the inside of the fridge with vanilla extract. To prolong the scent, soak a cotton-wool ball or a piece of sponge with vanilla extract and leave it in the refrigerator.

- **Deodorise the microwave** Is a strong fishy or spicy smell lurking in the microwave? You can get rid of the residual odour by pouring a little vanilla extract into a bowl and microwaving it on High for 1 minute.

- **Neutralise the smell of fresh paint** If you are not a fan of the smell of fresh paint, mix 1 tablespoon vanilla extract into the paint when you open it. The newly decorated house will smell as good as it looks.

- **Use as a perfume** Put a dab of vanilla extract on each wrist; you will smell delicious and many people find the scent of vanilla very relaxing.

- **Repel bugs** Almost everyone likes the smell of vanilla, but most insects hate it. Dilute 1 tablespoon vanilla extract in 200ml water and wipe the mixture on your exposed skin to discourage mosquitoes, flies and ticks.

- **Relieve minor burns** If you've accidentally picked up a hot pan or been splashed with grease from a frying pan, use vanilla extract to give quick pain relief. The evaporation of the alcohol in the vanilla extract will cool the burn.

- **Sweeten the smell of your home** Estate agents and property stagers who specialise in making homes appealing to buyers recommend this tip. Put a drop or two of vanilla extract on a light bulb, turn on the light, and your house will be filled with the appealing scent of fresh baking.

Vegetable oil

- **Help to remove a splinter** When a stubborn splinter won't come out, don't keep poking at it. Instead soak it in vegetable oil. The oil should soften up your skin, perhaps just enough to be able to ease the splinter out with tweezers.

- **Remove labels and stickers** Used jars, both plastic and glass, are always useful. But removing the old labels invariably leaves a sticky residue. Soak the label with vegetable oil and the label will slide off. It works well for sticky price tags as well.

- **Separate stuck glasses** When stacked drinking glasses get stuck together, it seems like nothing you can do will separate them without breakage. But the solution is simple: just pour a little vegetable oil around the rim of the bottom glass and the glasses will pull apart with ease.

- **Smooth your feet** Rub dry feet with vegetable oil before you go to bed and put on a pair of socks. When you wake up, they will be soft and smooth.

- **Prevent clippings from sticking to a mower** The next time you turn over the lawnmower to remove grass clippings that have stuck on, rub some vegetable oil under the housing and on to the blade. Next time, it will take a lot longer for clippings to build up again.

TIP oiling chopping boards

To restore and preserve dried-out wooden kitchen items such as chopping boards and salad bowls and tongs, use salad-bowl oil – a special mineral oil that is safe to use near food, won't go rancid and is designed to protect wood that comes into contact with food. It is best not to use ordinary vegetable oil, which will soak into dried-out wood and make it look much better, but never really dries and can get rancid after it has been absorbed by the wood.

Vegetable oil

- **Control mosquitoes near a birdbath** It is so satisfying to watch birds enjoying the garden bath you have provided. But unfortunately, still water can be a perfect breeding ground for mosquitoes. Floating a few tablespoons of vegetable oil on the surface of the water will help to keep mosquitoes from using the water and it won't bother the birds. But it is still important to change the water twice a week so that any insect larvae don't have time to hatch.

- **Season cast-iron cookware** After washing and thoroughly drying a cast-iron grill pan or wok, use a paper towel to wipe it down with vegetable oil. Just leave a very thin layer of oil. It will prevent the pan from rusting and season it for the next time you use it.

Vegetable peelers

- **Slice slivers of cheese or chocolate** When you need cheese slivers that are thinner than you can cut with a knife or want to decorate a cake with fine curlicues of chocolate, use a vegetable peeler.

- **Sharpen a pencil** When you don't have a pencil sharpener, a vegetable peeler will do just as good a job.

- **Soften hard butter fast** When you need to soften cold, hard butter in a hurry – to use in a cake mixture, for example – shave off what you need with a vegetable peeler. The butter will be soft in moments.

- **Renew scented soaps** When scented soaps start to lose their aroma, use a vegetable peeler to skim off a thin layer of soap, revealing a new, moist and fragrant surface.

Vinegar...

...around the house

- **Clean window blinds** For slatted blinds, put on a white cotton glove – the kind sold for gardening is perfect – and moisten the fingers in a solution made of equal parts white vinegar and hot water. Slide your fingers across both sides of each slat. Keep a container of clean water nearby to rinse the glove periodically.

- **Unblock and deodorise drains** The combination of vinegar and bicarbonate of soda is one of the most effective ways to unblock and deodorise drains. It is also gentler on your pipes (and your wallet) than commercial cleaners.

  - To clear blockages in sink and bath drains, use a funnel to pour in 100g bicarbonate of soda followed by 200ml vinegar. When the foaming subsides, flush with hot tap water. Wait 4 minutes and flush again with cold water. As well as clearing blockages, this also washes away bacteria that can cause odours.

  - To speed up a slow drain, pour in 100g salt followed by 400ml boiling vinegar, then flush with hot and cold tap water.

- **Clean computer equipment** Office electronics work better if they are clean and dust-free. Switch all equipment off. Mix equal quantities of white vinegar and water. Dampen a clean cloth in the solution (never use a spray bottle; you must not get liquid on the circuits inside). Squeeze it out and wipe. Use cotton buds to remove dirt on your keyboard and other tight spaces. Clean a

...around the house

computer mouse in the same way. Remove the ball, wipe, and let
it dry for a couple of hours before re-inserting the ball.

- **Wipe away mildew** To eliminate heavy accumulations of
  mildew, use vinegar at full strength. For light stains, dilute it with
  an equal amount of water. You can also prevent mildew forming
  on the bottoms of rugs and carpets by misting the backs with
  full-strength white vinegar from a spray bottle.

- **Give a shine to silver** Make silver shine like new by
  soaking in a mixture of 100ml white vinegar and 2 tablespoons
  bicarbonate of soda for 2-3 hours. Rinse in cold water and dry
  thoroughly with a soft cloth.

- **Burnish a pair of scissors** When scissor blades get sticky or
  grimy, wipe them down with a cloth dipped in full-strength white
  vinegar and then dry. This is effective and also helps to prevent
  them from rusting.

- **Get rid of the smell of smoke** Place a shallow bowl about
  three-quarters full of white or cider vinegar where
  the smell is strongest. Use several bowls if it
  permeates the house. The smoky residue should
  disappear in less than a day. You can also quickly
  get rid of fresh cigarette smoke by moistening a
  cloth with vinegar and waving it around.

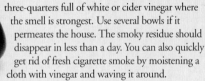

TIP buying vinegar

Vinegar comes in a surprising number of varieties: balsamic, Champagne, cider,
rice, and wine. For household chores, however, plain distilled white vinegar is the best
and least expensive choice. Cider vinegar runs a close second in practicality and is also
widely used in cooking and home remedies. All other types of vinegar should be used
only with food.

- **Clean chrome and stainless steel** Apply a light misting of undiluted white vinegar from a spray bottle. Buff with a soft cloth.

- **Polish brass and copper items** Make a paste of equal parts white vinegar and salt, or vinegar and bicarbonate of soda (wait for the fizzing to stop before using). Use a clean, soft cloth to rub the paste on until the tarnish has gone. Then rinse with cool water and polish with a soft towel until dry.

- **Unglue stickers and price tags** To remove a sticker or price tag from glossy surfaces, saturate the corners and sides with full-strength white vinegar and carefully scrape it off (using an expired credit card or similar piece of plastic). Leave for a minute or two, then wipe with a clean cloth.

- **Remove salt stains from shoes** Ice, slush and snow are hard on leather, and the salt used to melt it leaves a white stain and can cause your footwear to crack and disintegrate if it is left on indefinitely. To remove it, and prevent long-term damage, wipe fresh stains with a cloth dipped in undiluted white vinegar.

- **Clean piano keys** Dip a soft cloth into a solution of 100ml white vinegar mixed in 400ml water, squeeze it out, then gently wipe off each key. Use a second cloth to dry off the keys as you move along, then leave the keyboard uncovered for 24 hours.

- **Remove old smells from lunch boxes and car boots** Soak a slice of white bread in white vinegar and leave in the box or boot overnight. It should smell fresh by morning.

- **Freshen a musty wardrobe or cupboard** Remove the contents, then wash inside the wardrobe with a cloth dampened in a solution of 200ml each of vinegar and ammonia and 50g bicarbonate of soda in 4 litres water. Keep the door open and let the interior dry before replacing your clothes. If the smell persists, place a small tray of clean cat litter inside. Replenish every few days until the odour is gone.

...around the house

- **Erase ballpoint-pen marks** Dab some full-strength white vinegar on the marks using a cloth. Repeat until clean.

- **Brighten up brickwork** Use a mop dipped in 200ml white vinegar mixed with 4 litres warm water, for bright, fresh brickwork.

- **Conceal scratches in wooden furniture** To make a scratch less noticeable, mix some distilled or cider vinegar and iodine in a small jar and paint over the mark with a small artist's brush. Use more iodine for dark woods; more vinegar for light shades.

- **Get rid of white water rings on furniture** Mix equal parts vinegar and olive oil and apply with a soft cloth, moving with the wood grain. Buff with another clean, soft cloth. To remove rings from leather, dab with full-strength white vinegar.

- **Revitalise wood panelling** Mix 450ml warm water, 4 tablespoons white or apple-cider vinegar, and 2 tablespoons olive oil in a container, give it a couple of shakes, and apply to the panelling with a clean cloth. Let the mixture soak into the wood for several minutes, then polish with a dry cloth.

- **Remove candle wax** To remove hardened candle wax, soften it using a hair dryer on the hottest setting. Then blot up as much melted wax as you can with paper towels. Remove what is left by rubbing with a cloth soaked in a solution made of equal parts white vinegar and water. Wipe clean with a soft, absorbent cloth.

TAKE CARE

Don't use vinegar on marble table tops, worktops or floors. The acidity of vinegar can dull or even pit the protective coating and possibly damage the stone itself. Also, avoid using vinegar on travertine and limestone; the acid eats through the calcium in the stonework.

- **Wipe off wax or polish build-up** For wood, dip a cloth in equal parts vinegar and water and squeeze it out well. Then, moving with the grain, clean away the polish. Wipe dry with a soft cloth. For leather, wipe with a soft cloth dipped in 50ml vinegar and 100ml water.

- **Remove carpet stains** You can lift out a range of stains from a carpet with vinegar:

  - Rub light carpet stains with a mixture of 2 tablespoons salt dissolved in 100ml white vinegar. Let solution dry, then vacuum.

  - For larger or darker stains, add 2 tablespoons borax to the mixture and use in the same way.

  - For tough, ground-in dirt make a paste of 1 tablespoon vinegar with 1 tablespoon cornflour and rub it into the stain using a dry cloth. Let it set for two days, then vacuum.

  - To make spray-on spot and stain remover, fill a spray bottle with 5 parts water and 1 part vinegar. Fill a second spray bottle with 1 part non-foaming ammonia and 5 parts water. Saturate a stain with the vinegar solution. Let it settle for a few minutes, then blot thoroughly with a clean, dry cloth. Then spray and blot using the ammonia solution. Repeat until the stain has gone.

- **Restore a rug** Brush dingy rugs with a clean broom dipped in a solution of 200ml white vinegar in 4 litres water. The faded floor-coverings will look much brighter and you won't even need to rinse the solution away.

TAKE CARE

- Do not apply vinegar to jewellery containing pearls or gemstones because it can damage their finish or, in the case of pearls, actually disintegrate them.
- Do not attempt to remove tarnish from antiques, because removing the 'patina' could diminish their value.

...in the kitchen

- **Clean china, crystal and glassware** Put the sparkle back into glassware by adding vinegar to the rinse water or dishwater.

  - To make glassware gleam, add 50ml vinegar to the rinse cycle of the dishwasher.

  - Add 2 tablespoons vinegar to the dishwater when cleaning crystal glasses or fine china. Rinse in a solution of 3 parts warm water to 1 part vinegar and allow them to air-dry.

  - To remove coffee stains and other discolorations from china, try scrubbing them with equal parts vinegar and salt, followed by a rinse in warm water.

  - To rid glasses of the cloudiness that is caused by hard water, heat a pan containing equal parts white vinegar and water (use full-strength vinegar if your glasses are very cloudy), and soak them in it for 15-30 minutes. Scrub them well with a bottle brush, then rinse clean.

- **Cut the grease** Distilled vinegar is one of the best grease cutters around. It even works on frying vats used in many food outlets.

TIP vinegar and floor cleaning

Damp-mopping with a mild vinegar solution is widely recommended as a way to clean wood, vinyl or laminate flooring. But, if possible, check with the manufacturer first. Even when diluted, vinegar's acidity can ruin some finishes and too much water will damage most wooden floors. If you want to try vinegar on your floors, use 100ml white vinegar mixed in 4 litres warm water. Start with a trial application in an inconspicuous area. Before applying the solution, squeeze out the mop thoroughly (or just use a spray bottle to moisten the mop head).

Try these ways of using it in the kitchen:

● Pour 3-4 tablespoons white vinegar into a bottle of washing-up liquid and shake. The vinegar will increase its grease-fighting capabilities and you will need to use less.

● Boil 200ml vinegar in a frying pan for 10 minutes to help to keep food from sticking to it for several months at a time.

● Remove burned-on grease and food stains from stainless-steel cookware by mixing 200ml distilled vinegar in enough water to cover the stains (if they are near the top of a large pan, you may need to increase the vinegar). Let it boil for 5 minutes. The stains should come off with a light scrubbing.

● Remove blackened, cooked-on grease from a grill pan by softening it up with a solution of 200ml apple-cider vinegar and 2 tablespoons sugar. Apply the mixture while the pan is still hot and let it sit for an hour or so. Then watch in amazement as the grime slides off following a light scrub.

● If a hot plate is looking more like a grease pan, wash it with a sponge dipped in full-strength white vinegar.

● Stop grease from building up inside the oven by wiping down the inside with a rag or sponge soaked in full-strength white vinegar once a week. The same treatment will get grease off the grates on gas cookers as well.

● After frying, clean up grease splashes by washing them with a sponge dipped in undiluted white vinegar. Use another sponge soaked in cold tap water to rinse, then wipe dry with a soft cloth.

● Eliminate grease stains by wiping them down with a cloth dampened in a solution made up of equal parts white vinegar and water. In addition to removing the grease, the vinegar will neutralise any residual odours.

...in the kitchen

- **Disinfect chopping boards** Wipe wooden chopping boards or worktops with full-strength white vinegar after each use. The acetic acid in the vinegar is a good disinfectant, effective against such bugs as *E. coli*, salmonella and staphylococcus. Don't use water and washing-up liquid, because it can weaken the fibres of wood. To remove strong smells, such as onion or fish from wood surfaces, spread bicarbonate of soda over it and then spray on undiluted white vinegar. Let it foam and bubble for 5-10 minutes, then rinse with a cloth dipped in clean cold water.

- **Sterilise jars, containers and vases** Fill the container with equal parts vinegar and warm, soapy water and let it stand for 10-15 minutes. Close the lid and shake well or use a bottle brush to scrape off the remains before rinsing thoroughly.

- **Steam-clean the microwave** Place a glass bowl filled with 50ml vinegar in 200ml water inside the microwave and heat for 5 minutes on the highest setting. When cool, use the liquid to wipe away stains and splatters on the interior.

- **Deodorise a waste-disposal unit** Mix equal parts water and vinegar in a bowl, pour the solution into an ice-cube tray and freeze it. Drop a couple of 'vinegar cubes' down the waste disposal every week or so, followed by a cold-water rinse to keep it smelling fresh.

- **Wash out the dishwasher** To keep a dishwasher operating at peak performance and remove built-up soap film, pour 200ml undiluted white vinegar into the bottom of the unit or in a bowl on the top rack. Then run a full cycle without any dishes or detergent. Do this once a month, especially if you live in a hard-water area. Note: if there is no mention of vinegar in your dishwasher-owner's manual, check with the manufacturer before trying this.

- **Clean a coffee maker** If your coffee is consistently weak or bitter, your coffeemaker probably needs cleaning. Fill the decanter with 400ml white vinegar and 200ml water. Place a filter in the machine, and pour the solution into the coffee maker's water chamber. Turn it on and run through a full brew cycle. Remove the filter and replace it with a fresh one. Run clean water through the machine for two full cycles, replacing the filter again for the second brew. If you have soft water, clean the coffee maker after 80 brew cycles and after 40 cycles if you have hard water.

- **Clean a dirty Thermos** To get a Thermos flask clean, fill it with warm water and 50ml white vinegar. If you see any residue, add some uncooked rice, which will act as an abrasive to scrape it off. Close and shake well. Then rinse and air-dry.

- **Clean a tea kettle** To eliminate lime and mineral deposits in a kettle, bring 600ml full-strength white vinegar to the boil. Boil for 5 minutes and leave the vinegar in the kettle overnight. Rinse out with cold water the next day.

- **Make an all-purpose scrub for pots and pans** This can be safely used on all metal cookware, including expensive copper pots and pans. Combine equal parts salt and flour and add just enough vinegar to make a paste. Work the paste around the cooking surface and the outside of the utensil, then rinse off with warm water and dry thoroughly with a soft dish towel.

TIP homemade wine vinegar

Contrary to popular belief, old wine rarely turns into vinegar; it just spoils due to oxidation. To create vinegar, you need the presence of Acetobacter, a specific type of bacteria. You can make your own wine vinegar, though, by mixing one part leftover red, white or rosé wine with 2 parts cider vinegar. Pour the mixture into a clean, recycled wine bottle and store it in a dark cupboard. It will taste good.

...in the kitchen

- **Purge insects from your pantry or cupboards** Fill a bowl with 300ml apple-cider vinegar and add two drops washing-up liquid. Leave in your cupboard for a week. Dispose of the dead insects. Empty and wash the cupboard thoroughly with washing-up liquid or 400g bicarbonate of soda in 1 litre water. Discard all wheat products (breads, pasta, flour and similar). Wipe food cans.

- **Refresh a refrigerator** Vinegar is probably an even more effective safe cleanser than bicarbonate of soda. Use equal parts white vinegar and water to wash it, inside and out. To prevent mildew, wash with full-strength vinegar. Use undiluted vinegar to wipe off accumulated grime on top of the fridge.

- **Tenderise meat and fish** Soaking a lean or inexpensive cut of red meat in 400ml vinegar breaks down tough fibres and kills off any harmful bacteria. For fish, soak in full-strength vinegar overnight. Experiment with different varieties for added flavour or simply use apple cider or distilled vinegar if you plan to rinse it off before cooking.

- **Refresh an ice-cube tray** If your plastic ice-cube trays are covered with hard-water stains, soak them in undiluted vinegar for 4-5 hours, then rinse under cold water and let them dry.

- **Remove stains from pots, pans and ovenware** Nothing does a better job than vinegar when it comes to removing stubborn stains on cookware. Here is how to put the power of vinegar to use:

  - Get rid of dark stains on aluminium cookware (caused by cooking acidic foods) by mixing in 1 teaspoon white vinegar for each cup of water needed to cover the stains. Boil for a couple of minutes. Rinse with cold water.

  - To get cooked-on food stains off glass ovenware, fill with 1 part vinegar and 4 parts water, heat the mixture to a slow boil and let it boil at a low level for 5 minutes. The stains should come off with a light scrub once the mixture has cooled down.

- To remove stains from stainless-steel pots and pans, soak them in 400ml white vinegar for 30 minutes, then rinse with hot, soapy water followed by a rinse in cold water.

- For mineral stains on nonstick cookware, rub with undiluted, distilled vinegar. For stubborn stains, mix 2 tablespoons bicarbonate of soda, 100ml vinegar and 200ml water and boil for 10 minutes.

- **Get rid of berry stains and strong smells** Use undiluted white vinegar on your hands to remove dark stains from berries and other fruits or strong smells such as onion or garlic.

- **Make all-purpose cleaners** Keep two recycled spray bottles filled with these vinegar-based solutions:

  - For glass, stainless-steel and plastic-laminate surfaces, fill a spray bottle with 2 parts water, 1 part distilled white vinegar and a couple of drops of washing-up liquid.

  - For cleaning walls and other painted surfaces, mix 100ml white vinegar, 200ml ammonia and 50g bicarbonate of soda in 4 litres water and pour into a spray bottle. Spray onto spots and stains as needed and wipe off with a clean towel.

did you **KNOW?**

True balsamic vinegar comes only from Modena, in northern Italy, and is made from Trebbiano grapes, a very sweet white variety. Italian law mandates that the vinegar be aged in wooden barrels made of chestnut, juniper, mulberry or oak. There are only two grades of true balsamic vinegar, which typically sells for between £60 and £120 for a 100ml bottle: *tradizionale vecchio* vinegar is at least 12 years old, and *tradizionale extra vecchio* has been aged for at least 25 years (some balsamic vinegars are known to have been aged for more than 100 years).

...in the kitchen

- **Wash fruit and vegetables** Before cooking and serving fruit and vegetables, eliminate hidden dirt, pesticides and even insects, by rinsing them in 4 tablespoons apple-cider vinegar dissolved in 4 litres cold water.

- **Make better boiled or poached eggs** Vinegar does marvellous things for eggs. Here are the two most useful:

  - When you are hard-boiling eggs, add 2 tablespoons distilled vinegar for every litre of water. This will keep the eggs from cracking and make them much easier to shell.

  - When poaching eggs, add a couple of tablespoons of vinegar to the hot water. This will keep your eggs in a tight shape and prevent the egg whites from spreading too much.

...in the bathroom

- **Wash mildew from shower curtains** Clean off mildew by washing the shower curtain in the machine with a couple of dirty towels. Add 100g laundry detergent and100g bicarbonate of soda, and wash in warm water on the machine's regular cycle. Add 200ml white vinegar to the first rinse. Before the machine goes into its spin cycle, remove the curtain and hang it up to dry.

- **Shine ceramic tiles** If soap scum or water spots have dulled the ceramic tiles around your sink or bath, you can bring back the brightness by scrubbing them with 100ml white vinegar, 100ml ammonia and 50g borax mixed in 4 litres warm water. Rinse well with cool water and let the tiles air-dry.

- **Shine up shower doors** Wipe down doors and screens with a solution of 100ml white vinegar, 200ml ammonia and 50g bicarbonate of soda mixed together in 4 litres warm water.

- **Whiten tile grout** Has the grout between the tiles of the bath or shower enclosure become stained or discoloured? Restore it to its original shade of white by using a toothbrush dipped in undiluted white vinegar.

- **Clean the sink** Scrub porcelain sinks with full-strength white vinegar, then rinse with clean cold water. To remove hard-water stains from a bath, pour in 600ml white vinegar under hot running tap water. Fill the bath up over the stains and soak for 4 hours before scrubbing.

- **Disinfect shower-door tracks** Fill the tracks with about 400ml full-strength white vinegar and leave for 3-5 hours. (If the tracks are really dirty, heat the vinegar for 30 seconds in a microwave first.) Pour hot water over the track to flush away the debris. Use a recycled toothbrush to get rid of tough stains.

- **Remove mineral deposits from a showerhead** Remove the showerhead and place it in a litre of boiling water with 100ml distilled vinegar for 10 minutes (use hot, not boiling, liquid for plastic showerheads). When you take it out of the water, the obstructions should be gone. If you have a non-removable showerhead, fill a small plastic bag half full of vinegar and tape it over the fixture. Leave it for an hour before removing it and wiping down the showerhead.

- **Wipe down bathroom fixtures** Pour a little undiluted white vinegar onto a soft cloth and use it to wipe chrome taps, towel racks, bathroom mirrors, doorknobs, and to wash out dirty tooth glasses. They will all come up gleaming.

- **Fight mould and mildew** To remove and inhibit bathroom mould and mildew, pour a solution of 3 tablespoons white vinegar, 1 teaspoon borax and 400ml hot water into a clean, recycled spray bottle. Shake thoroughly. Spray on mould or mildew spots. Use a soft scrubbing brush to work the solution into the stains or just let it soak in.

...in the bathroom

- **Disinfect a toilet bowl** Pour 400ml white vinegar into the bowl and leave to soak overnight before flushing. Do this once a week to help prevent water rings appearing just above the water level in the toilet bowl.

- **Clean a toothbrush holder** Remove grime, bacteria and caked-on toothpaste with cotton buds moistened in white vinegar.

- **Wash out a tumbler** If several people in your home use the same tumbler to rinse after brushing their teeth, give it a weekly (or more regular if you prefer) cleaning by filling it with equal parts water and white vinegar or just full-strength vinegar and let it sit overnight. Rinse thoroughly with cold water before using.

...in the medicine cabinet

- **Control dandruff** Follow each shampoo with a rinse of 400ml apple-cider vinegar mixed with 400ml cold water or apply 3 tablespoons vinegar to your hair and massage it into your scalp before you shampoo. Wait a few minutes, rinse and wash as usual.

- **Condition limp or damaged hair** Combine 1 teaspoon apple-cider vinegar with 2 tablespoons olive oil and three egg whites. Rub into your hair, then keep it covered for 30 minutes using cling film or a shower cap. Shampoo and rinse as usual.

TAKE CARE

Combining vinegar with bleach or any other product containing chlorine, such as powdered bleach, may produce chlorine gas. Even in low concentrations, this toxic, acrid-smelling gas can cause damage to your eyes, skin or respiratory system, and high concentrations are often fatal.

- **Protect blonde hair from chlorine** Keep golden locks from going green in a chlorinated swimming pool by rubbing in 50ml cider vinegar and letting it set for 15 minutes before diving in.

- **Use as an antiperspirant** Splash a little white vinegar under each arm in the morning and leave it to dry. In addition to combating perspiration odours, you won't get deodorant stains on your clothes.

- **Soak away aching muscles** Adding 400ml apple-cider vinegar to a bath is a great way to soothe away muscle aches and pains or simply to take the edge off a stressful day. Adding a few drops of peppermint oil to the bath is also a great muscle relaxant and stress reliever.

- **Freshen your breath** Rinse your mouth with a solution of 2 tablespoons apple-cider vinegar and 1 teaspoon salt dissolved in warm water.

- **Ease sunburn and itching** Cool painful sunburn by gently dabbing the area with a cotton-wool ball or soft cloth saturated with white or cider vinegar. (This is especially effective if applied before the burn starts to sting.) The same technique will stop itching from mosquito and other insect bites.

- **Banish bruises** Speed healing and prevent black-and-blue marks by soaking a piece of cotton gauze in white or apple-cider vinegar and leaving it on the injured area for an hour.

- **Make a poultice for corns and callouses** This is a time-honoured treatment. Soak a piece of white or stale bread with 50ml white vinegar for 30 minutes. Then break off a piece big enough to completely cover the corn. Keep the poultice in place with gauze or adhesive plaster and leave it on overnight. The next morning, the hard skin will have dissolved and the corn should be easy to remove. Older, thicker callouses may require several treatments.

...in the medicine cabinet

● **Get rid of athlete's foot** Quell the infection and quickly ease the itching by rinsing your feet three or four times a day for a few days with undiluted apple-cider vinegar. As an added precaution, soak socks or stockings in a mixture of 1 part vinegar and 4 parts water for 30 minutes before washing them.

● **Soothe a sore throat** Here are three ways that you can make a sore throat feel better:

   ● Gargle with 1 tablespoon apple-cider vinegar and 1 teaspoon salt dissolved in a glass of warm water; do this several times a day if needed.

   ● For a sore throat as a result of a cold or flu, combine 50ml cider vinegar and 50ml honey and take 1 tablespoon every 4 hours.

   ● To soothe a cough and a sore throat, mix 100ml vinegar, 100ml water, 4 teaspoons honey and 1 teaspoon hot sauce. Swallow 1 tablespoon four or five times a day, including one just before you go to bed.
   WARNING: children under a year old should never be given honey.

did you **KNOW?**

The world's only museum dedicated to vinegar, the International Vinegar Museum, is based in Roslyn, South Dakota, USA. It is run by Dr Lawrence J. Diggs, an international vinegar consultant. You can visit him on-line at www.vinegarman.com

- **Treat an active cold sore** Quickly dry up a painful cold sore by dabbing it with a cotton-wool ball saturated in white vinegar three times a day. The vinegar will quickly soothe the pain and swelling.

- **Pamper your skin** Using vinegar as a skin toner dates back to the time of Helen of Troy. After you wash your face, mix 1 tablespoon apple-cider vinegar with 400ml water as a finishing rinse to cleanse and tighten your skin.

- **Fade age or sunspots** Before you take any drastic measures to remove or cover up the brown spots on your skin caused by over-exposure to the sun or hormonal changes, try vinegar. Simply pour some full-strength apple-cider vinegar onto a cotton-wool ball and apply it to the spots for 10 minutes at least twice a day. The spots should fade or disappear within a few weeks.

- **Make nail varnish last longer** Nail varnish will have a longer life expectancy if you first dampen your nails with some vinegar on a cotton-wool ball and let it dry before applying the varnish.

- **Clean a pair of glasses** If your specs have glass lenses, apply a few drops of white vinegar and wipe them with a soft cloth to remove dirt, sweat and fingerprints.

  WARNING: don't use vinegar on plastic lenses as it will damage them.

- **Soften your cuticles** Soak your hands or feet in a bowl of undiluted white vinegar for 5 minutes before giving yourself a manicure.

...in the medicine cabinet

- **Treat a jellyfish or bee sting** Pouring undiluted vinegar on the sting will quickly take away the pain and allow you to scrape out the stinger with a credit card. You can do the same for bee stings. Note: vinegar on stings inflicted by the Portuguese man-of-war is now discouraged because it may increase the level of toxin released under the skin.

   WARNING: if you have difficulty breathing or the sting becomes inflamed and swollen, seek medical attention at once; you may be having an allergic reaction.

...in the laundry

- **Clean the washing machine** An easy way to clean out soap scum and disinfect a washing machine is to pour in 400ml vinegar, then run through a full cycle without any clothes or detergent. If the machine is very dirty, fill it with hot water, add 8 litres vinegar and let the agitator run for 8-10 minutes. Turn off the machine and let the solution stand overnight. Then empty and run the washing machine through a complete cycle.

did you **KNOW?**

Recent research has shown that vinegar may be the most simple and inexpensive way to diagnose cervical cancer in women, in particular those living in impoverished nations. In tests conducted over a two-year period, midwives in Zimbabwe used a vinegar solution to detect more than 75 per cent of potential cancers in 10,000 women (the solution turns tissue containing pre-cancerous cells white). Although the test is not as accurate as a smear, doctors believe it will soon be an important screening tool in developing countries, where only 5 per cent of women are currently tested for this often fatal disease.

- **Soften fabrics, kill bacteria, eliminate static and much more** There are so many benefits to be reaped by adding 200ml white vinegar to the rinse cycle of a washing machine that it is surprising that it isn't mentioned prominently in the owner's manual of every washing machine sold. Here are the main ones:

  - 200ml of vinegar will kill off any bacteria present in a wash load, especially if it includes cloth nappies and similar items.

  - 200ml of vinegar will keep your clothes soft and smelling fresh, so you won't need to use fabric-softener liquids and sheets.

  - 200ml of vinegar will brighten small loads of white clothes.

  - Added to the last rinse, 200ml vinegar will keep clothes lint and static-free.

  - Adding 200ml vinegar to the last rinse will set the colour of newly dyed fabrics.

  - Adding 100ml white vinegar to your machine's wash cycle will brighten up colours in each load.

- **Whiten dingy cotton sports socks** Add 200ml vinegar to 1.5 litres water in a large pan. Bring to a boil, pour it into a bucket and immerse the socks. Soak overnight. Wash as usual.

- **Stop reds from running** Soak new garments in a few cups of undiluted white vinegar for 10-15 minutes before their first wash. They should not run in subsequent washes.

- **Remove yellowing from clothes** Soak the garments overnight in a solution of 12 parts warm water to 1 part vinegar. Wash them the next morning.

- **Soften blankets** Add 400ml white vinegar to the washing machine's rinse water (or a bath or deep sink filled with water) to remove soap residue from both cotton and wool blankets before drying. This will also leave them feeling fresh and soft as new.

...in the laundry

- **Flush out the interior of an iron** To eliminate mineral deposits and prevent corrosion on a steam iron, give it an occasional cleaning by filling the reservoir with undiluted white vinegar. Place the iron in an upright position, switch on the steam setting and let the vinegar steam through it for 5-10 minutes. Refill the chamber with clean water and repeat. Finally, give the water chamber a thorough rinse with cold, clean water.

- **Sharpen your creases** You will find the creases in freshly washed clothes will come out a lot more easily if you lightly spray them with equal parts water and vinegar before ironing. For truly sharp creases in trousers and smart shirts, first dampen the garment using a cloth moistened in a solution of 1 part white vinegar and 2 parts water. Then place a brown paper bag over the crease and start ironing.

- **Make old hemlines disappear** To make the needle marks from an old hemline disappear for good, moisten the area with a cloth dipped in equal parts vinegar and water, then place it under the garment before you start ironing.

- **Clean an iron's soleplate** Make a paste by heating up equal parts vinegar and salt in a small pan. Scrub the residue. Wipe with a damp cloth to clean away what's left.

- **Erase scorch marks** You can often eliminate slight scorch marks by rubbing the spot with a cloth dampened with white vinegar, then blotting it with a clean towel. Repeat if necessary.

TAKE CARE

Keep cider vinegar out of the laundry. Using cider vinegar to pre-treat clothes or adding it to wash or rinse water may actually create stains rather than remove them. Use only distilled white vinegar for laundering.

- **Remove cigarette smell from clothing** Add 200ml vinegar to a bath filled with the hottest water your tap can muster. Close the door and hang the garments above the steam. The smell should be gone after several hours.

- **Dull the shine in a skirt or trouser seat** Brush the area lightly with a soft recycled toothbrush dipped in equal parts white vinegar and water, then pat dry with a soft towel.

- **Reshape woollens** Shrunken woollen sweaters and other items can usually be stretched back to their former size or shape after boiling them in a solution of 1 part vinegar to 2 parts water for 25 minutes. Let the garment air-dry after you have finished stretching it.

- **Spray away creases** You can often get the creases out of clothes after drying by misting them with a solution of 1 part vinegar to 3 parts water. Hang the garment up and let it air-dry. You may find this approach works better for some clothes than ironing; it is certainly a lot gentler on the material.

(KIDS' STUFF)
Make a tie-dyed T-shirt

Making tie-dyed clothing is great fun for children of all ages. Start with a few white T-shirts, then use as many colours as the cold dye selection in the craft shop will allow. (1) Dissolve each dye tin or sachet in 20ml vinegar in its own bowl or container. (2) Use rubber bands to twist the shirts into unusual shapes, then dip them into the bowls (remember to wear rubber gloves). (3) After drying, set the colours by placing an old pillowcase or thin tea towel over each shirt and ironing it with a medium-hot iron. Wait at least 24 hours, then wash each shirt separately.

...for removing stains

- **Brush off suede stains** To eliminate a fresh grease spot on suede, gently brush it with a soft toothbrush dipped in white vinegar. Let the spot air-dry, then brush with a suede brush. Repeat if necessary. You can also generally spruce up suede items by lightly wiping them with a sponge dipped in vinegar.

- **Release old stains** Set-in stains will often come out in the wash after being pre-treated with a solution of 3 tablespoons white vinegar and 2 tablespoons liquid detergent in 1 litre warm water. Rub the solution into the stain, then blot it dry before washing.

- **Get the rust out** To remove a rust stain from cotton clothes, moisten the spot with full-strength vinegar and rub in a bit of salt. Let it dry in the sunlight (otherwise a sunny window will do), then put it in the wash.

- **Clear away crayon stains** Remove crayon marks from children's clothing by rubbing them with a recycled toothbrush soaked in undiluted vinegar before you put them in the machine to wash.

- **Remove rings from collars and cuffs** Give grimy collars and cuffs the boot by scrubbing the material with a paste made from 2 parts white vinegar to 3 parts bicarbonate of soda. Let the paste set for half an hour before washing. This also removes light mildew stains from clothing.

- **Make pen ink disappear** When a pen has leaked all over the front of a shirt, wet it with white vinegar, then rub in a paste of 2 parts vinegar to 3 parts cornflour. Let the paste thoroughly dry before washing the item.

- **Sponge out serious stains** Cola, hair dye, ketchup and wine stains on washable cotton clothing should be treated within 24 hours. Sponge with undiluted vinegar and launder immediately. For severe stains, add 200-400ml vinegar to the wash cycle as well.

- **Pat away water-soluble stains** You can lift out many water-soluble stains, including beer, orange and other fruit juices, black coffee or tea and vomit from cotton clothing by patting the spot with a cloth moistened with undiluted white vinegar just before placing it in the wash. For large stains, soak the garment overnight in a solution of 3 parts vinegar to 1 part cold water before washing.

- **Pre-treat perspiration stains** Pour some vinegar directly onto the stain and rub it into the fabric before placing the item in the wash. You can also remove deodorant stains from washable shirts and blouses by gently rubbing the spot with undiluted vinegar before laundering.

- **Soak out bloodstains** It is important to treat stains on clothing as soon as possible; bloodstains are relatively easy to remove before they set but can be nearly impossible to wash out after 24 hours. If you can get to the stain before it sets, pour full-strength white vinegar on the spot. Let it soak in for 5-10 minutes, then blot well with a cloth or towel. Repeat if necessary, then wash immediately.

did you **KNOW?**

If you have just come across an old, unopened bottle of vinegar and wonder if it is still safe to use, the answer is an unqualified yes. In fact, vinegar has a practically limitless shelf life. Its acid content makes it self-preserving and even negates the need for refrigeration (although many people mistakenly believe in refrigerating open bottles). You won't see any changes in white vinegar over time, but some other types may change slightly in colour or develop a hazy appearance or a bit of sediment. However, these are strictly cosmetic changes; the vinegar itself will be virtually unchanged.

...in the great outdoors

- **Use as insect repellent** Here is an old army trick to keep away ticks and mosquitoes – essential if you are going camping or walking. About three days before you leave, start taking 1 tablespoon apple-cider vinegar three times a day. Continue throughout your trek and, hopefully, you will return home bite-free. Another time-honoured approach is to moisten a cloth or cotton ball with white vinegar and rub it over exposed skin.

- **Maintain fresh water when hiking** Keep your water supply fresh and clean tasting by adding a few drops of apple-cider vinegar to your water bottle. You can also use a half-vinegar, half-water rinse to clean out the water container at the end of each trip to kill bacteria and remove residue.

- **Make a trap to lure flying insects** Keep gnats, flies, mosquitoes and other flying insects at bay by giving them their own VIP section in the garden when you are holding a garden party or barbecue. Place a bowl filled with apple-cider vinegar near some food, but away from you and your guests. By the end of the evening, lured by its inviting contents, most of the uninvited guests will be floating inside the bowl.

- **Give ants the boot** Serve ants on your premises with an eviction notice. Pour equal parts water and white vinegar into a spray bottle. Then spray it around areas where you see the insects. Ants hate the smell of vinegar. It won't take long for them to move on to better-smelling quarters. Also keep the spray bottle handy for outdoor trips or to keep ants away from picnic or children's play areas.

- **Clean off bird droppings** When birds have been using a patio or driveway for target practice, make the messy droppings disappear by spraying them with full-strength apple-cider vinegar. Or pour the vinegar onto a rag and wipe them off.

- **Clean outdoor furniture and decks** It is hard to keep mildew at bay on wooden decking and patio furniture. But before you attack it with bleach, try a milder vinegar-based solution:

  - Keep some full-strength white vinegar in a recycled spray bottle and use it wherever you see any mildew appear. The stains will wipe straight off most surfaces, and the vinegar will keep it from coming back for a while.

  - Remove mildew from wooden decking and patio furniture by sponging them off with a solution of 200ml ammonia, 100ml white vinegar and 50g bicarbonate of soda mixed in 4 litres water. Keep an old toothbrush on hand to work the solution into corners and other tight spaces.

  - To remove unpleasant smells and inhibit mildew growth on outdoor plastic furniture and patio umbrellas, mix 400ml white vinegar and 2 tablespoons washing-up liquid in a bucket of hot water. Use a soft brush to work it into the grooves of the plastic as well as for scrubbing seat pads and umbrella fabric. Rinse with cold water; then dry in the sun.

did you **KNOW?**

For a nontoxic alternative to commercial weedkillers, vinegar is an ideal solution. In field and greenhouse studies, vinegar has been proven to be effective at killing several common weeds within their first two weeks above ground. The vinegar was hand-sprayed in concentrations varying between 5 and 10 per cent.

But that is old news to seasoned gardeners who've been using undiluted apple-cider vinegar for ages to kill all kinds of weeds (and, regrettably, the occasional ornamental plant that grew too close to the target).

...in the garage

- **Keep car windows frost-free** If you park your car outdoors during the winter, a simple way to keep frost from forming on the windows is by wiping (or, better still, spraying) the outsides of the windows with a solution of 3 parts white vinegar to 1 part water. Each vinegar coating may last up to several weeks.

- **Clean carpets in a car** A good vacuuming will remove sand and other loose debris from carpets, but it won't remove stains or ground-in dirt. Mix up a solution of equal parts water and white vinegar and sponge it into the carpet. Give the mixture a couple of minutes to settle in, then blot it up with a cloth or paper towel. This technique will also eliminate salt residue left on car carpets during winter months.

- **Clean windscreen wiper blades** When a windscreen becomes more blurry after you turn on the wipers when it is raining, it is usually due to dirty wiper blades. Wet a rag with white vinegar and run it down each blade a couple of times.

...in the garden

- **Clean a bird feeder** Birds won't flock around a dirty, sticky or crusted-over feeder. Regularly wash feeders thoroughly in equal parts apple-cider vinegar and hot water. Rinse with cold water and air-dry outdoors in full sunlight before refilling them with food.

- **Keep cut flowers fresh** Mix 2 tablespoons apple-cider vinegar and 2 tablespoons sugar with the vase water before adding the flowers. Change the water (adding more vinegar and sugar) every few days to enhance the flowers' longevity.

- **Clean lawnmower blades** Before you put a mower back in the shed, wipe down the blades with a cloth dampened with undiluted white vinegar. It will clean off leftover grass on the blades, as well as any pests hiding in the clippings.

- **Speed germination of flower seeds** You can get plants with woody seeds off to a healthier start by scarifying them, that is, lightly rubbing them between a couple of sheets of fine sandpaper and soaking them overnight in a solution of 100ml apple-cider vinegar and ½ litre warm water. Next morning, rinse the seeds off and plant them. You can use the solution (minus the sandpaper treatment) to start many herb and vegetable seeds.

- **Test soil acidity or alkalinity** To test for excess alkalinity, add a handful of earth to a container and pour in 100ml white vinegar. If the soil fizzes or bubbles, it is alkaline. To test for high acidity in soil, mix the earth with 100ml water and 100g bicarbonate of soda. This time, fizzing indicates that there is acid in the soil. To find the exact pH level, have your soil tested or pick up a simple, do-it-yourself kit or meter.

- **Stop leaves from yellowing prematurely** The appearance of yellow leaves on plants accustomed to acidic soils, such as azaleas, hydrangeas and gardenias, may signal a drop in the plant's iron intake or a shift in the ground's pH above a comfortable 5.0 level. Either problem can be resolved by watering the soil around the afflicted plants once a week for three weeks with 200ml of a solution made by mixing 2 tablespoons apple-cider vinegar in 1 litre water.

- **Encourage blooms on azaleas and gardenias** Both bushes grow most successfully in acidic soils (with pH levels between 4 and 5.5). To keep them healthy and to produce more flowers, water them every week or so with 3 tablespoons white vinegar mixed in 4 litres water. Note: don't apply the solution while the bush is in bloom, as it may shorten the life of the flowers or harm the plant.

...in the garden

- **Eliminate insects around the garden** For a nontoxic trap, fill a 2 litre soft-drink bottle with 200ml apple-cider vinegar and 200g sugar. Next, cut a banana skin into small pieces, put them in the bottle, add 200ml cold water and shake. Tie a piece of string around the neck of the bottle and hang it from a low tree branch or place on the ground, to trap and kill any investigating insects.

- **Treat rust and other plant diseases** Use vinegar to treat rust, black spot and powdery mildew. Mix 2 tablespoons apple-cider vinegar in 2 litres water and pour some into a spray bottle. Spray the solution onto affected plants in the morning or early evening (when it is cooler) until the condition is cured.

- **Keep out four-legged creatures** Some animals, including cats, deer, dogs and rabbits, can't stand the smell of vinegar even after it has dried. You can keep these unauthorised visitors out of the garden by soaking several recycled rags in white vinegar and placing them on stakes around your vegetables. Re-soak the rags about every 7-10 days to keep them working effectively.

- **Exterminate dandelions and unwanted grass** Spray weeds with full-strength white or apple-cider vinegar. Early in the season, give each plant a single spray in its midsection, or in the middle of the flower before the plants go to seed. Aim another shot near the stem at ground level so the vinegar can soak down to the roots. Note: re-spray if it rains the next day.

...for pet care

- **Directly protect against fleas and ticks** Fill a spray bottle with equal parts water and vinegar and apply it directly to the dog's coat and rub it in well. You may have more trouble doing this with cats, because they hate the smell.

- **Clean your pet's ears** If your dog has been scratching his ears a lot more than usual lately, swab his ears with a cotton-wool ball or soft cloth dipped in a solution of 2 parts vinegar and 1 part water. This will keep them clean as well as helping to deter ear mites and bacteria. It also soothes minor itches from mosquito bites and similar.

    WARNING: do not apply vinegar to open lacerations. If you spot a cut in your pet's ears, seek veterinary treatment.

- **Keep cats away** If you want to keep your cats away from anything, sprinkle some full-strength distilled white vinegar around the area or onto the object itself. Cats don't like the smell of vinegar and will avoid it.

- **Add to pet's drinking water** Adding a teaspoon of apple-cider vinegar to a dog or cat's drinking water provides needed nutrients to its diet, gives it a shinier, healthier-looking coat and also acts as a natural deterrent to fleas and ticks, which hate the smell.

- **Get rid of a pet's territorial marks** When a puppy or kitten is being toilet-trained it will often wet previously soiled spots. After cleaning up the mess, it is essential to remove the scent from the floor, carpet or sofa so that they don't continue to use them. And nothing does that better than vinegar:

    - On a floor, blot up as much of the puddle as possible. Then mop with equal parts white vinegar and warm water. (On a wood or vinyl floor, test a few drops of vinegar in an inconspicuous area to make sure that it won't harm the finish.) Dry with a cloth or paper towel.

    - For carpets, rugs and upholstery, thoroughly blot the area with a towel or some rags. Then pour a little undiluted vinegar over the spot. Blot it up with a towel, then reapply the vinegar and let it air-dry. Once the vinegar dries, the spot should be completely free from odour.

...for the DIY-er

- **Wash concrete off your skin** Even though you wear rubber gloves when working with concrete, some inevitably splashes onto your skin. Prolonged contact with wet concrete can cause skin to crack and may even lead to eczema. Use undiluted white vinegar to wash dried concrete or mortar off the skin, then wash with warm, soapy water.

- **De-grease grates, fans and air-conditioner grilles** All air-conditioner grilles, heating grates and fan blades eventually develop a layer of dust and grease. To clean them, wipe with full-strength white vinegar. Use an old toothbrush to work the vinegar into the tight spaces on air-conditioner grilles and extractor fans.

- **Disinfect air-conditioner and humidifier filters** An air-conditioner or humidifier filter can quickly become inundated with dust, soot, pet dander and even potentially harmful bacteria. Every ten days or so, clean the filter with equal parts white vinegar and warm water. Let the filter soak in the solution for an hour, then simply squeeze it dry before using again. If the filters are particularly dirty, let them soak overnight.

- **Remove paint fumes** Place a couple of shallow dishes filled with undiluted white vinegar around a freshly painted room to quickly get rid of the strong paint smell.

- **Keep the paint intact on a cement floor** Painted cement floors have a tendency to peel after a while. Keep the paint stuck to the cement longer by giving the floor an initial coating with white vinegar before you paint it. Wait until the vinegar has dried, then begin painting. This same technique will also help to keep paint adhered to galvanised metal.

- **Peel off wallpaper** Removing old wallpaper can be messy, but you can get it to peel off easily by soaking it with a vinegar solution. Spray equal parts white vinegar and water on the wallpaper until it is saturated and wait a few minutes. Then whip the softened paper off the wall with a wallpaper scraper. If it is stubborn, try carefully scoring the wallpaper with the scraper before you spray.

- **Slow drying of plaster** To keep plaster pliable for a bit longer so that you can smooth it properly before it sets, add a couple of tablespoons of white vinegar to the plaster mix. It will slow down the drying process and give you the extra time you need for a perfect finish.

- **Revive your paintbrushes** To remove dried-on paint from a synthetic-bristle paintbrush, soak it in full-strength white vinegar until the paint dissolves and the bristles are soft and pliable, then wash in hot, soapy water. If a paintbrush seems beyond hope, before you throw it away, try boiling it in 200-400ml vinegar for 10 minutes, followed by a thorough washing in soapy water.

- **Get rid of rust** If you want to restore some rusty old tools that you have unearthed in the shed or picked up at a car-boot sale, soak them in full-strength white vinegar for several days. The same treatment is equally effective at removing the rust from corroded nuts and bolts. And you can pour vinegar on rusted hinges and screws to loosen them up for removal.

(**SCIENCE** FAIR)
Coat a nail with copper

Mix 100ml vinegar and ¼ teaspoon salt in a glass jar. Add 25 1p pieces to the solution and let them sit for 5 minutes. While you are waiting, take a large iron nail and clean it with some bicarbonate of soda applied to a damp sponge. Rinse off the nail and place it into the solution. After 15 minutes, the nail will be coated with copper, while the pennies will shine like new. This is a result of the acetic acid in the vinegar combining with the copper on the pennies to form copper acetate, which then accumulates on the nail.

Vodka

- **Make your own vanilla extract** Slice a dried vanilla pod open from top to bottom. Place in a glass jar and cover with 150ml vodka. Seal and leave for 4-6 months, shaking occasionally. Filter through an unbleached coffee filter or cheesecloth and it's ready to use.

- **Clean glass and jewellery** A few drops of vodka will clean glass or crystalline gemstones, such as diamonds or emeralds. Note: avoid getting alcohol on any gemstone that is not a crystal.

- **Kill weeds in the garden** For a quick and easy weedkiller, mix 30ml vodka, a few drops washing-up liquid and 400ml water in a spray bottle. Spray it on the weed leaves until the mixture runs off. Apply it at midday on a sunny day to weeds growing in direct sunlight, because the alcohol breaks down the waxy cuticle covering on leaves, leaving them susceptible to dehydration in sunlight. It won't work in shady spots.

- **Keep cut flowers fresh** To keep cut flowers fresh for as long as possible, you must minimise the growth of bacteria in the water and provide nourishment. Add a few drops of vodka (or any clear spirit) to the water to give anti-bacterial action and 1 teaspoon sugar. Change the water every other day, refreshing the vodka and sugar each time.

did you **KNOW?**

Essential to James Bond's Martini and so intrinsic to Russian culture that its name derives from the Russian word for 'water' (*voda*), vodka was first made in the 1400s as an antiseptic and painkiller. Classically, vodka starts as a soupy mixture of ground wheat or rye that's fermented (sugars in the grain are converted into alcohol by yeast), then distilled (heated until the alcohol evaporates and then condenses). Flavourings such as citrus were originally added to mask the taste of impurities, but are used today for enhancement and brand identification.

Wallpaper

- **Line drawers and shelves** Wallpaper remnants can be an excellent substitute for shelf lining paper when used to line dresser drawers or cupboard shelves, especially designs with raised patterns or fabrics, which may add a bit of friction to prevent things from moving around. Cut the wallpaper to fit the space.

- **Protect schoolbooks** If your child goes through book covers on textbooks on a regular basis, make use of unused rolls of wallpaper, especially vinyl or coated papers. Book covers made of wallpaper are typically stronger than even traditional brown-paper wrapping; they can hold their own against pens and pencils, and are much better at handling the elements.

- **Restore a folding screen** If you have an old folding screen that has become torn or stained over the years, give it a new look by covering it with leftover wallpaper. Use masking tape to hold the strips at top and bottom if you don't want to glue it on top of the original material.

- **Make a jigsaw puzzle** What can you do with leftover wallpaper? Why not use a piece to make a jigsaw puzzle? Cut off a medium-sized rectangular piece of patterned wallpaper and glue it onto a piece of thin cardboard. Once it has dried, cut it up into lots of curvy and angular shapes. It will give you or the children something to do on a rainy day.

super item **50 uses!**
WD-40...

...around the house

- **Treat your shoes** Spray WD-40 on new leather shoes before you start wearing them regularly. It will soften the leather and make the shoes more comfortable. Keep the shoes waterproof and shiny by spraying them periodically and buffing gently with a soft cloth. To stop shoes squeaking, spray WD-40 at the spot where the sole and heel join.

- **Clean, lubricate and prevent corrosion on guitar strings** Spray WD-40 on a rag and wipe over the guitar strings – don't spray or you will get a WD-40 build-up on the body and neck of the instrument. Apply a small amount of WD-40 after each session.

- **Separate stuck glassware** Stuck glasses will separate if you squirt them with WD-40. Wait a few seconds for it to work its way between the glasses, and then gently pull them apart. Wash the glasses thoroughly before you use them.

- **Tone down polyurethane shine** A new coat of polyurethane varnish can sometimes make a wood floor look too shiny. To tone down the shine and cut the glare, spray some WD-40 onto a soft cloth and wipe the floor with it.

- **Remove strong glue** To remove superglue from fingers spray WD-40 directly onto the fingers and rub your hands together until they no longer feel sticky.

- **Remove a stuck ring** A short burst of WD-40 will get the ring to slide right off. Remember to wash your hands after spraying them with WD-40.

- **Free stuck fingers** Use WD-40 to free a child's finger when he or she gets it stuck in a bottle. Just spray it on the finger, let it seep in around the finger, then pull the finger out. Always wash both the hand and the bottle afterwards.

- **Loosen zips** Stubborn zips will run with ease after you spray them with WD-40. Spray it on and pull the zip up and down a few times to distribute the lubricant evenly over the teeth. To avoid getting the WD-40 on the fabric, spray it on a plastic lid; then apply the spray with an artist's brush.

- **Keep puppies from chewing** To keep puppies from chewing on telephone and television-cable lines, spray WD-40 on the lines. Dogs hate the smell.

- **Get rid of cockroaches and repel insects** Don't let cockroaches or other insects get the upper hand in your home:

  - If you've had cockroach infestations in the past, keep a can of WD-40 to hand; a squirt kills them instantly.

  - To keep insects out of the house, spray WD-40 on windowsills and frames, and door frames. Be careful not to inhale the fumes when you spray and do not do this at all if you have babies or small children at home.

TAKE CARE

• Do not spray WD-40 near an open flame or other heat source or near electrical currents or battery terminals. Always disconnect appliances before spraying.
• Do not place a WD-40 can in direct sunlight or on hot surfaces. Never store it in temperatures above 50°C or puncture the pressurised can.
• Use WD-40 in well-ventilated areas. Never swallow or inhale it (if ingested, call a doctor immediately).

...around the house

- **Unstick wobbly shopping-trolley wheels** It may sound strange, but you could take a can of WD-40 with you whenever you go food shopping. So when you get stuck with a sticky, wobbly wheeled shopping trolley, you can spray the wheels to reduce friction and wobbling. Less wobbling means faster shopping. Note: spray the wheels outside the store, not inside.

- **Remove chewing gum from hair** Don't panic if you or the kids get gum in your hair – spray it with WD-40, and it will comb out with ease.
     WARNING: make sure you are in a well-ventilated area when you spray and take care to avoid contact with the eyes.

- **Keep wooden tool handles splinter-free** You can prolong preventing wooden handles from splintering by rubbing in a generous amount of WD-40. It will shield the wood from moisture and corrosive elements and keep it smooth and splinter-free for the life of the tool.

did you **KNOW?**

• In 1953, Norm Larsen founded the Rocket Chemical Company in San Diego, in southern California, USA, and, with two employees, set out to develop a rust-preventing solvent and de-greaser for the aerospace industry. On the fortieth try, they succeeded in creating a 'water-displacement' compound. The name WD-40 stands for 'Water Displacement – 40th Try'.
• In 1958, a few years after WD-40's first industrial use, the company put it into aerosol cans and sold it for home use – inspired by employees who smuggled cans out of the plant to use at home.
• In 1962, when astronaut John Glenn, Jr., circled the Earth in *Friendship* the space capsule was coated with WD-40 and so was the Atlas missile, which was used to boost it into space.
• In 1969, the Rocket Chemical Company renamed itself the WD-40 Company after its renowned product.

...for cleaning things

- **Remove scuff marks** Tough black scuff marks or tar on hard-surfaced floors can be quickly shifted if you spray them with WD-40. It won't harm the surface and you won't have to scrub as hard. Note: remember to open the windows if you are trying to clean a heavily marked floor.

- **Clean off dried glue** Remove dried-on glue from virtually any hard surface with ease. Simply spray WD-40 onto the spot, wait at least 30 seconds, and wipe clean with a damp cloth.

- **De-grease your hands** Spray a small amount of WD-40 into your hands and rub them together for a few seconds. Wipe with a paper towel and wash with soap and water.

- **Remove stickers from glass** Spray a little WD-40 on the sticker and glass, wait a few minutes, then use a no-scratch spatula or acrylic scraper to scrape the sticker off. The solvents in WD-40 will cause the adhesive to lose its stickiness.

- **Wipe away tea stains** To remove tea stains from worktops, spray a little WD-40 on a damp cloth and wipe the stains away.

- **Clean carpet stains** Spray the stain with WD-40, wait 2 minutes, then use a carpet cleaner or gently cleanse with a sponge and warm, soapy water. Continue until the stain has gone.

- **Clean a toilet bowl** You don't need a specialised product to clean filth and limescale from a toilet bowl. Use WD-40 instead. Spray it into the bowl for a couple of seconds and swish with a toilet brush. The solvents in the WD-40 will help to dissolve the gunk and limescale.

- **Condition leather furniture** Keep a leather chair or sofa in tip-top shape by softening and preserving it with WD-40. Spray it on and buff with a soft cloth. The combination of ingredients in WD-40 will clean, penetrate, lubricate and protect the leather.

...for cleaning things

- **Pre-treat blood and other stains** Spray WD-40 directly onto the bloodstains, wait a couple of minutes and launder as usual. The WD-40 will help to lift the stain so that it will come out easily in the wash. Try to treat the stain while it is still fresh, because it will be harder to remove once it has set. Use WD-40 to pre-treat other stubborn stains on clothing, such as tomato or sauce stains, lipstick, dirt, grease and ink.

- **Clean your hearing aid** To give a hearing aid a thorough cleaning, use a cotton bud dipped in WD-40. Do not use WD-40 to try to loosen up the volume control (it will loosen it too much).

- **Clean a blackboard** Spray WD-40 onto the blackboard and wipe with a clean cloth. It will look as clean and fresh as it did on the first day it was used.

- **Remove marker and crayon marks** Spray some WD-40 onto marks on the wall, furniture or appliances and wipe with a clean rag. WD-40 will not damage the paint or most wallpaper (test fabric or more ornate wall coverings first).

...in the garden

- **Protect a bird feeder** To keep squirrels from taking over a bird feeder, spray a generous amount of WD-40 on top of the feeder. Squirrels will slide off the top.

- **Keep animals off flowerbeds** Animals love digging up your favourite plants, but hate the smell of WD-40. To keep the animals out and your flowers looking beautiful, spray WD-40 evenly over the flowerbeds once or twice over the course of the season.

- **Remove cat-paw marks** To remove the paw marks off patio furniture or the bonnet of a car, spray some WD-40 on them and wipe with a clean rag.

- **Keep wasps from building nests** Mist some WD-40 under all the eaves of your house or wherever wasps like to settle in your home to deter their nest-building.

- **Relieve a bee sting** Spray WD-40 directly onto the bite site. It will soothe the pain at once.

- **Rejuvenate a barbecue grill** To make a worn old barbecue grill look like new again, spray it liberally with WD-40, wait a few seconds, then scrub with a wire brush. Only use WD-40 on a grill that has cooled off completely.

- **Keep a shovel snow-free** Make shovelling snow quicker and less strenuous by keeping the snow from sticking to your shovel and weighing it down. Spray a thin layer of WD-40 on the shovel blade, and the snow will slide straight off.

- **Waterproof boots and shoes** Give winter boots and shoes a coat of WD-40. It will act as a barrier so water can't penetrate the material. To remove salt stains, spray WD-40 onto boots and shoes and wipe with a clean rag.

did you **KNOW?**

Around a million cans of WD-40 are sold every week and it can be found in 187 countries around the world. The secret recipe, which has had the same basic ingredients for more than 50 years, is known only by a handful of people within the WD-40 Company. A lone 'brew master' mixes the product at corporate headquarters in San Diego.

The latest innovation from WD-40 is the 'No Mess Pen'. It is designed to be used for small jobs around the home, such as a squeaky drawer where using a spray can might be rather too messy. It is also highly portable, which is ideal if you need WD-40 on the move.

- **Renew faded plastic furniture** Bring colour and shine back to faded plastic patio furniture. Spray WD-40 on the surface and wipe with a clean, dry cloth. You will be surprised at the results.

- **Kill thistles** Don't let prickly weeds ruin your garden. Just spray some WD-40 on them and they will wither and die.

- **Remove dog mess from a shoe** Spray some WD-40 on the affected sole and use an old toothbrush to clean the crevices. Rinse with cold water.

...in the great outdoors

- **Remove old wax from skis and snowboards** Spray the base of your skis or snowboard sparingly with WD-40. Then scrape with an acrylic scraper. Use a brass brush to clean the base thoroughly and remove any oxidised base material.

- **Clean and protect golf clubs** Spray golf clubs with WD-40 after each use. Also use it to help loosen the spikes on golfing shoes.

- **Remove burrs** To remove burrs from a horse's mane or tail without tearing out or cutting its hair out, spray on some WD-40. You will be able to slide the burrs out of the hair with ease. This will also work for other animals with burrs or grasses stuck in their fur.

did you **KNOW?**

WD-40 is one of the few products with its own fan club. The official WD-40 Fan Club has more than 63,000 members and is growing. Over the years members have contributed thousands of unique uses for the product. The strangest use occurred in Hong Kong where a python was caught in the suspension of a bus. WD-40 was used to remove the unfortunate serpent.

- **Protect a boat from corrosion** To protect a boat's outer finish from salt water and corrosion, spray WD-40 on the stern as soon as you have pulled it out of the water. This will save you from having to replace parts and keep your boat looking like new.

- **Remove barnacles on boats** Use WD-40 to make removing barnacles from the bottom of a boat easier. Spray generously with WD-40, wait a few seconds, then scrape off the barnacles with a putty knife. Repeat as necessary. Use sandpaper to get rid of all of the remnants and corrosive glue still left by the barnacles.

- **Untangle fishing lines** Spray a tangled fishing line with WD-40 and use a pin to undo any small knots. Use WD-40 to extend the life of curled fishing lines. Pull out the first 3-6m of line and spray with WD-40 the night before you plan to use it.

- **Protect horses' hoofs** Winter horse riding can be painful for your horse if ice forms on its shoes. For protection, spray the bottom of the horse's hoofs with WD-40 before you set out.

- **Spray on fishing lures** Salmon fishermen spray their lures with WD-40 because it attracts fish and disguises the smell of humans that may scare them. Spray it onto lures or live bait before you cast your line. But first check local regulations to make sure the use of chemical-laced lures and bait is legal where you are fishing.

TIP the little red straw

'I've lost the red straw!' has been a common cry among countless users of WD-40 over the years. In response, the company introduced a notched cap, designed to hold the straw in place across the top of the can when not in use. Because the straw exceeds the width of the can by a substantial margin, the notch may be of little use to those with limited storage space. To save space, store the straw by bending it inside the lip of the can or simply tape it to the side as it was when first purchased. A snug rubber band will also work well.

...in the garage

- **Clean and restore a licence plate** To help to restore a licence plate that is beginning to rust, spray it with WD-40 and wipe with a clean rag. This will remove light surface rust and help to prevent more rust from forming and it won't feel greasy.

- **Remove stuck spark plugs** To save time replacing spark plugs, spray WD-40 onto stuck plugs so they can be removed quickly and easily.

- **Remove 'paint rub' from another car** If another vehicle has got a bit too close for comfort, leaving paint streaks on your car, you can remove the stains and restore the car's original finish by spraying the affected area with WD-40. Wait a few seconds, then wipe with a clean rag.

- **Revive spark plugs** When you can't get your car to start on a rainy or humid day, spray some WD-40 on the high tension leads before you try starting it up again. WD-40 displaces water and keeps moisture away from the plugs.

- **Stop insects from getting stuck on the car** Spray WD-40 on the grille and bonnet before driving and most of the insects will slide straight off. The few that are left can be wiped off easily without damaging the finish.

- **Clean oil spots from the drive** If oil has leaked onto a concrete driveway, spray it with a generous amount of WD-40 and then hose it down with water.

TIP don't overdo the WD-40

When you need to apply tiny amounts of WD-40 to a specific area, such as the electrical contacts on an electric guitar, an aerosol spray is overkill. Instead, use the pen version or store a little WD-40 in a clean nail varnish bottle (with cap brush) and brush on as needed.

Yoghurt

- **Relieve sunburn** For the quick, temporary relief of mild sunburn, apply cold plain yoghurt. The yoghurt adds moisture and its coldness soothes at the same time. Rinse with cool water.

- **Make play finger paint** Mix food colouring with yoghurt to make finger paints for the kids. Teach them about primary and secondary colours by getting them to put a few drops of yellow food colouring and a few drops of red in the yoghurt to make green finger paint. Or mix red and blue to produce purple.

- **Cure dog or cat flatulence** If your dog or cat has been producing a lot of noxious gas lately, the problem may be a lack of the digestive bacteria that prevent gas and diarrhoea. The active culture in plain yoghurt can help to restore the helpful bacteria. Add 2 teaspoons yoghurt to the food for cats or small dogs weighing up to 6kg. Add 1 tablespoon for medium-sized dogs weighing 7-15kg. Add 2 tablespoons for large dogs weighing 16-38kg. Add 3 tablespoons for dogs larger than that.

- **Make moss 'paint' for the garden** To encourage attractive moss to grow, put 200ml plain active-culture yoghurt into a blender along with a handful of moss and about 200ml water. Blend for about 30 seconds. Spread the mixture wherever you want moss to grow, as long as the spot is cool and shady. Keep misting the moss with water until it is established.

- **Make a face mask** You can give your face a quick boost by applying yoghurt:

  - To cleanse your skin and tighten the pores, put some plain yoghurt on your face and let it sit for about 20 minutes.

  - For a revitalising face mask, mix 1 teaspoon plain yoghurt with the juice from ¼ slice of orange, some of the orange pulp and 1 teaspoon aloe vera. Leave the mixture on your face for at least 5 minutes before rinsing it off.

Zips

- **Secure your valuables** Nothing ruins a holiday like reaching into your pocket and discovering it has been picked. To keep your wallet, passport and other valuables safe, sew a zip into the inside pocket of your jacket to keep items safe inside.

- **Make a sock puppet** Create a cheerful sock puppet that will keep young children amused for hours. Just sew on buttons for the nose and eyes and some wool for hair, and use a small smiling upturned zip to make the mouth.

- **Create convertible trousers** Here's a great idea for hikers and bikers who like to travel light. Cut the legs off a pair of jeans or other comfortable trousers above the knee. Then reattach the legs using zips. You can zip off the legs when it gets warm and zip them back on for cool mornings and evenings. Besides lightening your load, you won't need to search for a place to change.

- **Keep your keys safe** Have you ever lost your car keys in the sand at the seaside? Make sure it never happens again. Stitch a small zipped pocket – use matching terry towelling if you can – to one corner of the wrong side of your beach towel, just big enough for your keys, sunglasses and maybe a few coins.

Index

A

acidic foods 14, 43
acne, clearing up 207
address labels 8, 71;
waterproofing 200
adhesive plaster 9, 29
adhesives, removing 224
age spots, lightening 175, 359
air conditioners: degreasing
grilles 372; disinfecting filters
372; musty-smelling 39
air freshener, homemade 101,
131, 261, 292
Alka-Seltzer 10-11
allergic reactions: to aspirin 28;
to bee stings 51; to fabric
softener 357
aluminium cans 12
aluminium foil 13-21; DIY uses
20-1; garden uses 17-18;
household uses 15-16;
kitchen uses 13-14; laundry
uses 16; outdoor uses 19
aluminium pie dishes 22-3
ammonia 60
animals, deterring 380; see also
specific animals
ant control 63, 86, 133, 210,
227, 230, 261, 294, 309,
366
anti-perspirants 53, 357
aphids, deterring 38
apples 24; shrivelled apples
266
appliances: cleaning 330;
noisy 81
art: artist's palette 21, 161;
artwork holder 75; bowls
108; children's 78, 108;
finger painting 114, 163,
385
ashes 25, 317
aspirin 26-8
athlete's foot 52, 190, 358
azaleas 369

B

babies: baby bottles,
deodorising 331; baby
food 162, 166, 181; baby
shampoo 280; bibs 94;
bleeding gums 320; bottles
44; changing tables 232;
clothing 54; cradle cap 51;
footprint paperweight 180;
high-chair drop cloth 249;
inoculation 320; nappies
119; nappy rash 50, 229;
shampoo for 229; vomit 49
baby oil 29-30
baby powder 31-2
baby wipes 33; homemade 273
baby-wipes containers 34
backs, aching 192
bacon, cooking 221
bacteria, killing 361
baking powder substitute 45
baking trays 117
balloons 35-6, 315
bananas 37-8
bandages: Band-Aid plaster 9;
DIY uses 35; keeping dry 35;
plasters, removing 278
barbecues: cleaning 19, 241,
381; drippings from 19;
hose, protecting 146
basins, cleaning 332
basters 39; substitute for 298
bathing: bubble baths 279;
citrus baths 323
bath oil 40
bathrooms: bath cushion,
homemade 276; bath
enamel, cleaning 269;
bath plug, stopgap 248;
bicarbonate of soda in 52-4;
childproofing 254; cleaning
29, 33, 116, 127, 164, 279,
307, 332, 355; mildew in
82; mirrors, foggy 82, 281,
332; salt for 269; smelly 53,

87; tidying 282; tumblers,
washing out 356; vinegar
for 354-6
batteries 16, 173, 312; see also
under cars
beanbags 41, 281
beans (dried) 41
bed linen see sheets
bedrooms, organising 282
beds 66; bed slats, securing
254; bed trays 75
beer 42
bees 51, 71; beeswax 71
belts: belt buckles 201;
storing 100
berries: keeping fresh 106;
stain removal 175, 353
bicarbonate of soda 36, 43-57;
bathroom uses 52-4; DIY
uses 55-6; garden uses
57; household uses 48-50;
kitchen uses 43-5; laundry
uses 54-5; medicine-cabinet
uses 50-2; pet uses 56-7;
shelf life of 56
bicycles: chain lubrication 111;
streamers 124
bin bags, closing 249
birdbaths 342
bird feeders: cleaning 368;
protecting 380
birds: attracting 38; deterring
18, 22, 36; droppings,
cleaning 366; feeding 72,
99, 188, 246
biscuits 117; biscuit dough 157;
cutting 165, 166
bites or stings 11, 28, 51, 89,
185, 208, 260, 360, 381
blackboard cleaning 380
blackheads, removing 128
blankets: softening 361; storing
195, 323
bleach 54, 58-60, 174
blinds: cleaning 132, 287, 307,
343; repairing 203

bloodstains, removing 115, 156, 309, 365, 380
boats 383
bookmarks, making 126, 136, 220
books: bindings, reinforcing 123, 144; cleaning 32, 85, 87; covering 124, 215, 240, 375; mould on 32, 87
boots *see* shoes and boots
borax 61-3
bottles: deodorising 293; gripping caps 310; smelly 192
bowls, artistic 108
brass 194; cleaning 134, 171, 258, 345
bread 64; baking 98, 135; dough, cleaning up 164, 263; keeping fresh 216; keeping warm 13
breakables, storing 275, 287
breath freshening 98, 175, 269, 357
brickwork, brightening up 346
brooches, homemade 120
brooms 179, 254, 260
broth, grease removal 221
bruises 357
bubble wrap 65-6
buckets 67-8
buff polishing 287
burns: blister prevention 160; burned tongue, soothing 306; razor burns 52, 319; relieving 51, 52, 340
burrs, removing 382
butter 69-70, 157, 342
butterflies: attracting 38; making 223
buttons: extending 254; preventing loss of 204; protecting pearl 204

C

cabinets *see* cupboards and wardrobes; medicine cabinets

cakes 117; decorating 13, 150; keeping fresh 24
cake tins: greasing 275; novelty 14
callouses, poultices for 357
camping 19, 23, 66, 67, 99; equipment storage 167; marking a campsite 35; showers 67; tents 85, 145
candles 71, 151, 187, 312; extending life of 137; lighting 335; outdoor candleholder 250; as table centrepiece 22; wax removal 137, 229, 346
candlesticks, removing wax from 137, 229
cane chair seats 55
canoes, repairing 145
can openers, cleaning 222
cans 72-4; hermetically sealed 73; *see also* aluminium cans
car-boot sale signs 242
cardboard boxes 75-6
cardboard tubes 77-80; from carpet shops 78; children's uses 80; garden uses 79; household uses 77-9; outdoor uses 79
carpentry, simplifying 178
carpet remnants 81
carpets and rugs 40, 104; cleaning 42, 48; dents, removing 159; freshening up 114; restoring 347; slipping 256; stain removal 33, 42, 49, 62, 114, 259, 281, 309, 347, 379; static shock 129
carrots 103
cars 368; batteries 26, 56, 128, 231, 288; boots 345; carpets, cleaning 368; changing tyres 287; chipped paint 203; cleaning 110, 131, 278, 287, 290, 297; dashboard, scratched 30; deodorising 286, 345; in icy weather 179, 218, 270, 368; key, secret 143; licence plate, restoring 384; lights

124; mats 81; mirrors 242; navigation aid 93; 'paint rub' removal 384; radiator leaks 227; repairing dents in 250; safety reflectors 314; spark plugs, reviving 384; spark plugs, stuck 384; tyres 105, 287, 338; *see also* windscreens
car wax 82
cast iron, rust-free 101, 151, 211, 222
castor oil 83
cat litter 57, 84-5, 239
cats: cat hair 148; deterring 103, 189, 210, 370, 371; flatulence 385; paw marks removal 381; scratching, deterring from 314; scratching post 81; *see also* pets
caulk 123
CDs *see* compact discs
ceilings: ceiling fans 220, 232; drilling holes in 250; marks on 86
cement floors, painting 372
chalk 86
chandeliers, dusting 148, 339
charcoal briquettes 87, 121
charity shops 238
cheese 69, 117; grating 110, 274; mould on 69, 265; slicing 342
cheesecloth 88
cherries, stoning 220
chest rub 89; *see also* vapour rub
chewing gum 90; removing 40, 160, 177, 224, 229, 289, 378
chicken pox 205
chicken, roasting 24
children: childproofing 315; children's artwork, protecting 154; children's sport 76; child safety 35; child's room, organising 282; lunch box for 182; mattresses 14, 237; medicine for 160; tape uses

D

dandruff control 26, 50, 176, 191, 269, 356
decking: cleaning 367; weathered look 55
deer, deterring 227, 281, 286, 328, 370
dehumidifier, homemade 87, 100
de-icers 55
delicate items, dusting 148
dental floss 117
dentures 53
denture tablets 118
desks, organising 74, 179
desserts, keeping fresh 306
detergent 44, 54; boosting 174
dishwashers: baskets for 138; deodorising 44; detergent, homemade 44; washing out 350
disinfectant spray, homemade 59
disposable nappies 119
DIY: aluminium foil for 20-1; bicarbonate of soda for 55-6; paper bags for 218; petroleum jelly for 230-1; plastic bags for 243; plastic bottles for 247; tape for 314-5; using tights for 326-7; vinegar for 372-3
dogs: deterring 189, 370; dog house 81; dog mess, removing 382; dog odour 131; flatulence 385; puppy-training aid 377; ticks 308; water for 276; see also pets
doors 75, 105; banging 256, 302; squeaky 71, 110, 231, 281
dough 157, 164, 263, 325; coloured 274
drains: deodorising 343; unblocking 44, 62, 118, 141, 269, 289, 343
drawers: freshening up 131; lining 179, 375; musty 48; sticking 71, 285

drill bits, storing 226
drying rack, improvised 339
dry shampooing 205; for pets 31, 114
duct tape see gaffer tape
dust 102, 317; dusting 64, 148, 213, 214, 232; repelling 129, 132
dust cloths 33
dyeing: fabrics 317, 363; hair 228, 319-20

E

earrings 113, 120
earwigs, capturing 141, 197
egg cartons 121
eggs 122; beating 267; boiled 354; egg separator 140; egg-stain removal 28; freezing 161; freshness of 264; hard-boiled 264; poached 72, 265, 354; spilled 267
electrical equipment 132; labelling 8; tangle-free cords 77, 336
electrical tape 123-4
electric grill, cleaning 330
emery boards 125; alternative to 271
envelopes 126; sealing 199
Epsom salts 127-8
extension cords, storing 68
eyebrows, wild 178
eyes: make-up removal 278; puffy morning 252; tired 83, 320; watering (from onions) 209

F

fabrics: bleaching 174; delicate 151, 174; dyeing with tea 317; frayed 204; grease removal 86; mildew on 58, 62; scraps 77; softening 361; stain removal 154, 155,

290, 309, 331; storing 151; tie-dyeing 363
fabric softener 129-30, 131
fabric-softener sheets 131-2; homemade 130
facecloths 276
facials see under skin care
fans blades, degreasing 372
feet: aching 69, 89; revitalising 278, 341; smelly 54, 292, 320
fertiliser see plant food
file folders 126
fingernails: mending broken 202; pampering 175; strengthening 184
fingers, stuck 377
fire extinguishers, improvised 47
fireplaces 25, 317; cleaning 49, 259
fires, starting 218
firewood 25
first-aid kits 34
fish (as food): fish smells 43, 69, 224; frozen 185; tenderising 352
fish (as pets): cave in tank 135; goldfish 261; tanks, cleaning 39, 261; tanks, vacuuming 322
fishing 11; bait worms 102; casting 111; fishing floats 112; lures 383; nets, homemade 88; sinkers 169; untangling lines 383
flatulence 90; in dogs 385
flea control 261, 285, 370
floors 226, 346; cleaning 177, 226, 299, 316, 348, 348, 379; patching 73, 164, 202; protecting 81, 112, 123, 287; squeaky 309; vinyl, cleaning 226, 348; vinyl, reattaching tiles 20
flour 133-4; flour-dusting 257, 325
flowerpots 135, 295
flowers: artificial, cleaning 214, 258; cut flowers 27, 35, 59,

Picture credits

Additional photography:

Shutterstock: 8, Marcel Mooij; 9, Shapiso; 10 bot, marylooo; 14 bot, Aaron Amat; 15, Matt Antonino; 18, Kairos; 19, Tatuasha; 26, EML; 28, Subbotina Anna; 30, terekhov igor; 32 left, Sandra Cunningham; 35, Melanie DeFazio; 36 top, Leigh Prather; 37, Denis Pepin; 38, Neo Edmund; 44, Elnur; 45, Brett Mulcahy; 50, lev dolgachov; 51, Ronald Sumners; 54, Wolfgang Amri; 55, Margo Harrison; 60, Roman Sigaev; 62, ultimathule; 71, kmiragaya; 73, maniacpixel; 76, WilleeCole; 78, Jacek Chabraszewski; 80, Kristina Stasiuliene; 82 left, Semjonow Juri; 85 bot, Gladskikh Tatiana; 86, Serg 64; 90, marylooo; 92, Monkey Business Images; 95, Arvind Balaraman; 97, Noam Armonn; 100, Blaz Kure; 101, Fotocrisis; 103, Paul-Andre Belle-Isle; 106, Ivonne Wierink; 107, Marcel Mooij; 110, Stukkey; 113, sban; 118, didden; 120, Elnur; 127, Tereza Dvorak; 131, Milushkina Anastasiya; 132, Picsfive; 134 left, Aaron Amat, right, Gaby Kooijman; 142, Kaptelova Yulia; 145, Avava; 150 bot, Aaron Amat; 153, M Dykstra; 154 bot, Flashon Studio; 159, Charlene Bayerle; 160, Julian Rovagnati; 164 bot, Galina Barskaya; 169 bot, Gorilla; 172, Lasse Kristensen; 173, 2happy; 174, Thomas M Perkins; 175, Diana Lundin; 177, Yuri Arcus; 180 right, ryasick photography; 181 top, bluehill; 182 top, Fotocrisis, bot, James Steidl; 195, c; 196, Anthony Harris; 200 Irina Rubanova; 206, Daniel Krylov; 212, pixshots; 216, Oliver Hoffmann; 217 top, Ozankutsal; 226, slavapolo; 230, PhotoNan; 233, Elena Elisseeva; 234, SasPartout; 240 top, Richard Peterson; 241, Elena Elisseeva; 242, Sandra Kemppainen; 245, Shcherbakov Ilya; 250 bot, Raphael Daniaud; 261, MattJones; 263, Kristof Degreef; 265 left, David P. Smith, right, Velychko; 266, George Dolgikh; 267, Sandra Cunningham; 269, kristan sekulic; 279, Monkey Business Images; 280, Lori Sparkia; 282, Adi; 289, Monkey Business Images; 290, Nicholas Rjabow; 292, spe; 295 top, Jaimie Duplass, bot, 2happy; 296, Grant Terry; 301, Letizia Spanò; 303, fotohunter; 312, newphotoservice; 313, Elanamiv; 315, newphotoservice; 317, PaulPaladin; 318, Svilen G; 319, Sergey Toronto; 323, Bronwyn Photo; 325, Norberto Mario Lauraa; 326, Lorraine Kourafas; 332, trucic; 344, Alona Photo; 345, Monkey Business images; 346, ericlefrancais; 347, Ali Mazraie Shadi; 349, Daniel Rajszczak; 350, R; 351, Khomulo Anna; 352, Karin Lau; 353, Pavel Drozda; 355, Danielbotha; 356, Misza; 358, Danny Smythe; 359, Yanik Chauvin; 360, Curtis Kautzer; 361, Karkas; 362, Alexey Chernitevich; 367, sprinter81; 368, Tito Wong; 369, Cico; 371, Tischenko Irina; 371, Tomasz Wieja; 372, Chiran Vlad; 375, Baloncici; 378, Adisa; 379, Bruce Shippee; 380, Michael Rolands; 383, Aliaksei Lasevich; 384, Keith Levit; 385, Valua Vitaly.

For Toucan Books
Senior Editor Antonia Cunningham
Editor Jane Hutchings
Art Editor Thomas Keenes
Picture Research Jane Lambert
Proofreader Marion Dent
Indexer Michael Dent

For Reader's Digest Books
Editorial Director Julian Browne
Art Director Anne-Marie Bulat
Managing Editor Nina Hathway
Head of Book Development Sarah Bloxham
Picture Resource Manager Sarah
  Stewart-Richardson
Pre-press Technical Manager Dean Russell
Product Production Manager Claudette Bramble
Senior Production Controller Katherine Tibbals

Origination ImageScanhouse
Printed and bound in China

Note The information in this book has been carefully researched and all efforts have been made to ensure accuracy and safety. Neither the authors nor Reader's Digest Association Limited assume any responsibility for any injuries suffered or damages or losses incurred as a result of following the instructions in this book. Before taking any action based on information in this book, study the information carefully and make sure you understand it fully. Observe all warnings and Take Care notices. Test any new or unusual repair or cleaning method before applying it broadly, or on a highly visible area or valuable item. The mention of any product or web site in this book does not imply an endorsement. All product names and web sites mentioned are subject to change and are meant to be considered as general examples rather than specific recommendations.

Extraordinary Uses for Ordinary Things was created by The Reader's Digest Inc., USA and is published by The Reader's Digest Association Limited, 11 Westferry Circus, Canary Wharf, London E14 4HE

This edition is adapted from **Extraordinary Uses for Ordinary Things** published by The Reader's Digest Association Limited in 2007.

We are committed both to the quality of our products and the service we provide to our customers. We value your comments, so please so contact us on **08705 113366** or via our website at **www.readersdigest.co.uk**

If you have any comments or suggestions about the content of our books, email us at **gbeditorial@readersdigest.co.uk**

ISBN 987 0 276 44583 5
Book code 400-480 UP0000-1
Oracle code 250014692H.00.24